# PRAGMATICISM

## Theory and Application

### Ellyn Lucas Arwood
Texas Tech University
Lubbock, Texas

AN ASPEN PUBLICATION®

Aspen Systems Corporation
Rockville, Maryland
London
1983

Library of Congress Cataloging in Publication Data

Arwood, Ellyn Lucas.
Pragmaticism: theory and application.

Includes index.
1. Language acquisition.  2. Semiotics.
3. Speech acts (Linguistics)  4. Child development.
5. Language disorders in children.  I. Title
P118.A75    1983    401'.9    83-9982
ISBN: 0-89443-885-9


Publisher: John Marozsan
Editorial Director: R. Curtis Whitesel
Executive Managing Editor: Margot Raphael
Editorial Services: Jane Coyle
Printing and Manufacturing: Debbie Collins

Library of Congress Catalog Card Number 83-9982
ISBN: 0-89443-885-9

*To Tom*

# Table of Contents

# Foreword

Language-disordered children do not "fit" the research models proposed by psycholinguists and linguists. However, there is data to suggest that these children have certain characteristics in common. It is from these characteristics coupled with many years as a clinician and supervisor of "difficult to manage" language cases, that I have developed a "working" description of *how* children acquire language, *what* children learn in this process, and, to some extent, *why* it's learned.

The system that explains the "how," "what," and "why" is analogous to other natural processes, but to understand it the reader will have to shed all preconceived notions of "language." Academic language arts, using color, shape, and size, as well as structural analyses of words, phrases, morphemes, and turn taking, for example, will need to be put aside. The reader will need to forget about language as the goal and focus on communication as the purpose of any education.

This book is not about language as language has come to be known; it is not about pragmatics as the current psycholinguists and linguists have used that term; this book is a pragmaticism methodology in practice. The reader will be called upon to build a new understanding, as if creating a mobile with principles about communication. These active principles of communication will be presented as consequences of an act to be studied by the pragmaticism methodology explained in the text.

The author has written this text as an attempt to get the reader to recognize these consequences as the goal in dealing with language disorders—as an attempt to get the reader to put aside linguistic and psycholinguistic rigidity in dealing with a language-disordered child's changing system—as an attempt to "clean up" the misguided efforts of the modern users of "pragmatics"—in hopes that more flexible, purposeful, and effective intervention and assessment strategies for dealing with language-disordered children and adults might be utilized.

*Ellyn Lucas Arwood*

# Preface

Educators have long advocated the use of theoretically valid and consistent bases for evaluating, diagnosing, and treating language disorders. Even though theoretically valid bases have been advanced, the author has found a considerable discrepancy between theoretical discussions and actual therapy procedures. These discrepancies include

- applying information about normal development to deviant developing systems
- assuming a normal progression of skills after the system has been determined to be disordered
- equating a delay in skills with a system that is disordered
- using milestones to determine process functioning
- assuming that cognitive skills are the only underpinnings to communication
- measuring components not related to language in order to assess how well a child uses language
- teaching splinter skills with the knowledge that language cannot be taught.

Theoretical answers cannot be simplistically created. Answers can only be developed from a logical analysis of how the total system functions. Such an analysis is referred to as a pragmaticism methodology—a study of the way that ''signs'' are used to produce given consequences.

Pragmaticism includes the following principles:

- In any given context the situation is totally novel.
- Any similarities or differences detected between contexts are determined by interpretation.

- Interpretation of recognized features is based on the meaningfulness of the features.
- Features are semantic in nature and increase in complexity over periods of use and recognition.
- Semantics governs the way that the interpreter may understand any given communicative act.
- The value of the act for communication is totally dependent on the active process of the interpretant.
- The communicative value dictates the type of effect on the interpretant so that a performance is an act that changes the hearer's attitudes, beliefs, and/or behaviors.
- The hearer, according to pragmaticism methodology, may also be the speaker.
- The effects on the hearer and speaker are not expected to be the same but there should be shared semantic elements.
- Shared semantic elements are the conventions of the society for verbal and nonverbal information.
- The semantic elements include the propositional content, the preparatory set, the sincerity, and the essential components of the speech act.
- The speech act is the unit of analysis for a pragmaticism methodology.
- The pragmaticism methodology is a study of the sign consequences.
- The complexity of the signs may be divided into icon, index, and symbol.
- The three types of signs may in turn be analyzed according to the functional and perceptual properties of the organized semantic features.

Each of these principles will be discussed in the following chapters of this book, beginning with the development of a need for such a methodology in Chapter 1, followed by an explanation of semantics in Chapter 2. A paradigm for the semantic phases of development is established in Chapter 3 and the three phases are described in Chapters 4, 5, and 6. Once the phases are described the reader will be taken through assessment, remediation, and intervention application of the paradigm, followed by a discussion of the pragmaticism methodology as it is used in other disciplines.

The purpose of this text is to direct the reader through the pragmaticism methodology so that a model of semantic development may be developed. The working model presented in this text is an integration of not only what is known about language development but also what is known about language disorders. Unlike psycholinguistic theoretical models developed from the observation of task performance, this model is created from a presentation of processes escalating in a logarithmic fashion. And, unlike linguistic theoretical models developed from the products of native speakers, this model is a *description* of how a person's communication unfolds.

The support for such a descriptive model comes from the logic of the methodology, the known variables of a human system, and from clinical cases the author has used as research. The methodology is a form of study as well as a way to understand human consequences. The variables include those meaningful (semantic) constituents of a context between a speaker and a hearer. The clinical cases represent a wealth of untapped theoretical knowledge.

Since this model is a process-oriented description of semantic principles, the reader is asked to consider the following three points as the text is being read:

1. The constantly changing processes are "dynamic" in nature;
2. The communication products represent an integration of underlying social and cognitive interplays; and
3. The changes are operating on a continuum of consequences called a synergistic system.

The pragmaticism methodology will be most effective for the reader who considers these semantic principles. Changes in the way in which language is viewed, analyzed, and remediated will occur. The author expects these changes to be in attitude, belief, and behavior, with positive consequences for those children and adults who have communication disorders in prelanguage, language, and linguistic development.

# Acknowledgments

I wish to thank the friends and family members who have contributed to this work, especially my husband, Tom, who has challenged my ideas and typed my thoughts, and my sister, Mabel, whose work with children has been an inspiration. In all honesty, this book would not have been started had it not been for the insistence of one very kind editor, Curtis Whitesel, who is no longer with us but whose memory will live in the books that have already come to fruition. Mr. Whitesel recognized the need for clinicians, like myself, to write about the many children who have taught us so much. Parents of those children, I thank you for your patience in our attempts to learn what might be the most effective way of serving your children. My many students, I thank you for believing in my methods enough to try them with your clients.

## Chapter 1

# A Pragmaticism Approach to Language

*Let the utterance exist*
*Not as speech, but as an act!*

## Chapter Objectives

1. Discuss the various components of the psycholinguistic approach to the study of language.
2. Explain what is meant by the ''native-speaker assumption.''
3. Explain the rationale for developing a synergistic language model for the study of sign usage.
4. Explain the difference between an adult's language product and a child's language acquisition.
5. Discuss the limitations of the historical, psycholinguistic approach to the study of language.
6. Explain the types of evidence used to develop a synergistic language approach based on a pragmaticism methodology.
7. Compare the synergistic approach with the psycholinguistic approach for dealing with language disorders.
8. Explain the difference between linguistic properties and language skills.
9. Discuss the components of a pragmaticism methodology.
10. Compare the pragmaticism methodology with the psycholinguistic methodology.

## LANGUAGE THEORY TODAY

To determine an appropriate theoretical framework for language intervention, an overview of the current state of the art is necessary. As in many fields, the atmosphere is one of struggle between educators who apply ideas and researchers who research ideas. In this dichotomy the educator rejects certain theoretical assumptions held to be significant by the researcher because the theoretical tenets are not supported by the behavior of language-handicapped children. On the other hand, the researcher finds support for his or her assumptions from normal-language populations that do not represent those with language disorders. Thus the educator is taught to believe there is no choice but to apply the normal-language data to the language-disordered populations. The situation is further complicated by a psycholinguistic methodology that pertains not to people but to products only.

The psycholinguistic approach to the study of language is the current trend in the field of speech and language pathology. This approach utilizes a methodology of analyzing the components of a spoken, representative segment of language (Aram & Nation, 1982; Bloom, 1978; Carrow-Woolfolk, 1982; Clark & Clark, 1977; Lahey, 1978; Muma, 1978; Prutting, 1979; Wood, 1982) in an attempt to compare how one child's language is similar to what would be expected at a particular chronological age. The psycholinguists also consider the way the child's thinking or cognition affects his or her language acquisition. Research from Piaget (1971), for example, is incorporated into the study of the child's production.

The major fallacy with the psycholinguistic approach is that the emphasis is always on products. Even when research incorporates the thinking influence, the psycholinguist analyzes how a child does on a specific task. For example, a child might quickly point to a task given a verbal model, suggesting the child is an impulsive learner. Or sometimes, the child might be asked to select a picture in response to a given verbal model. When the child randomly responds, first to one type of picture and then to another, the psycholinguist may conclude that the child is an impulsive learner. The psycholinguist has considered "thinking style," but only for the task performance. The finding that the child is an impulsive learner does not tell the educator why the child is functioning as an impulsive learner. Furthermore, the attention to thinking style is artificial since the psycholinguist attended only to the child's performance on a given task. The given task is a product approach, not a systems or processes approach.

Although the psycholinguistic approach to the study of language is the current state of the art, there is an alternative—a pragmaticism approach to the study of semantic development. The purpose of this chapter is to present the psycholinguistic approach and the pragmaticism approach, and then to make a comparison of the two for use in developing appropriate remediation and assessment for language-disordered children. Chapter 2 will explain the semantic basis of the pragmaticism approach, often referred to as "synergistic," and Chapter 3 will explain how the synergistic system can account for the effects of audition, cognition, and socialization. These chapters will be followed by application.

## THE PSYCHOLINGUISTIC APPROACH

The psycholinguistic methodology that has been used to study language could be characterized for the most part by the term "static." "Static" is being used to refer to the isolation of specific language characteristics of a speaker. These characteristics are demonstrated through speech and are consequently structural in nature. Furthermore, the characteristics are assumed to be additive in nature; that is, the more discrete units or characteristics that are demonstrated by the speaker, the more complex is the speaker's language. The assumption suggests that a speaker acquires components. For example, if a psycholinguist is studying morphemes, the child's production of certain morphemes is believed to represent the complexity of the child's language. The assumption is that the more morphemes the child produces, the more complex is the child's language.

Following the additive principle of discrete units is a second assumption: the more complex the child's language system appears, as indicated by the use of certain discrete units, the more intact is the child's language system. This latter assumption might be referred to as the "discrete complexity assumption." Neither the additive assumption nor the complexity assumption is valid in the study of how children use language, under what conditions children use language, or why some handicapped children have difficulties in using language.

The limitations of the psycholinguistic assumptions of additive discreteness and discrete complexity might be explained best by addressing the following questions: (1) How can a psycholinguistic methodology of discrete units be applied to the dynamics of the language process? (2) How can the psycholinguistic methodology explain the differences between the adult's product and the child's product? (3) How can a psycholinguistic methodology account for the interplay between cognition and socialization in language acquisition? (4) How can the psycholinguistic model account for differences in the typical child's system when compared with a language-handicapped child's system? (5) How can individual differences be incorporated into an approach that considers only the products? Each of these questions will be discussed in the following sections.

### The Dynamics of Language Acquisition

Historically, the psycholinguistic procedure for studying language acquisition has been to collect the language samples of children either longitudinally or cross-sectionally and then to describe the characteristics of the child's utterances. The descriptions were controlled by the researcher's notion of what constituted language. If language was thought to consist of morphemes, the research analyzed the child's production of morphemes and explained how the child progressed from the use of some morphemes to other morphemes. This use of morphemes, for example, would then be considered according to the child's cognitive development, with Piaget's works usually cited as the basis for cognitive comparison.

The descriptions of the child's language have changed from old forms such as word classes and parts of speech to new psycholinguistic forms such as morphemes, constituents, allomorphs, etc. The methodology, however, has remained the same. The psycholinguist still collects language samples and describes the data. There has been an increased interest in describing this data according to the context in which the child is functioning. However, the constituents of the context have been limited to what the researcher thinks is important. For example, if the researcher thinks the caregiver's spoken words are important in analyzing the child's utterance, then the adult's words are transcribed.

The problem with the collection of data according to what the psycholinguist thinks constitutes language or what the psycholinguist thinks constitutes the context is that the researcher uses an adult frame of reasoning to decide the constituents. The adult frame of reasoning relies heavily on definitions—definitions of what the adult as a "native speaker" can produce. The native speaker is assumed to be an expert in his or her own language and therefore "knows" how language is defined. This introspective type of study has not been used with children as much as with adults because some psycholinguists have found the product of children to be different from the product of the adult (e.g., Brown, 1973). Based on this data, the child is assumed to be operating differently from the adult. Unfortunately, psycholinguists have not incorporated this assumption of difference between children and adults when explaining the child's language. They have historically looked at products that are definitional components of an adult mode of thinking.

These products or constituents of the psycholinguistic product may represent underlying processes but not necessarily in one-to-one correspondence with the child's language behavior. Thus the change in products of a child's language may represent changes in the underlying system that are not product based. In fact, there has been increasing interest in the child's processes of acquisition rather than in the child's product. However, until a method that analyzes the dynamics of the system is recognized and used, the analyses of child language will continue to consider products only.

The question "How can a psycholinguistic approach consider the dynamics of language acquisition?" can be answered simply. A psycholinguistic approach cannot account for the dynamics of language acquisition. In fairness to the psycholinguists, one must point out that most really have not been interested so much in the dynamics of the system as in the relationship between cognitive acts and language production. Therefore, perhaps the answer to the question is to look at another methodology—the pragmaticism methodology.

## The Child's Language and the Adult's Language

If the psycholinguistic approach is primarily interested in the discrete units of a speaker's production as it relates to the cognitive processes, the difference in cognitive processes between the adult and the child should explain the differences between the adult's language and the child's language product. This comparison between the child and the adult according to cognitive differences has shed light on the field of language study. Researchers (e.g., Clark & Clark, 1977; Moore, 1973; Ochs & Schieffelin, 1979) have recognized the importance of language usage from analyzing the differences in cognitive development in relationship to the differences in product.

Current research in semantics derives from the psycholinguistic approach of examining the differences in meaning between the child's product and the adult's interpretation. Unfortunately, much semantic research has relied heavily on the adult interpretation to the exclusion of what the child really may have intended. There must be some criteria that examines the child's output compared with the adult's production. The reader must look to pragmaticism methodology to overcome the limitations of the current psycholinguistic approach.

## Cognition and Socialization

Since the psycholinguistic approach really does not deal with socialization, there has been a tendency to attach the child's social need for using language to the rest of the psycholinguistic field like an appendage. There has been sufficient research in language (e.g. Bruner, 1975; Halliday, 1973; Halliday, 1975; Lucas, 1977) to suggest that the child's social interaction with his or her caregivers is a significant contribution to language acquisition, but the psycholinguistic methodology has difficulty dealing with the social aspects of language acquisition because more than products must be analyzed in order to understand the social relationship between the child and the adult.

Some researchers have put social use and language function as topics at the back of the book. Others have tried to apply the psycholinguistic methodology to the child's language use. The result of the latter approach has been numerous studies that deal with different components all under the heading of social development, or "pragmatics." For example, the author might list certain "social functions" at the age of two for development and then for the age of seven use the "indirect speech act" as the unit, and at the adult level "communicative competence." None of these units can be traced over time to the adult level of development. None of these units are pragmatic in nature. Terms like "communicative competence" or "turn taking" are the psycholinguists' constituents of social development, but these constituents still do not explain the way the child functions. The psycholinguistic methodology cannot adequately explain or describe the interplay between socialization and cognition in the acquisition of language because the constituents do not describe relationships.

## Typical and Atypical Language Development

The psycholinguistic approach to the study of language has provided the field of speech and language pathology with numerous studies that deal with what is typical in a child's language development. These studies present lists of when a specific skill might emerge and when it might be mastered by a child. The list is believed to be sequential in nature, with the child acquiring the first skill on the list before the second skill. These skills are believed to be systematic in development. That is, there are varying rates of acquisition among children but the same sorts of constituents are observed in most children at certain age levels. (For information regarding the typical systematic and sequential ordering of constituents see Bloom, 1978; Bloom, Lightbown, & Hood, 1975; Brown, 1973; Clark & Clark, 1977; Dale, 1976; Leonard, 1976; Menyuk, 1969; Muma, 1978; Trantham & Pederson, 1976; and Wood, 1976).

The sequential and systematic regularities observed in a child's language represent the conventions of the society. The conventions are those constituents that formulate the language constructions so that a child who is from an English-speaking home acquires English conventions whereas a child in a Spanish-speaking home acquires Spanish conventions.

These conventions are often the center of the psycholinguist's research. For example, if a child consistently demonstrated the use of a long vowel preceding a voiced consonant, the psycholinguist would say that the child was adhering to that specific rule. If the psycholinguist observed that a particular language marked or distinguished a plural noun from a singular noun by adding an ''-s,'' the psycho-linguist would say that the language marks plurals by ''-s.'' Therefore, the psycholinguist would investigate a child's production to determine whether or not the child produced the ''-s'' and at what age and under what circumstances. The assumption here is that the child will have a more complex system when the plural is marked that way (assumption of discrete complexity) and that the system will be more intact. The fallacy here is the assumption that the marking of the plural was the child's goal, that the child wanted to produce the plural marker like the adult's product. The fact may be that the child produced the plural marker when his or her *semantic system* was complex enough to support the production.

Research with language intervention (e.g., Gray & Ryan, 1973) indicates that conventional regularities such as the ''-s'' can be added by using specific tech-niques with the child. However, the child's ability to function with that newly added unit is not any better than before the intervention. Clearly, the goal is much more dynamic than the constituents can demonstrate when added together and that dynamic component is semantic or meaningful in nature. With a focus on the conventions, the similarities and differences between children are related to form and not function. The components of the conventions have no meaning by themselves and when taught in a discrete manner, there is no increase in language functioning outside the realm of adding the discrete unit.

When the psycholinguistic notion of systematic and sequential ordering of constituents is emphasized, the result is a sophisticated ordering of milestones. The milestones indicate when a child should be performing certain tasks, such as the production of a word or the production of a plural form, etc.

The majority of intervention studies propose that normal developmental data should be used as the basis for planning language intervention. This suggestion has some validity in that one needs to understand what children do in the acquisition of language to be able to recognize what a specific child is not doing. However, there are some problems with using normal developmental data as the primary set of criteria for developing assessment instruments and for planning intervention.

The main problem is that children who are not acquiring language as expected are not using the same assumed systematic, sequential progression. In fact, for some children the progression of milestones may be so deviant that working on the products may not be a suitable intervention approach (see Chapters 9, 10, and 11). The psycholinguistic approach of comparing a child to specific constituent milestones ignores possible differences in the systems. A deviant product may mean a deviant system, which is remediated most efficiently through examination of the system as it functions rather than by analyzing the difference in products. Normative data collected from normal developmental systems cannot be compared with deviant systems if the remediation plan is to be the product of such an assessment. When the child's system appears to be intact, the normative tests measure how that child does in comparison with other children. This information may be useful for some academic purpose. However, when the child's system is not intact, such a comparison is similar to comparing two different items such as an apple and an orange from a categorization of fruit.

Furthermore, the psycholinguistic practice of utilizing normative data or psycholinguistic developmental data with a language-handicapped child does not tell the educator how the language-disordered child is functioning. Only a methodology that examines the child's entire communication system will explain how he or she is functioning.

Normal developmental data cannot be used for comparing language-disordered children with children that are developing language in a systematic, sequential way. Language-disordered children are different! The clinician, diagnostician, and educator must be able to develop a data base from which to plan remediation. Language-disordered children have more in common with other language-disordered children than any given language-disordered child has in common with the normal developmental data. Once this data pool regarding those with language disorders is determined, remediation programs may be individualized for better treatment. Therefore, a psycholinguistic approach of relying on products and milestones cannot be used for determining how a language-disordered child is functioning.

## Individual Differences

The primary means of considering individual differences from the psycholinguistic point of view has been to derive cognitive differences in learning from examining the products of non-language-handicapped children. In order to examine the products, various tasks have been developed (e.g., Muma Assessment Program [MAP], 1979) to elicit the strategies that children use to solve the tasks or to approach the solution of the task. This psycholinguistic approach is one way to study the differences that two children might exhibit.

If the educator wants to know what the differences are between the children's overall functioning, responses to individual tasks for specific strategies will not answer that global question. Each child's system must be approached from a different methodology—instead of looking at the products, the methodology must have a framework that considers the products to be representative of a more dynamic system. The methodology for dealing with the dynamic system must have a more synergistic way of approaching the study of language so that individual differences within a typical scale of development as well as individual differences outside what is typical can be considered. Pragmaticism methodology is the answer. The following section will describe the synergistic variables of the pragmaticism approach.

## THE PRAGMATICISM APPROACH

To review, the psycholinguistic approach has several limitations, including the following: (1) not being able to account for the dynamics of language acquisition, (2) falsely assuming discrete additive properties for language acquisition, (3) not being able to account for the social factors in language acquisition, (4) not being appropriate for determining a language-disordered child's means of functioning, and (5) not being able to account for system differences as opposed to discrete individual differences.

The pragmaticism approach described in the following section will consider each of these psycholinguistic limitations by addressing the strengths of the pragmaticism system. These include the following points:

- The pragmaticism approach deals with the study of the sign (semiotics) as a dynamic process.
- The pragmaticism approach is synergistic in that it considers the interplay between cognition and socialization.

- The pragmaticism methodology considers acquisition processes as part of the child's total communication system.
- The pragmaticism methodology can be applied to language-disordered children and it can be based on what is known about the typical language system.
- The pragmaticism methodology can account for patterns of difference and not just differences in products.

A table of comparisons between the psycholinguistic and pragmaticism methodologies may be found at the end of this section.

**Semiotics—A Dynamic Process**

Charles S. Peirce is often considered the father of pragmatics. Peirce, who wrote between 1850 and 1900, came to distinguish the notion of pragmaticism, a study of semiotics, from pragmatics, a study of life. It is his notion of pragmaticism that is important to the study of signs or semiotics. Whereas other pragmatists, such as William James, were more concerned with answering questions about the practical consequences of life, Peirce's notion of pragmaticism dealt with the consequences of signs. When we hear of "pragmatics" in the study of language today it is really a notion of pragmaticism that deals with the consequences of language. The speaker's utterance is seen as the practical consequence of the signs that the speaker uses. Therefore, pragmaticism as a methodology deals with language use as the study of semiotics or sign users' effects or consequences on other speakers.

Several principles were developed from the works of Peirce:

- Signs do not exist independently of their use.
- Signs cannot be created—their origin must be derived from other signs.
- Conventionality refers to the state of awareness of sign relations.
- Signs come from objects affecting other objects.

These pragmaticism principles provide the basis of a methodology for studying the dynamic process of semiotics. Each of these principles will be discussed in the following section.

Signs, which Peirce divided into three types (see Chapter 2), do not exist independently of their use. This principle immediately rejects the psycholinguistic notion of sign discreteness. The sign can only exist as a sign if it is used; otherwise, the component is a part of an analysis separate from its representation.

Pragmatists suggest that the sign represents the moment of the utterance and nothing else. Therefore, separated from use, there is no sign. The act of using signs in a language signals the existence of language. The product components, which are not signs, cannot add up to form a system. The system acts as its own creator. Each sign is created from the use of a sign—the sign's existence is the sign's creation.

Whether or not a hearer can recognize a production as a sign depends on the conventionality of the system, not on the use. The hearer will recognize the conventionality if the hearer is aware of the system's conventions. A speaker cannot be made aware of the system by demonstrating the signs. In other words, if a researcher examines a child's product and discovers that the child does not use a plural ''-s,'' making the child aware of the ''-s'' will not ensure that the child will use the plural marker. The child will use the ''-s'' only when it represents a sign for which the child has such awareness.

That signs come from objects affecting other objects is a principle of relationship. It is the relationships between and among people, actions, and events that necessitate the production of signs. If the relationships did not need to be represented by a speaker, there would be no development of signs in a language system. The members of society would not have a need to communicate about such relationships. There would be no social interaction. This point brings the reader to the next strength of the pragmaticism methodology—the ability to account for the synergistic quality of cognition and socialization.

**The Synergistics of Cognition and Socialization**

Peirce's theory of semiotics considered how the mind represents the object for use of the sign. Ransdell (1979) stated Peirce's assumptions as follows: (1) ''. . . all cognition is mediated by ideas or representations''; (2) ''. . .the object is always other than the idea of it''; (3) ''. . .the consequential proposition [is] that the idea or representation must always be itself an object of knowledge cognized independently of the cognition of the object'' (p. 53). These assumptions suggest that the speaker's signs or effects on the hearer are separate from the actual object. According to these assumptions, the sign only represents the idea of the object.

This interaction between the ideas and the effects is really a theory of cognition based on the meaning or semantics (see Chapter 2). Oehler (1979) listed four basic principles inherent in Peirce's theory of cognition: (1) ''. . . all knowledge of the internal world is derived by the hypothetical reasoning from our knowledge of external facts''; (2) there is ''no power of intuition, but every cognition is determined logically by previous cognitions''; (3) there is ''no power of thinking without signs''; and (4) there is ''no conception of the absolutely incognizable'' (p. 67). The reader will be directed through each of these principles as it relates to the interplay between cognition and socialization.

Knowledge is a description of semantic development extracted from external stimuli. Chapter 2 will discuss the development of such knowledge from the organization of semantic features. The ability to alter a thought rests on the ability to alter past knowledge from a present change in external information. In this way, the speaker's use of signs alters thoughts, just as external stimuli may alter thoughts. This concept is quite different from the psycholinguistic assumption that the use of signs (language) is the product of cognition. This pragmaticism principle of cognition suggests that the signs are not only a product of their own use, but that their use can alter the knowledge representative of cognition.

Chapter 2 describes the semantic complexity of signs, but, for the immediate purpose of explaining the relationship between cognition and socialization, it is accurate to say that the ability to use signs is a catalyst for further learning. Peirce's principle that there is no power in thinking without signs refers to a person's inability to manipulate another person's or the speaker's own attitudes, beliefs, and behaviors without the use of signs. The signs create consequences that could be considered as control or power over the immediate environmental circumstances. The act is immediately synergistic in that it is not a sign or representation of a thought unless such consequences or effects are created.

The final principle that there is ''no conception of the absolutely incognizable'' represents the ultimate synergistic value of a pragmaticism approach to the study of signs. This principle means that nothing can exist or be created without the ability to think of such a beginning or such a creation. The representation of such a creation is the sign, which functions to affect the hearer so as to have consequences that also exist as signs, thus repeating the pattern of sign usage. The ability of a child to use a language system begins with the child's ability to affect a hearer so as to have consequences that had their beginning in cognition.

## Pragmaticism Methodology and the Language Disordered

If the pragmaticism methodology is concerned with the system of the child and not with the child's products, there is no need to compare and contrast similarities and differences in the products. The application of the pragmaticism methodology is an attempt to determine how the child's system is functioning, not an attempt to ascertain what products are present.

A child's total system must be assessed and if any part of that system is nonsystematic or nonsequential in nature, the child's language system is said to be disordered. The term ''language-disordered'' has been used with caution and preference over ''language-deviant'' or ''language-delayed.'' If the child exhibits any of several specific disorders such as echolalia (Lucas, 1980), the child can be said to be demonstrating language products as a result of a deviant system. Only a few children who begin life at a slower productive rate are actually ''language-delayed,'' but even these children will present a disordered system if allowed to progress through to chronological, cognitive ages in which certain processes should be used but which cannot be used by the child. Language-delayed children are the exception and not the rule; therefore, ''language-disordered'' is the more accurate term. Examples of diagnoses for language disorder as opposed to delay will be presented in Chapters 7 and 8 on language assessment and intervention.

In physiology, a synergistic system is the cooperative action of parts of the body to enhance or produce a desired effect. A synergistic model representative of a pragmaticism methodology is one in which the dynamics of the individual's physiology is represented through certain cognitive, social, or language types of behaviors. Thus, any breakdown in the system represents a deviation in the functioning of that system. The child with a breakdown in the system is a child with a language disorder. Furthermore, the disordered system cannot function synergistically.

One of the most important application principles of a synergistic model is that it must account for the orderly, systematic changes that a child demonstrates from birth to adulthood without a change in what constitutes the system. The products may change, but the pragmaticism methodology must account for the regularity between and among systems. The child's behavior in early stages of development represents the system that will produce other behaviors in later development. For example, many clinicians and researchers refer to "semantic relations," but when the child begins to demonstrate syntax and forms more like the expected adult form, the clinician changes units and begins to work on personal pronouns without any consideration for the same underlying semantic principles producing consequences in the child's development. Sometimes the clinician seems to think semantic relations are being taught simply because he or she is working with two-word combinations. A pragmaticism methodology restricts the educator or clinician to the child's semantic development, a system of synergistics between cognition and socialization. This restriction does not allow the clinician to slip back into an analysis of units.

The basic theoretical premise of a synergistic model when applied to the language-disordered is that the language moment is representative of the child's underlying sociocognitive processes. According to Peirce's semiotics, a given instance of sign usage or language production reflects the entire process of development. Unlike static, psycholinguistic models, the product exists as a unique moment and the underlying semantic processes allow for that moment. Whereas milestones or normative data are imposed inspections of how the processes have been functioning, they do not reveal the means by which the products have been created. The synergistic model attempts to locate the processes used to acquire those characteristics of the product, whether in a typical system or a disordered system.

## Systems of Difference

Because pragmaticism methodology considers the child's use of signs as a representation of social and cognitive influences, a disorder in the sign system reflects a breakdown in social and/or cognitive development. Such breakdowns reflect differences in disordered systems separate from the individual variations within a system. The pragmaticism methodology when applied to the language-disordered child has provided an invaluable source of information for assessing and intervening in the language-disordered child's system. From this information a paradigm about how a child's language system functions for language acquisition may be developed. Chapter 7 discusses how the synergistic model accounts for possible breakdowns in the system.

The data base about language-disordered children has increased to the extent that similarities suggest certain common deviations in their language systems. Children that have interrupted or impaired systems for acquiring language also have a progression of development, but the development is unlike that of the normal developing language system. The product for both systems often shows many similarities that confuse or confound the educator's attempt to provide the most effective remediation. For example, two children who are producing the plural marker ''-s'' have the same product but may have very different systems. In fact, one of the children may have a disordered system. Information about how the child uses the signs rather than what constitutes the product of the signs provides the educator with clues not only about how the system functions but also about what happens when the system is disordered. Examining the constituents of the product will never give that type of information.

If the clinician or educator is able to identify the impairment in the system and thus the language disorders, the assessment procedures and remediation programs will also become more effective. The ability to change or alter the functioning of the system for better use of signs to affect a hearer's attitudes, beliefs, or behaviors is an experimental control. If the intervention is effective, the system must have had a breakdown in what was changed. Data obtained through clinical intervention (see Lucas, 1980, and Chapter 7 of this text) indicates the greater effectiveness of a pragmaticism methodology in dealing with systems of difference over the limiting psycholinguistic methodology of discrete differences.

In summary, the pragmaticism methodology deals effectively with the dynamic process of semiotics, the synergistic quality of sociocognitive processes, the acquisition phenomenon of the total child, and the systems of differences rather than discrete differences. The pragmaticism methodology enables us to arrive at a paradigm of semantic development that explains the acquisition of the various phases of semiotics from prelanguage communication through language to an adult linguistic system. Chapters 4, 5, and 6 will discuss those phases in detail.

The last section of this chapter provides an overview of the pragmaticism methodology used to explain semantic development, which is the subject of Chapter 2. First, however, the reader is directed to a graphic comparison of the pragmaticism and psycholinguistic methodologies (Exhibit 1-1).

**Exhibit 1-1** Comparison of Methodologies

| *Psycholinguistic Study/*<br>*Intervention* | *Pragmaticism Study/*<br>*Intervention* |
|---|---|
| 1. Examines the consistency of the child's morphological, phonological, and syntactical performance, sometimes referred to as the linguistic domain for using morphemes, morphophonemic rules, morphological co-occurrence, etc. | 1. Examines the development of semiotics (signs) through a refinement of semantics with the *adult* product being linguistic in nature. |
| 2. Examines the meaning of words in relationships such as the role of the word "iron" in "The man used a seven iron." | 2. Semantics does not deal with words. Words do not exist in this methodology. Representations of meaning occur within the speech act framework. |
| 3. "Ideas are called semantic functions and relations" (Muma, 1981, p. 83). | 3. Ideas are products of underlying semantic coding of stimuli. These underlying thought objects are then represented by a sign interpreted by a hearer. Semantic relations such as an agent with an action are defined by semantic acquisition of a caregiver's verbal attachment. |
| 4. Intents are purposes for coding information, such as the desire to get a drink. | 4. Interaction is coded semantically when processed so that the purpose of communication stems from a need to refine semantics. |
| 5. Mental processes of the cognitive domain are assessed (memory, processing capacity, etc.) through tasks such as repeating digits, responding to stimuli changes, etc. | 5. The notion of a pragmaticism methodology precludes any measure of a process by a task. If the system is synergistic, task performances cannot measure the system, only the products. |
| 6. Communicative domain deals with topic changes, turn taking, etc. | 6. Pragmaticism does not separate a sign from its representation or interpretation. Therefore, turn taking, topic changes are not studied as separate entities. These separate components do not equal the whole system. |
| 7. Some psycholinguists do not separate linguistic from cognitive domains. | 7. Pragmaticism methodology deals with the system and the sociocognitive development of sign representation at prelanguage, language, and linguistic phases of semantic development. Therefore, there is a progression of semantic complexity related to cognition but certainly separable from specific linguistic principles. |

**Exhibit 1-1** continued

| *Psycholinguistic Study/ Intervention* | *Pragmaticism Study/ Intervention* |
|---|---|
| 8. Some psycholinguists use "language delay" and "language disorder" synonymously to mean a deviation in the mastery of certain skills. | 8. Since pragmaticism forces the examiner to consider the system rather than its manifestation, a change in representation *is* a change in the system. The changed system is no longer synergistically functioning as expected. Therefore, the products reflect a disordered system, not a delayed system. Consequently, such representations are atypical of expected developmental patterns. |
| 9. Assessment of the separate psycholinguistic components is considered content valid. | 9. Assessment of *how* the system functions to represent changes in the context is the *only* content-valid method. |
| 10. Intervention is aimed at developing what is typically observed in normal language development as defined by the psycholinguist. | 10. Intervention is based on the quality of the system's functioning for changing attitudes, beliefs, and behaviors in a hearer for maximum flexibility and productivity in learning. |

## PRAGMATICISM APPLICATION

The pragmaticism methodology used in this text to explain semantic development or semiotics makes the following assumptions:

- The child is an active pursuer of sensory stimuli for building knowledge.
- The organization of these stimuli into semantic features provides the basis of knowledge.
- Knowledge is the representation of thought through sign.
- Signs exist only as the expression of a speech act within a speech event.
- Assessment of a child's signs is the measurement of the child's ability to socially coordinate cognitive development.
- Signs are not limited to language but include nonverbal behaviors, but language is limited to verbal behavior.

Each of these assumptions will be explained in the remaining part of this chapter and then expanded in the other chapters of this text.

## The Child and Sensory Stimuli

The active strategy of the child as a pursuer of sensory stimuli allows the child to develop adequate information from the environment so as to create signs for acting upon new situations. For example, a two-year-old child might be expected to role play answering the telephone by picking up the receiver, waiting until someone else said "Hi!" and then hanging up the receiver, with the act being repeated. The ability of the child to demonstrate this symbolic representation is the result of active development of his or her internalization of the environment, not the result of cognitive skills in a vacuum. The child's telephone act represents many experiences and learning situations that had been recorded for retrieval.

As the child's information base becomes great enough, retrieval and subsequent use become more efficient with an increased ability to represent those ideas through signs. Information is added to the use of signs so that the signs actually assist to develop thoughts. This system of thought and language interaction provides the basic semantic information for further learning.

If the child were not an active pursuer of sensory stimuli, he or she would not be capable of creating sign production for representation of thought from environmentally acquired knowledge. Some severely multiply handicapped children are so incapable of seeking sensory stimuli that the sociocognitive processes for developing sign usage never occur beyond the minimal phase of prelanguage (nonverbal) development.

## The Basis of Knowledge

The author assumes that there are physiological changes in the reception and organization of sensory stimuli that alter the ways in which future receptions are organized. This hierarchy of sensory reception and organization develops features of information that are meaningful to the speaker so that there becomes a shared basis of knowledge between the speaker and the hearer. Chapter 2 explains the semantic basis in more detail.

## Thought and Sign

The pragmaticism methodology used in this book to construct a paradigm about semantic development assumes that the principles worked out by Charles S. Peirce are credible. The principles state that there are no signs without consequences or effects on a hearer even if the hearer is also the speaker. The signs exist as the act of presentation exists, much like the modern unit of the speech act. The speech act will be explained in Chapters 2 and 3.

## Speech Act and Speech Event

Because the speech act is a unit of semiotics, it is dictated by semantic constituents much like Searle (1969) and other philosophers of language have suggested. These semantic constituents exist as part of several successfully executed speech acts between a hearer and a speaker within a given set of conditions. These conditions are considered real only when the signs are interpreted as such by a hearer and are therefore called "felicity conditions."

## Assessment of Sociocognitive Development

The purpose of using a pragmaticism methodology to explain the use of signs as a semantic phenomenon of interplay between a speaker's cognition and consequences as dictated by social conventions is to be able to apply the information to the assessment and intervention of language disorders. Following a theoretical development, the application of this information to the assessment and intervention of language disorders will be presented for the three phases of semantic development: prelanguage, language, and linguistic.

## Language and Nonverbal Behavior

Communication of a spoken message is dependent on nonverbal behavior such as body orientation, eye contact, and gesture. It has been estimated that 60 percent of communication is nonverbal, leaving only 40 percent to be exchanged through verbal or language means. Furthermore, the majority of nonverbal conventions are acquired during the first phase of semantic development. Therefore body language—like the language consisting of phonology, syntax, and morphology—has its roots in early nonverbal semantic development.

The speech act, governed by semantic rules, includes nonverbal ways to assist communication through language. The semantic interplay between verbal and nonverbal conventions of communication results in the use of speech acts to alter the attitudes, beliefs, or behaviors of a hearer. Chapter 4 presents these constituents of the speech act.

## SUMMARY

The psycholinguistic approach to language and language disorders is limited to the examination of products assumed to be additive in complexity and generative in creating "normal" development. Because these assumptions are invalid, psycholinguistically based assessment and remediation must be questioned. The proposed alternative is to use a pragmaticism methodology to explore language acquisition and intervention. Pragmaticism approaches the child's system as synergistic—semantic in nature and social in origin. This synergistic system develops in complexity across three semantic phases: prelanguage, language, and linguistic.

---

## REFERENCES

Aram, D.M., & Nation, J.E. *Child language disorders*. St. Louis: C.V. Mosby, 1982.

Bloom, L. *Readings in language development*. New York: John Wiley & Sons, 1978.

Bloom, L., Lightbown, P., & Hood, L. Structure and variation in child language. *Society for Research in Child Development*, 1975, 40(2), 1-97.

Brown, R. *A first language: The first stages*. Cambridge, Mass.: Harvard University Press, 1973.

Bruner, J.S. From communication to language—a psychological perspective. *Cognition*, 1975, *3*(3), 225-287.

Carrow-Woolfolk, E. *Language disorders in children*. New York: Grune & Stratton, 1982.

Clark, H.H., & Clark, E.V. *Psychology and language*. New York: Harcourt Brace Jovanovich, 1977.

Dale, P.S. *Language development* (2nd ed.). New York: Holt, Rinehart & Winston, 1976.

Gray, B., & Ryan, B. *A language program for the nonlanguage child*. Champaign, Ill.: Research Press, 1973.

Halliday, M.A.K. *Explorations in the functions of language*. New York: Elsevier North Holland, 1973.

Halliday, M.A.K. *Learning how to mean*. New York: Elsevier North Holland, 1975.

Lahey, M. *Readings in childhood language disorders*. New York: John Wiley & Sons, 1978.

Leonard, L.B. *Meaning in child language*. New York: Grune & Stratton, 1976.

Lucas, E.V. The feasibility of speech acts as a language approach for emotionally disturbed children (Doctoral dissertation, University of Georgia, 1977). *Dissertation Abstracts International*, 1978, *38*, 3479B-3967B. (University Microfilms No. 77-30, 488)

Lucas, E.V. *Semantic and pragmatic language disorders: Assessment and remediation*. Rockville, Md.: Aspen Systems, 1980.

Menyuk, P. *Sentences children use*. Cambridge, Mass.: M.I.T. Press, 1969.

Moore, T.E. (Ed.). *Cognitive development and the acquisition of language*. New York: Academic Press, 1973.

Muma, J.R. Language: A new year. *Journal of Childhood Communication Disorders*, 1981, 5(2), 83-89.

Muma, J.R. *Language handbook*. Englewood Cliffs, N.J.: Prentice Hall, 1978.

Muma, J.R., & Muma, D.B. *Muma Assessment Program*. Lubbock, Tex.: Natural Child Publishing Co., 1979.

Ochs, E., & Schieffelin, B.B. (Eds.). *Developmental pragmatics*. New York: Academic Press, 1979.

Oehler, K. Peirce's foundation of a semiotic theory of cognition. *Peirce Studies* (Edited by members of the Institute for Studies in Pragmaticism, Lubbock, Tex.), 1979, *1*, 67-76.

Piaget, J. *The language and thought of the child*. New York: World Publishing Co., 1971.

Prutting, C.A. Process pra ses n: The action of moving forward progressively from one point to another on the way to completion. *Journal of Speech and Hearing Disorders*, 1978, *44*(1), 3-30.

Ransdell, J.M. The epistemic function of iconicity in perception. *Peirce Studies,* Edited by members of the Institute for Studies in Pragmaticism (Lubbock, Tex.), 1979, *1,* 51-66.

Searle, J.R. *Speech acts: An essay in the philosophy of language.* Cambridge, England: Cambridge University Press, 1969.

Trantham, C.R., & Pederson, J.K. *Normal language development.* Baltimore: Williams & Wilkins, 1976.

Wood, B.S. *Children and communication.* Englewood Cliffs, N.J.: Prentice-Hall, 1976.

Wood, M.L. *Language disorders in school-age children.* Englewood Cliffs, N.J.: Prentice-Hall, 1982.

## SUGGESTED READINGS

Brock, J.E. Principal themes in Peirce's logic of vagueness. *Peirce Studies* (Edited by members of the Institute for Studies in Pragmaticism, Lubbock, Tex.), 1979, *1,* 41-50.

Brock, J.E. *Peirce and Searle on assertion.* Paper presented at Bicentennial Peirce Conference Proceedings, held in Hague, Holland, June 1976.

Esposito, J.L. On the origins and foundations of Peirce's semiotic. *Peirce Studies* (Edited by members of the Institute for Studies in Pragmaticism, Lubbock, Tex.), 1979, *1,* 19-24.

Ketner, K. *Charles S. Peirce Newsletter.* Lubbock, Tex.: Peirce Institute, 1981.

Lucas, E., & Sparks, J. *Speech act theory.* Unpublished research project, Texas Tech University, 1981.

Martens, E. *C.S. Peirce on speech acts.* Paper presented at Bicentennial Peirce Conference Proceedings, held in Hague, Holland, June 1976.

Oehler, K. Peirce's foundation of a semiotic theory of cognition. *Peirce Studies* (Edited by members of the Institute for Studies in Pragmaticism, Lubbock, Tex.), 1979, *1,* 67-76.

Peirce, C.S. M.S. 292.00009; M.S. 295.0002, 3; M.S. 599.RR40 (1850-1890). Institute for Studies of Pragmaticism. Texas Tech University, Lubbock, Tex.

Ransdell, J.M. The epistemic function of iconicity in perception. *Peirce Studies* (Edited by members of the Institute for Studies in Pragmaticism, Lubbock, Tex.), 1979, *1,* 51-66.

Smith, M.D. Peirce and Piaget: A commentary on signs of a common ground. *Semiotica,* 1977, *19*(3/4), 271-279.

## Chapter 2

# The Integration of Semiotics and Function

*The strangest song is one*
*Of linguistic code—*
*Sweet, subtle, and profound!*

## Chapter Objectives

1. Explain the synergistic quality of meaning or semantics.
2. Define the relationship between semantics and linguistic properties.
3. Describe the relationship between pragmatics and semantics.
4. Explain the historical difference between turn-of-the century pragmatics and the current use of the term "pragmatics."
5. Explain the importance of meaning to assessment and intervention application.
6. Explain the difference between semantics and language as it pertains to the development of a linguistic system.
7. Relate semantic properties and principles to the notion of conventions.
8. Explain the various properties of semantics cited in this chapter.

## INTRODUCTION

Chapter 1 dealt with the historical trend of viewing language from a psycholinguist's perspective of discrete constituents and dealing with language disorders from data based on normal development.

It was suggested that these historical trends examine language as consisting of static entities. Therefore, language acquisition is often described as the addition of such entities in a linear fashion. The psycholinguist thinks of language development as a graded increase in complexity through a series of steps much like climbing an increasingly difficult staircase. This analogy might be appropriate if one is interested in the structural components rather than the function of the stairs. However, if one wants to know how the child's language system is functioning, the plans for the staircase to be built need to be considered. Planning considers all aspects synergistically functioning to achieve the final product. If any one area is treated independently, the final product will not be functional. For example, considering the size of the boards for the steps of the staircase without consideration for the size of the support will not result in a functional staircase.

Language acquisition is best viewed like the preceding planning problem and not like the linear development of stairs without support. Without consideration for the effect of various language aspects on each other and on the output, linguistic systems cannot be predicted. From the literature regarding children's language and from clinical observation, it appears that the language product is an ''end'' without consideration for its meaning (semantics) in terms of the speaker's intent, purpose, and resulting effect.

However, semantics must be seen in the light of its pragmatic influence on the development of sociocognitive processes for a semiotic, linguistic system. The purpose of this chapter is to discuss semantics or meaning as it relates to the synergistic concepts of semiotics.

## WHAT IS SEMANTICS?

Katz (1973) asked the following questions about semantic properties and relations:

(1) What is the difference between meaningfulness and meaninglessness?
(2) What is the sameness of meaning? What is the difference between synonymy and nonsynonymy?
(3) What is multiplicity of meaning or ambiguity?
(4) What is truth by virtue of meaning and what is falsehood by virtue of meaning?

(5)    What is semantic redundancy?
(6)    What is entailment by virtue of meaning?
(7-9)  What is presupposition, superordination, incapatibility?
(10)   What is a self-answered question? (p. 38)

It should be apparent from looking at the philosophical complexity of these questions that semantics must include a wide variety of "functions" in the language skills. Semantics includes not only the preverbal set (presupposition) before an utterance but also the intended message (hearer's meaningfulness) and the effect on the hearer. This last point, the effect on the hearer, includes the hearer's ability to rule out conflicting messages (redundancy, truth, ambiguity, synonymy) and to be conventionally compatible with other speakers. Thus the speaker could be his or her own hearer and answer his or her own questions.

Other researchers and theorists have attempted to define semantics and have derived often a narrow, adult-interpreted orientation to semantics in terms of referents or even more simplistically in terms of "vocabulary." This attempt to narrow the broad concept of semantics undermines the complexity and synergistic value of the field. Moerk (1977) attempted to capture the value of semantics for the purpose of understanding early language development when he described semantics using "matrix algebra." Unless one understands matrix algebra, this conceptualization of semantics is difficult to comprehend. However, Moerk did explain the *extension* of a term as part of a temporal continuum in which the components of a set would be the continuum. According to Moerk, the *intension* of a term would include the semantic features or the "variety of situational specifications that this concept [term] has undergone" (p. 5).

It is difficult to grasp a three-dimensional set in motion but basically that seems to be the best way to view semantics. Moerk's use of extension and intension helps set boundaries on a dynamic system, but only for the unit of analysis of the system, not for a quantifiable set. Therefore, imagine the semantic set as a mobile, changing with time and by environmental influences on internal structures so that there are an infinite number of configurations and effects possible. Although the mobile branches also create an infinite number of structures, the branch material remains unchanged. In other words, even though semantics is the purpose, intent, change, meaning, and effect, the ways in which semantics is expressed include the conventional phonology or sound system, the morpheme or morphology system interacting with sound and structure by the ordering of syntax.

Moerk pointed out that Wittgenstein (1953) referred to meaning as use. Today when "use" is mentioned, readers may immediately call to mind the notion or area called pragmatics. It should be noted that the pragmatists at the turn of the century were seeking truth or what appears to be meaning. However, it is evident by looking at Charles Peirce's manuscripts that he developed a pragmatic logic as a way to ask and answer questions about meaning. Peirce's notion of semantics as described in Chapter 1 was a philosophy of pragmaticism.

When considering language notions, Peirce would use the same methodology as he did to answer other philosophical questions. Peirce's pragmaticism methodology was the performance of utterance acts to establish the truth or falseness of a question. Language was the act of uttering just as semantics was the existence of a notion represented by the utterance.

Another way of looking at semantics would be to consider the relationship between "semantics" and thinking or cognition, that is, the difference between what constitutes "meaning" and "thinking that is meaningful." One way to approach these differences is to consider some sort of breakdown of semantics. As discussed earlier, questions about semantics raise more complicated questions, which cannot be answered without some criteria or framework. Since the early pragmatists were using a methodology aimed at logically looking at a total picture of existence, their views are preferable to those of the static psycholinguistic approach described in Chapter 1. The total approach is much more suitable to application since the purpose behind language intervention is to help the language-disordered child use a communication system.

## COMMUNICATION

Communication refers to the conveyance of an intended message so as to act to alter a hearer's attitudes, beliefs, or behaviors. Although improving language skills is one way to improve the mode of communication, a total approach is probably the best way to improve the speaker's ability to affect other persons in the environment. Therefore, methodologies such as those used by the pragmatists to examine semiotics will probably provide new information to the person working with language disorders, more so than further examining the language components from a psycholinguistic perspective.

Peirce's manuscripts (although his longhand is often difficult to read) logically worked through the development of "meaning." According to Peirce's initial writings, as reviewed by Esposito (1979), Peirce began viewing semantic development or meaning as having to distinguish "representation" from "images." The more Peirce struggled to separate these ideas, the more his theory of signs (semiotics) was developed. In this process, Peirce had to establish refined distinctions in the classification of signs, the structures of interpretation, and the processes of relation.

From these refinements, it was apparent that signs (representations, etc.) could exist only if there were "sign makers," and the impression of the sign could only have impact if there was a universal use considering both the interpretations and the relationships among the "maker," the environment, and others. Several communication principles came out of Peirce's work:

1. Signs cannot exist independently of their use.
2. Signs cannot be created; their origin must be built from other signs.
3. Conventionality refers to the state of awareness of sign relations.
4. Signs come from objects affecting other objects.

Through the development of these semantic communication principles, Peirce observed a universe that exchanges information by consequences which are represented as signs. According to Peirce, "the essence of a sign leads to a proof that every sign is determined by its object by first partaking in the character of the object [as a diagram does] or second by being actually determined by that object, regardless of any representation that it is . . . or by being connected with that object for given interpretants . . ." (MS 292.000008; Lucas & Sparks, 1981).

Peirce's distinction between objects like diagrams or maps and their representation results in the first distinction of signs—the icon. The icon, or thought, is similar to the actual diagram of an object. However, the diagram is not the object, therefore it exists independently of interpretation. Looking at the diagram and recognizing its surface features would be the next level of meaning in Peirce's theory of semiotics—the index. Finally, if the observer represented whatever meaning was interpreted from the diagram with an advanced sign, then a symbol sign would have been created. Because these signs are semantically based, communication is refined by a speaker as the speaker's semantic development increases.

## Meaning and Semiotics

As is evident from the previous discussion of communication principles, Peirce's theory of semiotics was really one of meaning or semantics, including inference (referring specificity), knowledge, and truth. Peirce established the icon, the index, and symbol signs for his theory of semiotics.

The first of these, the icon, is discussed by Ransdell (1979) using Peirce's logic. According to Ransdell:

> . . . perception cannot *in general* be identified with the object itself toward which perception is directed since the entity which appears immediately sometimes fails to be consistent in character with what the object is otherwise known or found out to be; hence, that which appears is called an 'idea' ('representation,' 'sign'), and it is supposed that our perceptual knowledge of an object is always mediated through an appearance or idea of it. A three-term distinction is thereby set up, consisting of knowing mind, known object, and intervening or mediating idea through or by means of which the knowing is put in connection with the known object. (pp. 52-53)

From the previous explanation of the relationship of object, mind, and representation comes three assumptions:

1. . . . all cognition is mediated by ideas or representations;
2. . . . the object is always other than the idea of it; and
3. . . . the consequential proposition that the idea or representation must always be itself an object of knowledge cognized independently of the cognition of the object.'' (p. 53)

With reference to Aristotle, a Greek philosopher, Ransdell illustrates the difference between the signs as cognitive representations of the perception of an object. According to Ransdell, Aristotle distinguished signs (semia) from objects (pragmata) and the objects' likenesses (homoiomata or perceptions by the viewer). This notion of the image being a likeness of the object is similar to the "imagist" theory of meaning with which Ransdell credits John Locke. From the interpretation of Ransdell and the contribution of Peirce, it appears that the spoken sign has a mental likeness to the object only when it functions as such.

According to Peirce, the term *object* need not be limited to the real object, but may refer to the object of thought. The first level of this thought object is the iconic sign if it has a likeness or representation. Ransdell states, "There is iconic representation in *every* case of sensory perception in virtue of the fact that a form . . . is referred to some object as the form (quality, character, phenomenal structure) of that object" (p. 57).

This level of sign, the icon, is so similar in likeness to the thought (object) that there is little displacement in time, so exact likenesses such as a map representing topography are considered iconic in nature. It is the perceptual representation that is iconic, not the map itself. According to Ransdell, Peirce would say, "all cognition is perceptual in the sense that it always involves an iconic presentation of the cognized object" (p. 61). It appears that the mere perceptual memory or direct perceptual act is iconic in that it has representative likenesses.

The second level of the likeness representation involves the index sign. The third level, distinguished by Peirce in 1867, is the symbol (MS. 292.00009). Although the icon is the perceptual likeness, the index sign is dependent on the interpretant. Thus the index represents the sign only as interpreted. Finally, the mental association with the object is the symbol (MS. 292.00002).

In other words, the perception of a thought (object) is the icon and there is no way for another person or the speaker to use an iconic representation for meaningful communication. The index refers to the likeness, thus establishing a relationship between a speaker and the interpretant (either the speaker or the hearer). Finally, the association between the recognition of thought and the intended representation results in symbols.

For example, observing a cat drink is a perception of the act and is termed iconic until an interpretant recognizes the relationship of the thought with the act, then it is meaningful and an index. When the act is mentally associated with a mode, then symbolic representation, such as that expressed by an utterance such as "Look!" is evident.

Peirce thought that once the representation or symbol of a sign was established, further thinking would only provide more truth—that is, more information about the object. Thus the index of an object was the many characteristics, or what today may be called "perceptual and functional semantic features," of the symbol. The index was also referred to as an object but not as exact as a symbol. For example, "Look at the table!" might induce everyone who is listening to turn their gaze to the table, which would be an index sign (event). However, if the person said, "Oh, my gosh, the table is turning purple!" there would be a more exact representation or symbol for the sign (event). If the speaker walked into the room, gasped, and pointed toward the area of the table, the listeners would look in that direction. The speaker's ability to get the listeners to look is an "icon." The icon is a sign by relationship, but it does not refer generally to a specific event.

It should be possible to observe from the previous examples that there are tenses (other than morphological) in the representation of a sign. The speaker's ability to be more specific with a symbol than an icon or an index indicates that there are various levels of refining or specifying a message. In an overgeneralized sense, it could be said that the icon represented a sign at a communicative level. However, the hearer had to do a maximum amount of interpretation so the burden of the message was with the hearer. The index was an ability to represent the sign with language skills, but again the burden of receiving the complete message rested with the hearer. The use of a symbolic act, however, gave the message as the speaker intended, and through language the act could specify the desired effects on the hearer. This latter usage (symbolization) represents maximum linguistic development.

The breakdown of general semantics into icons, indices, and symbols allows for a better understanding of the dynamic relationship of meaning betweeen the speaker and the hearer so that one can represent thought in order to facilitate new thoughts about a sign. Although the breakdown of semantics into icons, indices, and symbols increases the range of usage to include influences and effects, semantics includes relationships and not just a system between the speaker and the hearer.

If icons are signs of basic communication content, they represent relationships between an object (this includes actions and events) and the characteristics shared about that icon between the speaker and the hearer. The way in which such characteristics are acquired is explained in the material in Chapter 4 on pre-language semantic acquisition.

Indices increase the characteristics so that purposeful utterances later referred to as "speech acts" may be used. Indices are represented primarily through basic language skills that are conventional for a given population. The way in which indices are acquired and represented with language skills is explained in the material in Chapter 5 on language development.

Finally, the messages are refined so that the speaker accepts primary responsibility for conveying intent. The hearer or interpretant need only have the same level of conventions to understand more complex messages.

## Semiotic Theory of Cognition

The relationship between sign usage or semiotics and meaning or semantics is what Peirce called a semantic theory of cognition. Oehler (1979) described the basic principles of Peirce's semiotic theory of cognition:

1. . . . all knowledge of the internal world is derived by the hypothetical reasoning from our knowledge of external facts;
2. [there is] no power of intuition, but every cognition is determined logically by previous cognition;
3. [there is] no power of thinking without signs;
4. [there is] no conception of the absolutely incognizable (p. 67).

These four contentions are logically presented by Peirce through a series of manuscripts that argue for existence of thought only by sign, with the complexity or type of sign relating more to the type of referring. In other words, the further away the referent is in relationship to the thought, the more complex the sign. Another way of viewing this hierarchy of cognition is to define the icon as a pure image. The more specific the sign, the more representative is the referring resulting in more meaningfulness in the sign.

An example (MS. 599 RR40) of an icon would be the existence of an image of an event in which a man in a town sees a balloon and he begins to stare at it. He is forced by his natural "instincts" to gaze and so others begin to gaze. The man's upward gaze points out the basic referent. Therefore, the gaze is an index. As the man is staring at the balloon, a bicyclist quickly passes by, almost running over the balloon gazer. The bicyclist automatically yells "Hi!" and automatically the balloon gazer exclaims, "Ah, a narrow escape!" The other observers turn and look in the direction of the escape. The man's "Hi" is again an index, but Peirce would say that it is a somewhat more perfect sign than just the upward gaze.

The reason that Peirce would say that the "Hi!" is a more perfect sign than the gaze is because the utterance added meaning to the context that the gaze couldn't. The "Hi!" could be accepted by the interpretant in a number of different ways, such as the "existence of danger" or "a friendly greeting." However, Peirce points out that the gaze cannot be interpreted falsely or truthfully. Only the "Hi!" can have such interpretations.

The mental image of the balloon gazer's situation is an icon; the gaze is an index sign as is the "Hi!"; but, an explanation of the balloon is a symbol since the interpretant can recognize the specificity of such an utterance. Peirce's separation of cognition into three levels of sign usage allows the language clinician to apply these levels to the semantic development of language-handicapped children. The assessment and remediation application allows for a semantic or cognitive distinction among communication (icon and index signs); language (icon, index, and symbol signs); and linguistics (a more perfect symbol usage). Peirce summarized the use of icon, index, and symbol signs for a cognitive theory of semiotics when he wrote:

> First by marking in the characters of that object when I call the sign an *Icon*, secondly, by being really connected with the object (interpretant), when I call sign an *Index*, third by being connected with that object for given interpretants, that is, by being mentally associated with the object, I call this a *Symbol*. (MS. 295. 00002,3)

## THE LANGUAGE SYSTEM

The semantic complexity of a message is increased by the application of several linguistic principles, including semanticity (refinement), displacement (referring), redundancy (structural development), productivity, and flexibility. These linguistic principles are explained in the following section. The application of these principles to language results in the most advanced level of development, discussed in detail in Chapter 6, "The Linguistic System."

### Semanticity

Brown (1973) discussed the fact that without meaningfulness nothing else would seem to matter in the study of language. The primary concern of this chapter has been to define meaningfulness in terms of semantics. Semanticity or meaningfulness is one of the most important linguistic aspects of language that seems to be critical to language acquisition and to the phenomenon of lexicalization.

Although icons, indices, and symbols of signs exist and allow for varying forms of referring, a speaker's ability to lexicalize, or add new items to his or her repertoire, is the result of semantic refinement. The refining of a sign eventually results in acquisition of more signs, each with slightly different information for new symbols to be created. Therefore, it is also possible that refinement is really the addition of thought or information about a lexical item until a new symbol is needed to represent the increased information. For example, "cat" may be used by a child to refer to an event, action, or object. The child's individual meaning is unique and specific to the child's use of "cat." The child's experiences surrounding the "cat" usage increase with the passage of time as the child acquires more information with each experience. Eventually, similarities and differences can only be expressed by adding a new symbol to represent the various signs. The acquisition of new symbols may be called lexicalization. The use of one term to represent others or the process of "overextension" is explained in the following chapters.

Lexicalization allows language skills to be refined and semanticity to be increased. For example, the child adds "cow," "dog," "milk," and "eat" to the earlier "cat" term, which in turn allows the child greater use of language skills. As more language is used, experience increases and so does the complexity of the child's system. Semanticity or meaningfulness supports any increase in the child's language complexity.

If a child stays at the icon and index levels, refining or semanticity probably does not occur as a real process. In order for a child to develop a linguistic system, semanticity needs to be apparent, especially during the second and third phases of development (see Chapters 4 and 5).

Pragmatists like Charles Peirce described semanticity according to various kinds of usage. Peirce suggested that the ways in which the terms are used also indicate the representations. Peirce illustrates this extension of semanticity with the example "cats and dogs." To say "It's raining cats and dogs" has no likeness to the terms "cats" and "dogs," but when combined in a particular usage, the meaning is extended and the concept is a perfect symbol.

In summary, semanticity is a property inherent in a true linguistic system. Without the ability to extend meaning in new contexts or situations, a person may express a sign with an icon or index but not with true symbols. The dynamic aspect of a true linguistic system is lost without semanticity—a way to increase meaning.

## Displacement

Brown (1973) added the principle of displacement to the other linguistic properties mentioned in his "Unbuttoned Introduction." In the literature the concept or notion of displacement has usually been treated as various forms of referring, or as related to time, space, or distance. The act of referring and the concept of space and time are related to each other. Referring is complicated by the extent to which an object, event idea, etc., is removed in time and/or space. Thus the further the sign is from "X," the more semantically complex is the symbol.

Peirce (MS 357.1866) suggested that there are three universal "conceptions" of reference: (1) reference to a ground; (2) reference to a correlate; (3) reference to an interpretant. Child development researchers suggest the same division as the child separates the event (ground) in relationship to the child's self; as the child separates himself or herself from others; and as the child separates others from a third person or interpretant.

Piaget (1955) discussed these notions in terms of egocentricity in which the child goes through various stages of relating the self to the environment. Researchers such as the Clarks (1971) viewed the three planes of spatial reference in terms of a child's acquisition of spatiotemporal markers, and clinicians (Lucas, 1980) viewed the reference planes in terms of remediation techniques for specific semantic language disorders. Whatever the perspective, it is apparent that there are various reference points and planes that are ways to refer to a sign by use of a symbol in relationship to the speaker and the speaker's reference points.

In order for an utterance to be truly symbolic and thus linguistic in nature, the principle of displacement must be met. For example, "Hi" does not add information to the setting and thus does not refer. When spoken, "Hi" represents a language skill but it does not meet the linguistic requirement of displacement. There is no separation of the sign and the act in space and time. There is no restatement of a common relationship and there is no joint relationship established. The greeting "Hi" seldom does anything but index a sign. Thus a child who is taught to greet may be said to have a language skill but certainly not a linguistic system. Neither the property of semanticity nor the property of displacement is present.

Some literature in psychology has dealt with displacement as a temporal concept (cognitive in nature) rather than as a linguistic principle. Stall (1982) attempted to study the acquisition of temporal concepts in deaf adolescents. She found that the separation between time as a psychological, cognitive ability and time as an acquired auditory language skill was impossible to make. Even when adolescent subjects who were deaf from birth said they knew what an "hour" or "minute" of time was, they still could not judge when a period of time had elapsed. The hearing adolescents who were matched on intelligence and vocabulary ability had no difficulty judging periods of elapsed time. The difference was so great between the hearing and deaf individuals that Stall thought there was something wrong with the tasks, and she went back and asked the adolescents about time concepts. For example, she asked, "What is an hour?" and the adolescent might reply, "Well, it's 60 minutes." Then Stall would ask, "How long does your math class last?" The deaf adolescent would reply that it was an hour long. It would seem that this adolescent was sure he had experienced the passing of an hour of time day after day in his hour-long math classes. However, when he was asked to perform a three-minute task, he said it took an hour to perform.

These deaf adolescents had the language skills but were missing something in terms of linguistic displacement, or perhaps it would be more accurate to say cognitive displacement. Stall (1982) discussed the relationship of time and space from several perspectives, since the literature is lacking in studies of the relationship between psychology and language as it pertains to the deaf population. From reading these perspectives, one can conclude that language skills were acquired through either visual or auditory channels but the ability to acquire the full potential of semanticity as it relates to displacement might be auditory in nature. Although not well tested at this time, some assumptions might be made.

It is possible that displacement could be visual, or in other words spatial in nature, as well as auditory or temporal in nature. For example, if an object is moved in position, only the position changes in relation to the speaker, not the object. Thus the relationship between the speaker and the object is a continuum through spatial distance. However, once an utterance is produced, time does not allow the same temporal relationship to ever repeat. For example, the utterance "Let's go to the store" has several types of referring or levels of linguistic displacement. "Let's" refers to more than one person in relationship to the speaker. "Go" is an act that will take place by the speaker and the hearer's interpretants. "To the store" refers to a place that is at a distance from the speaker but that can be reached by movement. The utterance "Let's go to the store" reflects a more sophisticated usage of referring or displacement by symbolic uses of sign than the utterance "Go store" even though the speaker's primary intent may be the same for both utterances. The utterance "Let's go to the store" when produced with other demonstrated linguistic properties suggests the acquisition of a linguistic system, whereas the utterance "Go store" represents the acquisition of early language skills.

The utterance "Let's go to the store" is more semantically complex and represents a certain ability to acquire the relationships between language and environmental acts, actions, and events. As stated in the principle of semanticity, the acquisition of additional information results in the speaker's ability to handle symbols that have no visual counterpart. The utterance "Justice is blind to those who are self-serving" may be understood by the sign-to-symbol conceptualization unique to the hearer. Without displacement of a sign through a symbol relationship, the hearer could not interpret this utterance. Furthermore, this type of displacement can no longer be coded visually but must include the multidirectional sense of audition. Further explanation of the auditory effects on language will be explained in Chapter 3.

## Redundancy

Linguistic discussion of redundancy in language is usually centered around two notions: (1) language is highly redundant and the message is kept intact by redundancy; and (2) language rules or principles are aimed at limiting redundancy. With the first notion, researchers view similar utterances as redundant in content. For example, "The men sailed ships" and "The men were sailors" might be considered to have the same general meaning. However, the two utterances are not equal in meaning since the referring in the two utterances is actually different. In "The men sailed ships" the sailing of ships or the function of the men is the important symbolic relationship. In "The men were sailors" the occupation of the men is the important symbolic relationship. No two propositions or ideas are ever equal in semantics since the underlying knowledge changes with each utterance and thus the referring relationship between sign and symbol also changes. This dynamic relationship between the speaker and the hearer in a context bound by past experiences will be discussed in terms of speech acts in Chapter 3.

The notion that language rules or principles are aimed at limiting redundancy is plausible. For example, ellipsis is the omission of redundant material which often results in an embedded structure. In "The man ate the beans" and "The man is sick," if both signs of "man" refer to the same person, this relationship is acknowledged by the speaker saying "The man who ate the beans is sick." The term "who" replaces the redundant term and becomes a place marker called a "constituent." It should be noted that children with good language skills but who exhibit problems acquiring a complete linguistic system demonstrate difficulty with embedded structures. In fact, sometimes these children do not recognize that the person is the same by perceptual characteristics so the child refers to the person as two separate people—one who eats the beans and one who gets sick. Sometimes if the child is asked if the person is the same, he or she will puzzle over the question and find characteristics that will make the person the same or will find characteristics that will make the person different. Usually if "different" is the answer, it is because the child sees the perceptual and functional characteristics of the person as different. Perhaps the person in one picture of a story book is wearing brown shoes and in the next picture the artist shaded the shoes so that they are closer to being black. The child who has difficulty with this redundancy is unable to organize the information in the pictures into conceptual relationships about displacement and semanticity.

Redundancy of meaning results in growth or development of language skills. In this way, redundancy is a linguistic process used to extend the semanticity and the displacement properties. Redundancy is actually necessary for a linguistic system to be developed. Another, perhaps more accurate, perspective is that a symbol's singular use for a multiplicity of signs is a form of redundancy that results in lexicalization by individuals and changes in societal conventions so that the symbol becomes more specific and less ambiguous. Thus redundancy appears to coordinate semanticity. The primary difference between the two processes is that semanticity is the result of some redundancy.

## Productivity

Productivity is a term often defined by the linguist as novel utterances produced by a speaker. However, that usage of the term is constraining. Productivity can be viewed not only as a variety of utterances, that is, quantitatively, but also as a variety of uses. As Austin (1962) suggested, "To say is to do." The utterances that are productive are those that perform a variety of functions.

## Flexibility

Flexibility is the counterpart of productivity. A language system is flexible when an utterance can be produced in a variety of situations. Productivity and flexibility may be viewed as functioning together. For a child to acquire a linguistic system, he or she must be able to produce a variety of novel utterances in a variety of situations to have a variety of effects on a hearer.

## THE LINGUISTIC SYSTEM

In the preceding section, five linguistic principles were discussed as being necessary to meet linguistic requirements. All of these linguistic properties are semantic in nature. In fact, the "normal speaking" adult's system may be viewed as linguistic in nature and based on an increasingly more complex semantic development. Semanticity, displacement, redundancy, productivity, and flexibility are found in the adult's system. Each of these principles may be traced from prelanguage development through language skills to the adult system by observing the semantic properties of the child's system. The early development of the sign is represented by relationships that are icons; increased knowledge allows for language to be represented in index; and the final sign-to-symbol relationship, capable of the highest level of displacement and resulting in semanticity, is truly symbolic.

Although the semantic components are being delineated, little has been said about the relationships of these components or the ways these components function. What determines when a system functions so that all linguistic properties are present?

## Language and the Linguistic System

It is not the semantic properties that trigger language skills. Language itself facilitates the acquisition of a linguistic system. The relationship between thought and language must be assumed in order to test hypotheses about the system. Assuming that language or a person's grammar is the product of physiological changes from incoming stimuli and organization of the stimuli, language may be viewed as a cortical act that provides the method to symbolize certain types of thought. Thoughts or concepts are hierarchically arranged in complexity so that a lexical item (concept) represents thought. As displacement through removal of the referent occurs and semanticity increases, the flexible and productive individual uses language to symbolize more complex thoughts, thereby limiting the language structure that might be redundant.

Clinical evidence supports the hypothesis that thought facilitates more language. The clinical evidence also suggests that the thought coded semantically is auditory for linguistic principles but may be represented visually for basic language skills. To support this hypothesis, semantics will be divided into the areas of presupposition, proposition, predication, and effects.

## Presupposition

Before a speaker's utterance, certain environmental information is available for processing. This information must match prior circumstances in some similar characteristics so that there is an identifiable relationship. This relationship represents what is known or is common with the speaker and the speaker's past. The identifiable information establishes the presupposition of the proposition and its arguments.

The presupposition is conceptualized in nature and this represents thought about the context as generated from past experiences coupled with a speaker's unique processing. Each person's active and passive organization of the information being received results in a slightly different set. This set provides the backdrop for communication and is sometimes referred to as the speaker's "preparatory set" (see Chapter 3).

The presupposition or conceptual information organized into a preparatory set allows the speaker to establish a relationship with a hearer. The presupposition includes the sources of reference either immediately available or displaced. As the reference sources become more available to both the speaker and the hearer, less specificity is needed in the message. However, information is increased if the presuppositions are not similar for the speaker and the hearer. Basically, the presupposition includes all thought prior to an utterance and establishes a cognitive preparatory set of semantic information.

## Proposition

Once the speaker has a presupposition about a context, the speaker uses a sign (icon, index, or symbol) to represent this notion. Whereas icons only show a relationship to a referent, the index may allow the speaker a chance to use language to show the relationship. For example, two strangers are walking down a hall. One of the strangers acknowledges the proximity of the other with "Hi!" Although the relationship is indexed, there is no new information added to the hearer's interpretation. However, the hearer may alter his or her belief set about the other stranger or generalize to other strangers. The hearer may think, "Gee, he is friendly'' or the hearer may automatically smile and not think anything more about the situation.

The hearer's own presupposition about the situation will determine the way in which the speaker's utterance will be utilized to alter beliefs, attitudes, or behaviors. If the ''Hi'' was an automatic greeting, the speaker may not have intended to alter the hearer's attitudes, beliefs, or behaviors. Thus the speaker's utterance was not a true proposition or idea. If the speaker intended to produce effects, the ''Hi'' was used to represent a nonspecified proposition. The proposition, often symbolized as ''X,'' is an idea that is purposefully conveyed. Unfortunately, the less specific an utterance is, the less likely it is that the intended proposition is conveyed. Every utterance that has a specified, intended effect on a hearer is said to have propositional content. The only utterances that are assumed not to have purpose and an intended proposition are echolalic, stereotypic, or automatic utterances.

Propositional content can be quite complex semantically. The complexity of the person's ideas increases with semanticity, redundancy, flexibility, and productivity. With the linguistic system, a speaker's utterance might consist of several propositions linked together by information about the idea, called the argument, which is often expressed as ''Y.'' Thus the argument explains the proposition. For example, a simple proposition-to-argument relationship would be ''X'' is ''Y,'' such as ''The dress is red.'' The information about the proposition or central idea defines the proposition, so the proposition and argument are relative to each other. Another example of ''X'' is ''Y'' would be ''She is not going.'' Remember, the structures do not determine the relationship, but the relationship is determined by the meaning.

The importance of being able to define semantic relationships by the use of propositional content affords the educator and clinician a method of determining semantic usage within a special event. If a child or adult is not able to stay on topic or to make transitions from topic to topic, the only way currently available to analyze this behavior is to look at the propositional content of the speaker. Specific errors are identifiable (Lucas, 1980) and remediation can be aimed at improving the semantic skills related to propositional content. However, it should be noted that analyzing a speaker's ability to stay on topic is still a method that just looks at part of the system. The reason why the symptom of not staying on topic is present must also be determined in order to theoretically understand *why* certain procedures are workable and why some are not.

## Effects

Given a presupposition about the preparatory set, the speaker produces an utterance act consisting of a certain propositional content given with sincerity, which is identified through a number of essential elements. These preparatory, propositional, sincerity, and essential elements constitute the speech act (Searle, 1969), which could be produced in a series to create a speech event. It appears that these semantic constituents are the units of structural analysis of a synergistic linguistic system when coupled with those previously described linguistic principles.

### Linguistic Principles and Speech Acts

Without these linguistic principles, speech acts may still be performed. For example, a three-year-old child might say, "Get me that digger!" The proposition of getting a digger is obvious to the speaker and the hearer, and the argument in terms of which digger is apparent, as is the function of who wants the digger. Furthermore, in a given preparatory content where it is assumed that the digger is available for the hearer to get and that the child will not or cannot get it, the sincerity of the conditions are met. When the child finally utters, "Give me that digger" and says it with the appropriate loudness, stress, and intonation while turned toward the hearer or the digger, the hearer responds by handing the digger to the child. The three-year-old child has met all of the conditions of a speech act.

The child has performed a speech act but probably has not met all of the conditions of a linguistic system. Although capable of very sophisticated language skills, the three-year-old's propositions are limited in displacement; properties of time, space, quantity, and quality; and, of course, there is reduced semanticity. Semanticity for lexicalization is observed through processes such as overextension (see Chapter 5). The three-year-old child in the above example was competent as a speech act performer but probably does not have access to a complete linguistic system so as to extend those speech acts to enable him to, for example, make promises, vows, swear oaths, make pledges, etc. The following section discusses communication, language, and linguistic systems in relation to the proposed model for language-handicapped populations.

### THE SEMANTIC SYSTEM

This chapter has discussed the complexity of semantics in terms of five linguistic properties and in terms of specific language skills for the production of a speech act in a given speech event. The underlying assumption is that semantics is the basis for language skills and the subsequently developed linguistic system. In order to support this assumption, data from the literature and from the language-disordered population must be noted. The rest of this chapter will briefly overview what is present in the normal development literature and the next chapter will incorporate the literature into a language model supported by data regarding language-disordered populations.

## Information/Knowledge

What a speaker "knows" about a situation is the speaker's knowledge. Knowledge of a situation and the speaker's knowledge are not the same as "linguistic knowledge." The speaker's linguistic knowledge has sometimes been referred to as a speaker's linguistic competence. Linguistic competence has to do with the speaker's ability to produce language skills and does not necessarily refer to content or to knowledge about the world. Knowledge can be viewed as the information that the speaker can talk about. In other words, there has to be some meaningfulness in a situation to set the stage for any utterance. The ability to produce the utterance comes from the conventions, that is, the code that is recognizable only by use and stored only when processed by the human brain.

This knowledge is the "stuff" out of which all aspects of semantics are made. The form that knowledge takes is probably biochemical in nature and the result of physiological transfer of neural impulses. The impulses must be organized for storage and retrieved in connection with novel situations, so some assumptions might be made about organization. It appears that normal language learners code two types of information—perceptual and functional.

The perceptual information is the sensory reception of how objects and events taste, touch, look, hear, or feel. The sign is attached when enough information of perceptual features has been acquired. For example, the two-year-old child calls all four-legged animals with tails "cats," not because they have four legs and a tail but because those perceptual characteristics configurate into a different shape which has been marked as "cats" by Mom.

Mom's symbol of cat had a different level of knowledge about animals, but the child related the animal with a sign for what the child had organized into an index. The fact that the child had limited knowledge may make the sign-symbol usage seem imperfect to the mother. She would then, presumably, proceed to correct the child's usage until the relationship seems semantically perfect.

The other type of early information is functional in nature. Although perceptual knowledge can be related to all senses, visual and tactile input play a significant role in providing size, shape, and color information. Remember that the size, shape, and color are not coded but rather the texture, configuration, organization, shade, hue, etc., are recorded in nonverbal types of code. The symbols that are acquired represent the vast amount of one's underlying knowledge. Semanticity adds to the organization so that lexicalization is rapid in the first years of development. Functional information is much like perceptual knowledge except that the senses by which it is coded may be limited.

Functional knowledge represents information about displacement, that is, relationships between activity and events. A simple functional piece of information is the activity related to an object. For example, a person *cuts* with a knife and *drinks* with a cup. Evidence from language-disordered children suggests that functional information is poorly coded for this population, and that the means of coding is primarily auditory. Based on this information from language-disordered populations coupled with a logical analysis of displacement, it seems possible that the functional information is coded auditorily, and as it is reorganized by semanticity, the reorganization is auditory and retrieval becomes auditory in nature.

Wernicke's area of the left temporal lobe of the cortex has typically been labeled as the auditory language portion of the brain. It might be that the linguistic principles, semantic in nature, may be attached to the auditory symbolic coding. This conclusion, if appropriate, has a significant contribution to the literature about what distinguishes human auditory language from other systems such as sign language systems used by the deaf population or symbol systems used by animals.

## SEMANTICS AND COGNITION

The purpose of the next section is to describe the relationship of Peirce's sign system to cognition. An operational definition of cognition might be simply "thinking." Although generalized, this operational definition allows more freedom in terms of eventually relating how cognition or "thinking" overlaps with language. In order to discuss this semantic-cognitive relationship, several questions must be addressed: What is thinking? How is thinking done? When does thinking occur? Where does thinking take place?

### What Is Thinking?

Thinking may be considered as beginning with sensory images constructed from organization of the external and/or internal reception of sensation in the receptor organs such as the eyes, ears, nose, mouth, skin, etc. Sensory impulses are organized into perceptual clusters. For example, "house cat" probably begins with sensory images but certainly is not confined only to sensation. The sensory images must be incorporated into other forms. Perhaps the senses organize information. For example, a cat will run when the auditory stimulus of barking is heard even though the cat is totally protected from the dog that is outside. In the cat's previous experience there has been enough organization of the sensory input (barking) to signal a change in its behavior. If the cat's behavior is changed by such repetitive association of the auditory message with the cat's experience, then in a classical sense the cat has demonstrated learning.

It is by logical assumption that learning may be seen as a product of the association of organized sensory input and experience through thinking or cognition. The basic thinking of the cat is a cortical act that requires more than integration at the lower peripheral nervous system. Perceptual clusters are cortically associated to experiences, resulting in predictable acts in the cat to demonstrate consistent responses.

Although the basic integration of sensory input into sensory images allows animals to show changes in behavior representative of learning, change is the simplest form of communication represented by the icon. The cat can demonstrate the change in behavior and thus the person watching assumes responsibility for the message and describes the relationship using a higher system of signs. Children who have experienced a serious deficit in the performance of the cortical areas of the brain responsible for sensory integration will demonstrate the corresponding level of thinking. For some children, the iconic sign system may be the highest level attained. The basic iconic sign is useful only as it relates to a hearer's willingness to interpret. Therefore, basic thinking or cognition begins with a person's internal organization of sensory input into images that are represented by the basic iconic sign. The thinking process must increase in complexity in order for higher level signs to be demonstrated.

**How Is Thinking Done?**

If signs are hierarchical and the first level of signs, the icons, represents the basic integration of sensory input, then the next higher level of signs must represent the way in which the thinking process is additive. Based on what is known or assumed about sensory input organization, there must come a time when the sensory input organization has no more meaning unless the person can attach a higher level of sign to represent the meaning.

Therefore, in order for meaning to occur, there must be a series of levels of processing. Studies of memory indicate three levels of processing. The first level is the sensory level of input that is short term in nature. This short-term memory appears to have no real meaning for the person since there is no retrieval. The second level of memory is the rehearsal stage, which is a transition between the sensory level and the way in which meaning becomes a reality. The third level is a recall-of-retrieval stage in which the sensory organization becomes recognized, that is, the person's past experiences have been attached to the present experience so as to make meaning or recognition of the past organizations.

It seems logical that at the last level of memory, the storage and subsequent retrieval of sensory organizations is synonymous with the term ''semantics.'' In other words, if the thinking is meaningful, the sensory organization has been processed until there is an attachment with previous organizations. The ability to utilize this retrieval level is directly correlated with a person's ability to learn, that is, to process incoming stimuli about an experience. The higher the level of sign, the more organization has occurred, which is representative of more learning.

How does the sensory input become a reality? This is really a physiological question. Research suggests that learning involves a change in the status of a cell.

If a person's cells are normal, the number of biochemical changes that could take place is probably infinite, allowing for an infinite representation of changing behavior, which is learning. The three levels of processing occurring above basic sensory integration must allow for meaning through retrieval recognized at the cortical areas of the brain.

### Where Does Thinking Occur?

Thinking takes place wherever the sensory organization can occur so as to be represented by a sign. Since the peripheral nervous system allows only for sensory integration of reflexive behavior, the central nervous system must be responsible for the represented signs. Furthermore, since these signs must link meaning with sensory organization, the cortical regions of the brain must be responsible. Evolution has allowed the human species to have a cortex expressly ready for the specification of higher levels of sign integration. Such a capacity is absent in the lower species.

Even though the human being can do tasks that other animals cannot, there must be an effort to understand the hierarchy of development within the human. The iconic sign of the human infant or severely, profoundly mentally handicapped person has many of the same characteristics as the signs in other species. Learning and communication are occurring at the same level but with very different expectations. The following section describes the person's higher levels of thinking.

### Cognition and Language

At some point of learning, an individual's cognition overlaps with his or her language. This overlap occurs when the sign representation has increased beyond the basic integration of sensory images to images that are represented by a sign that is more referential in nature—the index. At the point where a group of sensory experiences has become so closely organized that another sign can refer and predict its image, language becomes a product of the cognition.

Is language innate or learned? Obviously, according to the assumptions already presented in this chapter, the product of language is the result of learning. But are the language *skills* learned?

Learning appears to occur along with processing of the sensory information into organized units. This processing allows for the attachment of meaning when the experiences are frequent and related in time or proximity. The attachment occurs as the organized units become recognizable. These recognized units are representative of previous experiences and thus are usable.

The person who uses these units acquires the attachments of tags to the experience by other significant persons marking the experience. In other words, the parent talks to the child using conventions of the society. This talking attaches the tag to the experience for the child. The experience may now be referred to by the tag that the parent used. When the child who is physiologically capable of producing the tags has had frequent experiences that have had the temporal marking, the child uses the tag.

As relationships between the basic icons are developed, the child is able to assimilate the organized units into more advanced signs that represent more and more of the child's experiences. Finally, an index is used that is truly symbolic in nature and the sign is uttered as the product.

The original question was "Is language learned or is it innate?" Based on the hypothetical development presented in the preceding paragraphs, it appears that the conventional system is learned. However, the ability to attach signs to the processed sensory input varies according to the genetic endowment of the species. The human has cortical development for utilizing advanced types of signs. Furthermore, there are individual physiological differences that are a result of each person's heredity. These differences also result in differences of ability to acquire, store, and utilize sensory units.

The systematic and sequential development of each individual can be explained. Most of the structures follow principles inherent in the conventional system. However, certain qualities are found in most if not all languages that are studied. If the representation occurs through the utilization of cognition, the signs though different in convention should represent the same type of meaningfulness. For example, all languages show a "negative." How well could one represent the absence or presence, the denying of an act, or the rejection of an object if there were no way to represent these experiences?

The universal types of meaning across languages must be an inherent part of cognition rather than language. In other words, the members of the species are programmed physiologically to produce similar neural responses to stimuli and to organize them into perceptual units that are attached by the members of the species through language experiences. The species' uniqueness must account for the similarities of cognition or thinking and the differences among cultures is accounted for by the necessity of the conventions in that society. Finally, individual differences must be accounted for in part by individual differences in heredity.

## COGNITIVE SIMILARITIES

Those similarities in thinking based on shared human physiology are represented through signs by the use of language often referred to in the literatures as "universals" or "rules" or "principles." If the human species' way of thinking is responsible for these similarities, they should be separated from the differences found across the languages in various cultures. The following section describes some of the similarities.

## Negation

Bloom (1970) described three different meanings related to the use of negative forms of language usage. These include (a) the rejection of an act, (b) the denial of an event, and (c) the nonexistence of an object.

Although language signs are used to express these various types of cognitive negation, their meaning is really the recognition of actions, events, or objects in the environment as previously marked or tagged by another speaker for the language-acquiring child. Therefore, the cognition represents an organization of stimuli with the attachment of language to the organized perceptual units until the child thinks about sending the action away, denying that the event happened, or expressing the lack of presence. Since these are cognitive skills, the child's ability to do this type of organized thinking should be represented by a hierarchy of more complex signs.

The negation forms of thinking do express themselves through a higher, more complex set of signs as the child gets older. Prelinguistically, the child expresses the iconic representation through facial and body communication that is nonverbal. As the child attaches perceptually organized experience to the adult-modeled tags, he or she represents the thinking through basic signs that are usually indexed for the hearer. For example, the child points and says, "No!" Finally, the child expresses the referent as a predication about a proposition: "No, I don't want that stick!"

Whether or not the child's cognitive negation increases in complexity is debatable. Is the child's refinement of the sign system also a refinement of cognition or does the refinement in cognition represent a refinement of the representative sign system? Both of these possibilities exist.

Although negation is a cognitive act that is represented by a basic iconic sign, as the child's thinking expands through every sensory input, so does the child's level of organization for sign representation increase until there is enough organization of experience to be represented as a higher level sign. Therefore, the child who uses the symbolic level of signs actually refers and predicts a higher level of effect in the hearer than the child who is using iconic signs for basic "sender" communication.

Of course, the opposite of all the negation types is the actual existence, the action, or presence of an event or object. These are all present in the languages representing the basic forms of referring and predicating. Negation, like the linguistic principles mentioned earlier, is really a product of the thinking experience. Language and cognition overlap when the semantics or meaningfulness of an experience is recognized by the speaker, then coded and sent to the hearer.

**Modifiers**

All languages show the refinement and specification of referring and predicating through basic qualifiers that reflect the cognitive act. Clark and Clark (1977) present a table of various modifiers based on the work of Vendler (1968). The Clarks' list demonstrates some of the underlying cognitive meanings expressed through language by the various modifiers.

Articles were first on the Clarks' list. Articles ("a," "an," "the") distinguish between a specific and nonspecific referent, for example, while size modifiers distinguish between the overall mass, weight, and/or volume of an object. The essential point of this list of modifiers is that they represent basic ways that the human codes incoming stimuli. Some of the most obvious ways include the perceptual attributes of the objects, such as size, shape, color, texture, and material. For the functional attributes of actions and events, the incoming stimuli might be coded as to the time of the activity, the origin of the activity, or the manner in which the activity is completed.

Perceptual organization of thinking into various groupings allows for the development of new signs. In this case, the new signs are all modifiers. The basic referents are modified or specified in some way. The way in which the present relates one notion to another provides the point of reference for the development and subsequent use of a particular sign. For example, in order for a person to represent the "upness" of an object, the reference point would have to be the absence of "upness" or what is later marked with the sign as "downness."

Many modifiers are obviously marked as polars to show this opposition in learning. Spatiotemporal markers such as "before," "after," "next," "tomorrow," etc., are in opposition to their reference point. Other types of qualifiers such as "hot," "cold," "big," "little," etc., are also recognizable polars. It seems logical that these terms are relationships with obvious reference points, the opposition of the term. Therefore, the learning of such terms is really the acquisition of the underlying cognitive development that is the thinking and learning from experience.

**SUMMARY**

Meaning is the interplay among relationships, the relationships of persons, objects, actions, and events. As meaning develops in a child so does the complexity of cognitive representation through icons, indices, and symbols. This ability to represent relationships is pragmatic in nature. That is, it represents the meaningfulness of the speech act within a speech event. Even though the conventions of the representation are learned, the child's ability to encode, store, and retrieve the sensory organization or perception is species specific. Therefore, the representation of cognition is the organization of perceived properties. Given these theoretical notions of semantics, the form of language skills is conventional, whereas the meaning is a hierarchical acquisition of knowledge about relationships. The ability to represent complex relationships results in a linguistic, adultlike system of communication identifying the similarities and differences in what is perceived. Chapter 3 will describe the proposed synergistic system.

### REFERENCES

Austin, J.L. *How to do things with words*. London: Oxford University Press, 1962.

Bloom, L. *Language development: Form and function in emerging grammars*. Cambridge, Mass.: M.I.T. Press, 1970.

Brown, R. *A first language: The early stages*. Cambridge, Mass.: Harvard University Press, 1973.

Clark, H.H., & Clark, E.V. *Psychology and language*. New York: Harcourt Brace Jovanovich, 1977.

Esposito, J.L. On the origins and foundations of Peirce's semiotics. *Peirce Studies* (Edited by members of the Institute for Studies in Pragmaticism, Lubbock, Tex.), 1979. *1*, 19-24.

Katz, J.J. The realm of meaning. In G.A. Miller (Ed.), *Communication, language, and meaning*. New York: Basic Books, 1973.

Lucas, E.V. *Semantic and pragmatic language disorders: Assessment and remediation*. Rockville, Md.: Aspen Systems, 1980.

Lucas, E.V., & Sparks, J. *Speech act theory*. Unpublished research project, Texas Tech University, 1981.

Moerk, E.L. *Pragmatic and semantic aspects of early language development*. Baltimore: University Park Press, 1977.

Oehler, K. Peirce's foundation of a semiotic theory of cognition. *Peirce Studies* (Edited by members of the Institute for Studies in Pragmaticism, Lubbock, Tex.), 1979, *1*, 67-76.

Peirce, C.S. MS. 292.000008; 357.1866; 292.00009; 295.00002,3; 599.RR40. Institute for Studies in Pragmaticism. Texas Tech University, Lubbock, Texas.

Piaget, J. [*Language and thought of the child*] (M. Gabain, Trans.) Cleveland: Meridian Books, 1955. (Originally published 1926.)

Ransdell, J.M. The epistemic function of iconicity in perception. *Peirce Studies* (Edited by members of the Institute for Studies in Pragmaticism, Lubbock, Tex.), 1979, *1*, 51-66.

Searle, J.R. *Speech acts: An essay in the philosophy of language*. Cambridge, England: Cambridge University Press, 1969.

Stall, C.H. *The effect of early auditory deprivation on time estimation ability*. Unpublished doctoral dissertation, Texas Tech University, 1982.

Vendler, Z. *Adjectives and nominalizations*. The Hague: Mouton Publishers, 1968.

Wittgenstein, L. [*Philosophical investigations*] (G.E.M. Anscombe, Trans.) Oxford, England: Blackwell, 1953.

## Chapter 3

# Synergistics and Audition, Cognition, and Socialization

*A child's hour is but a tune, laughing, playing*
*Back from the past, learning for the future—*
*A way to find the new in the old.*

## Chapter Objectives

1.  Explain a theoretical relationship between cognition and socialization.
2.  Explain the relationship between audition and linguistics.
3.  Explain the relationship between linguistics and cognition.
4.  Explain how socialization and language interact with cognition.
5.  Explain the relationship between speech acts and synergistic principles.
6.  Explain how the speech act can be used to account for various relationships.
7.  Explain how the transition into the use of linguistic principles affects the speech act moment.
8.  Explain how semantics is considered the basis for prelinguistic, language, and linguistic development.
9.  Explain the relationship between pragmaticism and speech acts.
10. Describe the synergistic components of a speech act.

## INTRODUCTION

The purpose of this chapter is to describe the interaction among cognition, socialization, communication, language, and linguistics in a synergistic system of acquisition for learning. The basis for this system was established in Chapter 2 with an explanation of semantics. This chapter will relate the semantics to a workable unit, the speech act. The speech act will be used as the overall framework from which to consider the assessment and remediation of the language-disordered population. The available literature about atypical as well as typical acquisition of speech act development across the prelanguage, language, and linguistic phases of semantic development will be reviewed (also see Chapters 4, 5, and 6).

## THE SPEECH ACT

The pragmatists (e.g., Austin, 1962; James, 1952; Peirce, 1850-1890) established a framework from which was developed the modern notion of the speech act (e.g., Searle, 1969). For example, in writing about sign consequences, Peirce would tell the reader what he was going to discuss and the surrounding conditions for the discussion. This initial information would provide the preparatory set of the modern speech act. Then Peirce would state that a particular notion were true if its existence would prove the truth. This would establish the sincerity component of a speech act. Peirce would then describe the notion, the propositional content, by using the conventions or essential elements. (These semantic constituents will be discussed more fully later in this chapter.) Peirce's writing would parallel the performance of speech acts within a speech event. His arguments were logical and understandable because Peirce included all aspects of a speech act within the speech event. From Peirce's writing, it appears that if meaning were to be conveyed using the same pragmaticism methodology comparable to the performance of a series of speech acts, there would be more messages better received by the hearer and fewer disruptions than if only components of the speech act were available to the hearer.

The development of the speech act notion comes *not* from the idea that the communication event is necessarily logical but that to perform the speech act is to change the speaker and the hearer's attitudes, beliefs, and/or behaviors. These changes in both the speaker and the hearer result in a system that is believed to be synergistic. The psycholinguistic units (discussed in the preceding chapters) that describe the speaker's production cannot explain anything about how the synergistic system *between* the speaker and hearer is functioning. The changes within and between the speaker and hearer represent a dynamic system that allows the speaker to be an active part of a context in which the hearer's presence is of utmost importance.

The speaker's ability to communicate can only be evaluated in terms of the hearer's change rather than according to what the speaker utters. This change reflects the meaningfulness of the sign usage in context. Therefore, the speaker's utterances as part of the context are meaningful to the hearer under the specified conditions of the speech act. It seems unimportant to consider anything but the speech act in assessing or remediating language disorders. Considering anything but what is meaningful would result in a psycholinguistic approach to a synergistic system. In other words, with all that is meaningful, why settle for an incompatible approach to evaluating a child's system?

The following sections discuss how these meaningful aspects of the speaker and hearer in context result in acquisition and learning of meaning by the child. It should be noted that in considering the shared component between the speaker and hearer, the speaker's ability to receive and to make meaningful incoming auditory stimuli as well as the hearer's ability to interpret the speaker's product must be viewed in terms of social interaction.

## Cognition

How does the speech act fit into the realm of cognition? Perhaps a more appropriate first question would be "What is cognition?" Probably every educator has an "idea" of what cognition is "all about." For the purposes of this book, cognition refers to the person's ability to organize external stimuli at the cortical level into meaningful units that may be used for future experiences of learning (see Chapter 2). How does the speech act fit into this system of organization, retrieval, and future use?

The speech act is the unit that attaches meaning to the cognitively organized notions shared between speaker and hearer. The speaker organizes incoming stimuli received from the senses into meaningful units stored at the cortical level. But to use this information to affect the attitudes, beliefs, or behaviors of a hearer, the speaker must organize, retrieve, and use the meaningful units. The meaningfulness of the unit depends on the hearer's interpretation and marking of what is meaningful. The speech act or shared system between the speaker and hearer *is* the *use* of the organized information. Cognition is the general set of processes that allows for the speech act to exist.

## Socialization

Why would a speaker have a need to organize the information being received into a set of processes referred to as cognition? To be social, that is, to be involved in an interaction with another person, means to be able to share meaning. Thus, socialization is a primary reason for the speaker organizing incoming stimuli into meaningful units that could be used to affect the attitudes, beliefs, and/or behaviors of another person. In this way, the speaker may be able to request physical assistance or to share an experience that the hearer has not experienced.

The human species appears to have a need like all primates to be social (Hinde, 1972), to interact in expected or predicted ways with other members of society. The expected behaviors form the conventions of society. These conventions include not only verbal means but also nonverbal kinesics, proxemics, and paralinguistics. For example, a predicted behavior might be to stay within three feet of a speaker in order to convey warmth and friendship. In most North American cultures, however, if speaker and hearer are within three feet of each other the situation would be considered intimate and very uncomfortable for business associates and strangers (Fast, 1970). These nonverbal situations are part of the conventions expressed in the essential elements of the speech act along with the expected language skills of the society. The conventions of the language system would be shared by the hearer if the speaker is going to have a given intended effect.

The expected effect is really part of societal expectations. Where does a speaker get these expectations? The cognitive framework of the speaker determines his or her ability to utilize incoming information about the conventions. In other words, the speaker will not use conventions if he or she does not have the ability to organize the incoming stimuli—stimuli that provide the speaker with information about the constituents of conventions.

It should be apparent that the social aspects of conventions can only exist if the cognitive abilities are present. The cognitive abilities are organized by the semantic information input. If the speaker is able to receive and process nonverbal information as meaningful, the person will probably not present problems with social skills. Children who have problems with knowing whether or not to give eye contact or when or when not to talk are *not* experiencing social "imperception" problems, as was suggested by Yoder (1983). The problem that these children demonstrate in the nonverbal areas is also evidenced in their language or verbal skills. They are experiencing an overall problem in organizing what is processed (see Chapters 7 and 8). What about the cognitive abilities being present but not the social skills? What is the relationship between cognition and social abilities? That relationship is part of the synergistics of language acquisition and will be explained in the following section.

## SOCIALIZATION AND COGNITION

The relationship between socialization and cognition has been considered under several different theoretical frameworks. Probably the best-known framework for cognition has been the Piagetian interpretation of what a child could do based on different levels of ability. The child's ability also provided parallel advances of the social areas of development. Although the Piagetian framework (e.g., Piaget, 1955; Sinclair-de Zwart, 1973) is well researched and will be discussed to some extent later in this chapter, it is important to note here that the social aspects of development are *not* completely considered in the Piagetian interpretation of children's behavior. There are other frameworks that consider the social aspects from a different perspective.

The pragmatists' attempt to incorporate the nature of society with the individual's thought and subsequent consequences views social development as a product as well as a catalyst of learning. A Russian counterpart to Piaget considered the purpose of cognition as it is affected by language use. This Russian, Lev Semenovich Vygotsky, was born in 1896. He wrote *Thought and Language* in 1934. It was suppressed in 1936 shortly after his death and resurfaced in 1956 with an English translation and discussion provided by Hanfmann and Vakar (1962). Vygotsky considered the acts of a speaker to greatly affect cognitive thought. Since acts are influenced by societal conventions and thus social in purpose, Vygotsky's work is really a treatise on how language and thought are related in a synergistic process between effects and being affected.

**Thought and Language**

The primary consideration in discussing the relationship between thought and language is the effects that each has on the other. ''Thought'' and ''cognition'' are being used synonymously in this text but they are not necessarily the same. Thought may not be processed beyond the reception and recognition of sensory stimuli. For example, Peirce refers to this basic organization as the ''thought object.'' Any mammal by neurological disposition would be capable of a thought object. The ability to organize thought objects into meaningful units would require some other physiological skills and skills other than basic discrimination and recognition. Advanced processing of incoming stimuli would require retrieval and use according to conventional codes. One sophisticated way of doing this type of advanced processing would be to use language skills—a conventional verbal and nonverbal system developed through thought.

A person's ability to incorporate thought objects into a language system that would be capable of advancing language skills into a more sophisticated system (linguistics) could only be interactive in nature. The thought object is facilitated by the language skills but the language skills begin only by the cognitive processes that existed through neurological readiness coupled with environmental stimulation. This explanation of thought and language is primarily based on Vygotsky's presentation. The following section will discuss the importance of the Piagetian contribution to the development of cognition. The term ''development of cognition'' will be used to represent the series of semantic processes that are utilized by the child in the learning system.

## Piaget and Cognition

According to Piaget, a child's thought differs in quality from an adult's thought but not necessarily in quantity. The qualitative difference appears to be in what encompasses the thought. This difference appears logical when one examines the performance of children at various ages on various tasks. However, the Piagetian literature does not explain what is responsible for the differences at various ages, except to say that a child learns differently at different ages, therefore performance reflects the cognitive learning process at that particular age.

There appears to be a social need for the child to develop a more sophisticated way of interacting in the environment, and, from this social need, the child organizes his or her thought objects into more sophisticated groups of semantics or information for other uses. Thus the changes in the child's performance on tasks are the result of changes in the social need and subsequent cognitive need to refine the system. For example, a three-year-old child has different information about what constitutes "table" than an eight-year-old child or an adult speaker.

Piaget's classification of developmental changes as observed by an adult represent perceptive recognition of the product of semantic refinement. The child who does not show these changes in task performance has a less refined semantic system. The development of meaning through a shared social speaker-hearer context requires significant social purpose as well as cognitive processing. The product is one of sociocognitive integration and *not* one of cognition.

Utilizing the Piagetian stages of cognitive development without consideration of the social importance of the child's performance is comparable to the psycholinguistic analysis of a speaker without consideration of the hearer's importance. The significant contribution of social purpose is well presented in the description by Vygotsky (1962) of an autistic child. According to the Piagetian stages, the autistic child would be performing at the earliest level of social development, with the egocentric child somewhere between the autistic child and the adult.

The autistic child may not evidence many social skills by either verbal or nonverbal means. But the lack of these social skills is not the same as describing the aberrant social behavior that the autistic child may evidence. Likewise, the three-year-old child, who is described as being egocentric or self-centered, is capable of language skills that autistic children may structurally present without the ability to utilize flexibly or productively. An autistic child may repeat the sentence structures heard in a television commercial but not be able to ask for a drink of water. However, a ten-month-old infant will be able to demonstrate how to get an adult hearer to provide a drink of water. The discrepancies between the autistic child's social development and the egocentric child's social development is related to the interaction between cognition and socialization.

The Piagetian notion that the ability to perform certain tasks is reflective of cognitive ability is logically acceptable. However, the notion that these abilities are reflective of a parallel development in social skills is less so. Data collected from children at all ages indicates that even the youngest infant is an active aggressor on the environment as long as the environment is affected. The child's purpose for interacting is social, with the ability to perform more advanced tasks contingent on the child's ability to affect others' behaviors. The child who is developing typically never seems to be a passive, uninterested child. The child seeks information only as part of the adult-created speech event.

When the child is an active participant there is little opportunity for the child to *develop* social skills. The child must come with the social need to refine the interaction between the speaker and hearer through cognitive development. The child's ability to perform tasks or to respond to a situation according to societal conventions is based on the child's use of the social purpose to develop cognitive processes for refinement of meaning or semantics. The term ''through cognitive development'' refers to the acquisition of semantics by the child's ability to receive sensory information, organize the information into bits, and then use the information so as to refine the system.

The human or primate need to be social affects the child's ability to organize the information in his or her environment. The child aggressively seeks out the components of the information so as to refine the system of social interaction. For example, the three-year-old child whose play behavior reflects his or her own interests in the ''here and now'' is not necessarily *un*interested in other people or other environmental activities. The three-year-old child is using the same socially motivated acts to acquire knowledge about more than just his or her ideas or situation as the eight-year-old child or the adult.

From the social need to interact in ways that become more refined by societal requirements, the child develops information that is used to facilitate new ways to process information. The new ways to process information are evidenced in the child's qualitatively different ways to solve problems, to do tasks, to represent underlying information. These qualitatively different ways to demonstrate underlying information may be organized into four basic stages consistent with the stages of Piaget: sensorimotor development, perceptual invariants development, preoperational concrete development, formal operation development. Each of these stages as they represent the development of meaning out of social need will be discussed in the following sections.

### Sensorimotor Development

The first general stage of development is called the sensorimotor stage. According to the Piagetian framework, a child would be demonstrating such motor responses to sensory input as creeping, crawling, tasting objects, gathering information. According to a pragmaticism methodology, the child at this stage represents ideas by means of an icon or index. However, considering the importance of social requirements, these signs become more refined as the child processes more information during a shared speaker-hearer interaction. Sensorimotor activity is actually the primary mode of environment exploration used by the child to socially affect others. The way that others respond to the child attaches meaning to the experience for the child.

The child in this period of development is limited by his or her sensorimotor capacity. In order to demonstrate more advanced acquisition of information, the child would have to demonstrate other behaviors.

## Perceptual Invariants

During the second phase of development the child does demonstrate more advanced ways of organizing information received from the shared speaker-hearer context. The child during this phase organizes the attributes or perceptual features of objects, actions, and events with the functional features of relationships to form signs representative of not only icons and indices but also symbols. This child learns about the environment not only from the shared speaker-hearer context but also through incidental acquisition. In other words, a child who is chewing on a ball may be acquiring some stimulation from the act but the amount of learning is limited unless the child can also demonstrate a change in behavior. The only human consequences of sign development will occur as a shared product between speaker and hearer.

The child in this stage of organization utilizes previous shared experiences to recognize, organize, and manipulate similar agents, actions, objects, and events. The child's manipulation results in change in the child and change in the hearer. The hearer's interpretation and nonverbal response provides additional information for the child to further analyze and incorporate into past information. Thus the child in this stage of development is able to recognize the perceptual and functional attributes of water in a number of different vessels, a favorite Piagetian exercise.

Although the child in this phase of development is capable of demonstrating a refinement of information about how features relate to each other, these relationships are not well represented until the next set of behaviors are provided for observation. The next set of behaviors demonstrate that the child is able to relate features through the development of symbol signs that relate sets of signs. Thus the development of the next set of behaviors represents the child's ability to operate on symbols for limited uses.

## Preoperational Concrete Development

The preoperational phase of development is represented by the child being able to demonstrate how the signs or symbols are used to facilitate further learning about the symbols. This semantic phase of development is observed in children who use sophisticated language skills to learn about concepts of displacement, to acquire advanced semanticity, and to acquire a productive and flexible sign system.

The child during this phase will perform semantic tasks related to quantity and quality according to the principles of one or more dimensions. This child has not acquired enough information to manipulate symbols in a pure displacement using a symbol to learn about another symbol without consideration for any of the previously used perceptual or functional semantic attributes or features. It is not until the next phase of semantic development that the child is able to manipulate symbols.

## Formal Operations

The fourth phase of semantic development is characterized by the child's ability to manipulate symbols without consideration for the semantic features representative of the symbol. For example, the child in the previous phases of development was using signs to represent his or her relationships to the environment sensorily and perceptually. The child can now take a sign that represents this past sensory and perceptual information to define or learn about other symbols.

Through this ability to manipulate "pure symbols" the adolescent and adult are capable of deductive and inductive reasoning, analogous thinking, creating puns, analyzing jokes, and in essence creating new forms of symbolic use. The person capable of formal operations thinks in definitions since the symbols can now stand for other symbols with relating the sign use to concrete experiences. Definitions of nontangible concepts such as "justice," "endowment," "morning," "ethics," etc., are easily processed and demonstrated through linguistic skills.

From the previous discussion of the four phases of semantic development there should be some conclusions about the interaction between socialization and cognition:

- The child actively seeks ways to collect incoming stimuli for information processing.
- The information represents the semantic development of the child.
- The semantic development will not increase unless the child seeks the information.
- The child must be physiologically ready to represent the underlying semantics. The following section discusses the relationship among these four conclusions.

## SOCIOCOGNITIVE RELATIONSHIPS

The child has certain physiological prerequisites for the reception of incoming stimuli (e.g., Strand, 1978). These unfold through physical maturation during the first five to seven years of development. However, the social need to acquire semantic information continues until there is no more life. From the first day of life to death, a human being demonstrates the social need to interact with his or her environment. Although there are "closet cases" reported in the literature and instances of people who spent years with minimal social interaction, the ability to survive optimally is quite dependent on the opportunity to interact with others in the environment. Many "failure to thrive" children have severe medical reasons for not living, but most of them show little response to the environment because of neglect and lack of shared social interaction.

Observation of the caregivers with their "failure to thrive" children is really a lesson in physical manipulation without social attachment. The caregiver carries the child, feeds the child, and puts the child down without a synergistic act of sharing. The assumed nonverbal sharing of the context by gaze, smiles, and eye contact does not happen between these children and their caregivers. "Caregiver" is an overstatement of the situation and the term "parent" cannot hide the lack of nurturing and social bonding in these children.

In all fairness to the individuals who are responsible for the well-being of these children, the child has not given the parent or caregiver anything to share. The reciprocity of a shared speaker-hearer situation is not only contingent on the child's cognitive capability but also on the child's ability to physiologically demonstrate the ability. The child who cannot demonstrate through physiological development has limited ways to socially act on the environment. The caregiver cannot interpret the child's intent without those behaviors and so there does not develop a shared speaker-hearer event.

Working with children who have not developed any but the most rudimentary communication because of the lack of social, not cognitive, development is a challenge. Measuring their cognitive ability is almost impossible until they are provided social development through intervention so that there is a set of behaviors available to represent cognitive development. Many of these children make significant gains once an opportunity for social interaction through some behavior is provided and they develop skills comparable to what would be expected of a child of significantly more cognitive ability. For example, a child who showed little response to environmental stimuli (auditory, visual, or tactile) at the age of 18 months showed self-help skills of dressing and feeding by the age of 24 months when given the opportunity to interact under intervention. This child would have originally been diagnosed as severely, profoundly mentally retarded and in fact this child was placed in an agency for such children. Upon intervention, the child learned a number of skills that only children with more "cognitive" ability could have demonstrated. At 36 months the child was moved to an early childhood education classroom for handicapped but not mentally retarded children. At present this child shows significant variation in learning from what is typical. The ability to learn appears to be directly related to the amount of information provided in a social interaction.

This child's interaction with the environment is primarily based on how to get things (including people) to do things for him. He hasn't really gone beyond basic needs into more socially interactive events and his development is not expected to show an increase in learning until there is more evidence of a desire to interact socially. The teacher is going to have to impose this desire on the child if the child can be expected to perform tasks typical of older children.

The preceding example of a socially handicapped child provides evidence of the need of a child to be social prior to being able to demonstrate cognitive abilities. The stages of Piaget are related to a child's ability to act on the environment from a social need to learn or refine human interaction. Without that need a child will demonstrate few of the so-called tasks for cognitive assessment. A child who has no reason for interacting has no reason to explore the environment. Therefore, nonverbal as well as verbal abilities do not develop as expected. Such a child may show little response to the environment and may be assumed to be cortically blind and deaf, as was the child described in the preceding example. Without a consideration for the synergistic quality of social development affecting cognitive demonstration, that child could have been left without appropriate assessment and diagnosis. The child was provided with appropriate assessment because the evaluation team was interested not in what the child could demonstrate but *how* the child demonstrated behaviors representative of learning (see also Chapter 4). The synergistic system that affects sociocognitive development in the infant is the same system that affects linguistic development in the adolescent.

**Linguistic Sociocognitive Effects**

A developmentalist might say that a child must be able to act motorically on the environment to develop certain behaviors representative of cognitive development but in fact the child need not act motorically so much as act to affect the acts of others. The term "sensorimotor" represents the mode of expression as well as the mode of active pursuit for most children; however, children born with severe physical handicaps will develop a sophisticated system of concept use if given appropriate modes and provided that the child does not have other physiological limitations on cognitive development. The children who were considered "failure to thrive" babies or the children who show little response to the environment will not demonstrate cognitive development any more than a physically handicapped child who is not provided with a system or mode of interaction.

Incredible, positive changes have been observed in the "personality" of severely physically handicapped children, adolescents, and adults when a mode for active pursuit of information was provided by intervention. For example, a three-year-old child who was physically limited to eye gaze for indexing was never observed to initiate an interaction between an adult and the child until the child had a communication board with choices for requests to act upon the environment. Thereupon the child attempted to initiate through all sorts of behavioral and visual changes.

In another case, a thirteen-year-old adolescent was believed to have "cognitive abilities" comparable to his peers as assessed by the school diagnostician and as reported by the parents and aides. However, the child was limited by a system that could not provide for the flexible learning consistent with adolescent systems. He had a communication board that acted as a mode of communication once someone else had initiated an act. The child basically had a system of responding to others' speech acts. He could not perform a speech act and could only demonstrate learning through the use of an aide that would ask questions for the child to answer. It was a relationship much like Twenty Questions, the popular game of guessing what the other person is thinking about.

During the past year, this adolescent has received a microcomputer for use in learning at school and communicating with others. Athough the interfacing with various systems in the environment is taking time, the adolescent has shown an incredible difference in social participation. He tries not only through the board but through motor behaviors, speech (mostly unintelligible), and facial changes to communicate with people in the environment. Furthermore, the child has shown interest in learning how to feed and dress himself.

This child had had the best treatment in the schools and home since he was diagnosed as having brain damage at birth, but it was only when he received the opportunity to be an active participant in the *shared* act between a speaker and a hearer that he seemed to blossom. Reports from those who have known this child suggest that he now has purpose for being involved.

The child demonstrated enough behavior that the assumed "cognitive equality" with his peers was soon tested. By use of the microcomputer it was found that he was missing some of the linguistic properties that most adolescents would be able to demonstrate. He was unable to represent some of the displacement properties of the language, such as those related to space and time as well as quantity and quality. This lack of ability could be related to two factors: (1) the child had no way to receive advanced information about the properties since there was never developed a shared speaker and hearer relationship; and (2) the child had progressed for a number of years without the need to represent the notion of more than one by adding plurals, etc. These two factors will be discussed in more depth in Chapters 5 and 6.

The effects of social opportunity from the individual's need to be social appears to be like a catalyst for using physiological development to acquire information from the environment. Social development does not appear to be the product of cognitive thought. The thought becomes meaningful only as the child is able to manipulate or change the objects, actions, and events in his or her environment.

A child's unwillingness to be with a stranger or the demonstration of "stranger anxiety" is not a lack of social development but a representation of underlying semantic development. Such a child demonstrates unwillingness to be with a stranger because he or she has acquired sufficient information about the environment to recognize the voice as different, the touch as different, or even the person's perfume as different. Likewise, an older child will reflect his or her parent's anxiety to leave, not because the child is afraid to leave but because the parent is giving verbal and nonverbal cues that the parent is anxious. For example, the parent might say "Now you stay here and be a big boy. Mama will be back in a little while." Most children will willingly go with a stranger by three years of age if the adults in the context do not show their anxiety or if the person taking the child does not act anxious or secretive.

Children who are deficient in semantic development, that is, deficient in the ability to perceive changes in the environment, will limply go with strangers. Likewise, these children are often considered "fussy" because caregivers are unable to soothe or comfort them. The child continues to cry or fuss when the environmental stimuli change. The effect of this "fussy" child is that the caregivers are not being actively changed by the child. The child does not have the semantic development to respond to the environment in a way to change it. There is not sufficient cognitive development from incoming stimuli to be socially demonstrated. These children are not active learners.

## Sociocognitive Differences

There seems to be an interaction between what might be assumed to be social and what might be assumed to be cognitive. Social skills are usually those abilities that the child demonstrates for maintaining interaction, initiating interaction, and producing change in the interaction. Cognitive abilities are usually those skills that reflect the child's ability to think and act in novel situations. Although the ability to act or think and the ability to interact appear to be related, there are distinctions between the social and cognitive skills, as evidenced by children who are handicapped more in one area than the other.

The primary distinction between cognitive skills and social ability has to do with the purpose or intent of an act. It appears that a child will perform an act or respond to another's act for a variety of reasons that are social in nature. For example, a child may want an object or someone's attention. These desires are social in nature. However, the child's ability to communicate these desires is not only a product of the child's genetic endowment but also his or her ability to produce cortical changes demonstrating cognitive ability.

The relationship between the child's purpose for performing an act and the ability to perform an act may be described according to a number of sociocognitive processes. These processes affect the development of communication into language and finally linguistics. Because these social skills and cognitive abilities are related but separate, it seems appropriate to separate the child's product or tool called language from the child's sociocognitive processes. Many psycholinguists in the field of communication disorders do not make such a separation (e.g., Muma, 1978), which perpetuates a nebulous, hazy approach to the treatment of language-disordered children.

The treatment of language-handicapped children necessitates an understanding of the reason the child is not progressing as expected. The child's functioning may be a result of a problem with social or cognitive development. The resulting breakdown in the system will be different for the two types of problems (see Chapters 7, 9, 10, and 11). For theoretical purposes, the lack of distinction between cognition and language is unwarranted. There appears to be a distinction between the ability and the purpose to perform an act. The following section will discuss the relationship between language and sociocognitive properties.

## LANGUAGE AND SOCIOCOGNITIVE PROPERTIES

The interrelationship between the child's social need and the child's ability to continue to have needs and to be able to act on those needs is separate from the acquisition of tools for meeting those needs. In other words, the child's social and cognitive development is not the same as the child's development of tools for representing sociocognitive development. This representation or development of tools is the acquisition of language.

Language serves as a tool for meeting those needs and for facilitating the learning of new needs. Language is the form of the tool—represented by phonology, morphology, and syntax—whereas the underlying basis is cognitive in nature and determined by semantic development. The development of the semantic system is a result of the social need of the child created partly by the environment and partly by the child's physiology.

Language skills are measurable in discrete performance units according to psycholinguistic or linguistic variables such as words, grammatical morphemes, parts of speech, transformations, and so forth. The underlying system of semantics is measured by the overall context. The components of the context, including the shared referents, the message, the effects of the speaker and hearer, illustrate the use of language for social effects according to semantic or cognitive principles. This contextual act may be called a speech act. The speech act consists of semantic constituents called the preparatory set, the propositional content, the sincerity rule, and those essential elements of society's conventions necessary to have a specific effect on a hearer.

The speech act semantic constituents are not complete until the contextual act has been satisfied so that a hearer has been affected in some manner. Therefore, these semantic principles are not just constituents of the speech act but are also the processes of sociocognitive development. The effects and purpose for the effects are social in nature but the ability to perform the act is semantic or cognitive in nature. The speech act is the performance within the context or it is the contextual act, but it is *not* a product. The speech act is an active set of processes that allows participants to learn and grow through the use of utterance acts, or language.

In order to understand the dynamic system of processes that occur in the performance of any given speech act, each of the semantic constituents will be examined—the propositional content, preparatory set, sincerity, and essential elements.

## Propositional Content

A speaker's ideas originate from external stimuli received through the senses and sent as electrical or chemical impulses to the cortex, where the physiological changes of the cells allow the stimulation to be organized into semantic units. These semantic units could be called bundles of semantic features. The bundling of the features occurs automatically according to the person's past experiences. These bundled features become larger units that are attached by speakers in the child's environment to a lexical tag or referential meaning. The referring establishes the predications of the child's basic thought or proposition. The proposition and predications become part of the child's organization. In other words, as the child acts on the environment, the speakers of a language mark the acts with language. This marking by the use of language allows the child to increase his or her organization of the underlying semantic features being received and perceived. The lexical tags become part of the child's internal organization, not according to the adult speakers but according to the child's previous semantic development.

Previous semantic development becomes the basis for every way that the child could possibly organize new information. As the child acquires sufficient information to use language to refer to the underlying semantic knowledge shared with a hearer in a given context, the child has the ability to produce a verbal proposition. This proposition is the content of the utterance act that the child produces. For example, the child says, ''I want my bear.'' The context is interpreted by the adult hearer as a situation in which the child sees her bear and reaches for the bear. Therefore, the adult believes that the child wants the adult to hand the child the bear. The primary proposition of the child's uttered words is ''want.'' This child is also able to explain what is wanted and thus is able to refer to the object as ''bear.''

The proposition is expanded to include the "what" constituent. In this explanation the child has included something about the proposition, a primary predication.

These propositions and predications are part of the child's semantic development within his or her environment. The interpretation by the hearer represents the actual proposition of the speech act. If there were no effects on a hearer, the proposition would exist only in the child's mind as a thought object. However, the acquisition of language allows the child to produce changes in the environment according to the way in which the hearer interprets the child's utterance.

The interpretation of the utterance greatly depends on the amount of shared information the speaker and hearer utilize. Similar past experiences or similar semantic notions in a given situation produce a context that has more shared information than unshared information. This semantic notion of the context is called the preparatory set, which is part of the dynamic semantic system.

## Preparatory Set

A speaker's ability to refer requires shared information about the referent. To place the referent into a proposition as interpreted by a hearer requires shared information about the proposition. And for the speaker to produce certain desired effects in a hearer, he or she must say something about the proposition in a predication that is shared by the speaker and hearer according to past semantic experiences. This shared semantic system is the preparatory set.

Some researchers have estimated that about 60 to 65 percent of the shared semantic system comes from nonverbal stimuli in the environment. For example, the referents may be physically present or the notions (predications) about the referents might be present, as in the case of a given room. The speaker in the room is processing the contents of the room according to past experiences in this room or rooms similar in nature. The hearer also processes incoming stimuli about the room according to past experiences. The more information the speaker and hearer share about this room, the less verbal information must be provided in order to have a certain effect on a hearer. If there is enough shared semantic information, the speaker might say, "Hey!" And the hearer might say, "Yeh, I forgot to close the door!" The speaker and hearer shared sufficient information so that the preparatory set was as close as possible between two people. The preparatory set was so well understood or shared that the speaker didn't have to perform an utterance act with the proposition and predication. The hearer produced the utterance act instead.

The sharing of a preparatory set of semantic information allows the speaker to produce an intended effect on the hearer. The amount of responsibility necessary for the speech act to be performed is equally shared between the speaker and hearer by means of the preparatory set. Whenever the semantic information is not sufficiently shared or when there is not an adequate preparatory set established between two parties, the speech act will not be performed. An utterance act might be interpreted differently than intended so that a different speech act is performed.

The dynamic properties of this semantic system should be apparent. In the case of the preparatory condition of the speech act, the set is different for each individual since past experiences are also different. The amount that is shared allows for speech acts to be interpreted according to the preparatory set. A speaker cannot decide that the utterance act will have a specific effect—only the hearer can decide that interpretation. For example, the speaker wants the hearer to pass the saltshaker and says, "May I have the salt?" The hearer might have a different semantic set about the situation and say, "No, you have had enough salt today."

The speech act occurs only when it happens. One of the semantic conditions that determines the speech act is the preparatory set that exists as shared semantic information. Whether or not the speaker is interpreted as intended partly depends on the sincerity condition of the speech act.

## Sincerity Condition

When the speaker performs an utterance act, the hearer will assume that the speaker intends to perform the act as specified. This condition is called the sincerity constituent. The speaker says, "May I have the saltshaker?" and the hearer assumes that the speaker really does want the saltshaker. A violation of the sincerity condition occurs when the speaker intends something other than specified or when the conditions of the preparatory set dictate something other than intended.

Violations of the sincerity condition include indirect speech acts such as "Could you pass the salt, please?" It is obvious to both the speaker and the hearer that the hearer is capable of passing the salt. The real intent of this utterance act is that the speaker is requesting the salt. Most children have difficulty with indirect speech acts, which is why a teacher does not say to kindergarten children "Why don't you take your seats" if she wants them to sit down.

Other violations of the sincerity condition include the utterance act that is produced as a joke or in pretending. For example, "You be the man" when the hearer is a female teacher. In this role play situation, the speaker and hearer recognize the preparatory conditions and agree on the pretended intent. The ability of the hearer to understand depends on the shared semantic information from the context as well as sufficient semantic knowledge of conventions to know when to interpret the utterance act differently. Chapter 5 describes some of the violations that three-year-old children are capable of understanding if the system is developing according to what is expected.

The sincerity condition exists according to the speaker and hearer's ability to match the propositional content with the preparatory set that each has developed. Whether or not an utterance act is interpreted as the speaker intended depends on the two persons in a given context with a given shared background. The way in which the speaker may affect the hearer's attitudes, beliefs, and/or behaviors depends on the speaker's ability to use certain essential conventional elements.

## Essential Elements

The essential elements of a speech act are all of the nonverbal and verbal signs that are shared by a society. These shared meanings or signs are considered the society's conventions. Among the conventions are components of the speech act moment, such as paralinguistic features, gestures, facial postures, body positioning, language skills, gaze, eye contact, and the like. The use of language as a tool is determined by the conventions of the society so that the essential element is in part the use of language. However, the preparatory set, propositional content, and sincerity condition depend also on the way the language as well as all of the essential elements are used.

The child acquires the essential elements through interaction in the environment. The social requisite of the essential element is part of the dynamic system. The child's ability to acquire the social conventions is also part of the system. The combination of the social need and the cognitive ability results in an interactive system of acquisition. The child performs more and more acts upon the environment that are verbally organized so that the system by existing allows the child to actively learn. This sociocognitive process might be considered synergistic in nature.

## THE SYNERGISTIC SYSTEM

The synergistic system of speech act performances consists of an interrelationship among the social needs and cognitive abilities of an active learner. The conventions that are acquired through these sociocognitive abilities are representations of the underlying meaning that the child is acquiring. Such representation builds as semantic features through the basic icon to an index into the symbol.

Speech act development represents an interactive set of sociocognitive processes such that the child who cannot develop a social need does not continue to demonstrate active learning. Likewise, the child who has not been capable of organizing incoming stimuli into cognitive abilities does not demonstrate a social need for learning. The interrelationship between need or purpose and ability allows for language skills to develop.

The system that does not interact in this manner is incomplete and so is the representation. Unfortunately, the incomplete system does not continue to function as expected. Because the child's system *is* synergistic, the interruption of the system is also synergistic. In other words, if the child is not able to develop a social purpose for interaction so as to demonstrate cognitive abilities, the child's ability to learn is also changed. *The acquisition of the conventions for representation of the child's semantic learning is not linear.*

## Escalated Development

With an understanding of the dynamic significance of the speech act performance, one can recognize the importance of the synergistic concept. The synergistic system allows the child to acquire semantic information in a logarithmic fashion that escalates the development of ways to represent semantic development. Although there are many nonverbal ways of representing this semantic knowledge, the child's ability to manipulate symbols comes through the acquisition of language as a tool for representation.

When the system is disturbed the entire process of escalating the development is also disturbed. The child does not continue to develop the semantic system as previously expected. For example, a child might continue to acquire pieces of the semantic groundwork so that he or she acquires some language skills but the language skills may be disorganized. This disorganized language pattern is the result of an impairment in the synergistic system. However, whatever the system has been doing will continue. Therefore, the child who was typically doing "A" to get "BB" semantic development continues to get "CCC" or "DDDD." However, the child with an impairment in the system might go from "A" to "C" and then to "L" and back to "D." There is no linear progression in either system but the breakdown in the system results in a nonescalating type of development.

This nonescalating type of development is often seen in children as stereotyped utterances, utterances that are rigid in content, limited speech act performances, limited frequency of utterances, etc. The synergistic value of the system is often greatly impaired in a breakdown of the system or in a system that is not able to utilize social purpose for representing cognitive abilities.

Since the system functions as an integrated series of units, the representation is best described as the semantic conditions are met through the speech acts. An analysis of the speech act quickly discovers the problem with a system that is not unfolding as expected since the speech act is a dynamic notion. The pragmaticism methodology of studying the use of signs according to the meaningful or semantic conditions allows the educator to observe the functioning of a system so as to assess the system and plan remediation for an impaired system.

From this pragmaticism methodology it is also apparent that a child with an impairment in representation is also a child with an impairment in the system. This child's system is not the same system that typical development would predict. The outcome of impaired systems might also be predictable according to the problem. Chapter 7 discusses some of the predictions of disordered systems. When the system is truly synergistic and operates as expected, the child is capable of learning through the performance of speech acts.

## LEARNING THROUGH SPEECH ACTS

Although a child begins life as a hearer, the child's nonverbal system is quite actively organizing others' verbal systems. The system is unique to the child because each child organizes the system according to personal experiences. These experiences become part of the semantic system that allows the child to increase the amount of information that may be organized at any one time. The system, although unique to the child, is part of a greater system of contextual acts.

Within the context, caregivers are providing a tremendous amount of meaning through interpretation of the child's acts as well as the caregiver's acts. If the child is not able to join in the contextual system of the speech act, the effects on the hearer or caregiver become minimal. The caregiver does not continue to be stimulated or to learn from the context and, of course, the child's learning is already limited by the fact that he or she is not able to engage in the system.

The parent or caregiver begins to just meet the child's physical needs without adding to the enrichment of the child's system. This minimum set of actions cannot be called a true interaction since the two people are not involved in a system of exchange. Whenever there lacks a true interaction, the child is not learning from the environment. The problem is circular—the child is unable to provide the necessary set of behaviors for the parent to interpret and this keeps the parent from being able to add information to the child and thus facilitate the functioning of the child's system.

Parents of handicapped children often express how difficult it is to meet the child's needs. When these parents are observed, they are often quite capable of meeting the child's physical needs. It is the parent's social needs that are not being met. The child is not providing any feedback about the environment for the parent to comment on, to respond to, to understand the child, etc. The true synergistic system that produces the speech act is not in effect. The parent does not perform speech acts since the child cannot interpret and the child does not act on the parent's physical caregiving.

The physiological need to be stimulated and to be a part of this contextual system of synergistic development is real. Children who are not capable of establishing this system and parents who are not capable of providing this system do not get their social needs met for cognitive representation. They do not learn from the situation. There is a clinical way to investigate the validity of these statements. When the next child who is not interacting with a caregiver is brought for an evaluation, consider whether or not the semantic conditions are being met. Since there is no interaction, the conditions will not be met. The parent or caregiver is minimally learning from the situation if it is the child who is responsible for the lack of interaction. If it is the parent who is responsible for the lack of interaction, the parent will have minimal capability of performing speech acts. His or her utterances will be difficult to understand.

## Learning Systems

A child who is not capable of establishing a learning system with the environment may show minimal acquisition of self-help skills such as putting on clothes but the individual will not develop an advanced tool such as language for advanced learning purposes. Consider, for example, five individuals who for a variety of etiologies were restricted to prelanguage communication skills and had never been in a treatment program including school.

These five individuals had one thing in common—they were able to learn adaptive behavior for dressing or feeding or physically meeting needs if the need could be met in the immediate environment. They ranged in age from eight years old to adult and all demonstrated the ability to learn from the manipulation of the environment. For example, one person had acquired some visual configuration discrimination of words by watching television and another individual had learned how to take apart electronic equipment such as a stereo and put it back together.

Although these individuals had the cognitive ability to learn, a synergistic system between the social need and the cognitive ability had not occurred. Each of these individuals had been almost totally excluded from the speech act system somewhere in his or her early developmental history. For example, in one case the parents had not accepted the child and the child spent most of his first eleven years sitting in a watering trough on a ranch totally isolated from other people except when the child fed himself while others were around. The deprivation had resulted in tremendous problems physically as well as cognitively. Even with the physical deformities of the legs from sitting in the water trough, this child, like the other four individuals, grew into a fairly normal looking person with limited communication abilities.

When intervention was begun with each of these individuals, auditory symbols were not effective. The child or adult had not acquired a system in which semantic development could come from auditory input. Were these individuals the way they were because of an auditory inability to acquire the conventions rather than because of the social, speech act deprivation? This is a difficult question to answer except to say that for some of these individuals the auditory system was facilitated. In one case the adult learned to play a guitar and one of the younger individuals developed speech through visual signing.

From intervention through the use of visual cues (sign language or reading, for example), these five individuals were able to acquire more complex uses of signs. It appears that they were able to do more incidental types of learning through the unidirectional sense of vision and less through the multidirectional sense of audition. This is also logical from the point of view of pragmaticism methodology, since the auditory component of the contextual system is the most displaced and the most meaningful component when interpreted—most meaningful because the auditory sign-to-symbol relationship allows the active learner to develop more semantic information until there is what Peirce would call a "perfect symbol." An example of a perfect symbol might be "government" or "justice" or "synergistic." The ability to understand or to interpret these perfect symbols rests on the user's ability to acquire sufficient information about the underlying semantic features. The only way to acquire these features is through a marking system between a speaker and a hearer in which the referent need not be present. This can occur only through audition that can hold the referent in place even though the referent can't be touched, held, or manipulated.

When sufficient auditory information has occurred, the user is able to interpret the perfect symbol—one that does not have referential meaning but rather meaning through experience in the oral-aural system. The relationship between cognition and socialization is developed to its maximum level through audition. The primary means of auditory development comes through the established interaction of a caregiver and child in an interaction. This interaction develops the child's ability to learn because there is a need to learn about the context. Each piece of sensory information that is received and acted upon becomes part of the child's system that facilitates the need for more learning.

When the speech act dynamics become a part of the child's synergistic learning system, the child shows tremendous growth in the language tool. More and more sophisticated means of representation are needed as the child learns more and more about the environment.

## SUMMARY

The synergistic system is a speech act paradigm between a child and a caregiver that have a need to interact so as to express semantic development about the environment. As long as there exists this need between the two individuals and as long as the child's *and* the parent's system is functioning in a *truly* synergistic way, the child will develop a number of verbal and nonverbal tools for representing semantic development.

The first semantic development is represented through basic communication or prelanguage skills (see also Chapter 4), which is then used to facilitate certain sociocognitive processes for language development (see also Chapter 5). Finally, the information becomes so refined through audition that the child has facilitated the maximum use of linguistic representation (see also Chapter 6).

The interrelationship between audition, cognition, and socialization is one that can best be described as synergistic. An interruption in any of the three parts of the system—audition, cognition, socialization—will result in a different functioning system. The next three chapters will describe the development in each of the three phases of semantic acquisition—prelanguage, language, and linguistic.

## REFERENCES

Austin, J.L. *How to do things with words*. London: Oxford University Press, 1962.

Fast, J. *Body language*. New York: Evans, 1970.

Hinde, R.A. (Ed.). *Non-verbal communication*. Cambridge, England: Cambridge University Press, 1972.

James, W. Some principles of philosophy. In M.J. Adler (Ed.), *The Principles of Psychology* (Great Books of the Western World). Chicago: The University of Chicago, 1952.

Muma, J.R. *Language handbook*. Englewood Cliffs, N.J.: Prentice-Hall, 1978.

Peirce, C.S. Collection of manuscripts at the Peirce Institute, Lubbock, Texas (Texas Tech University) (M.S. 292.00009; MS 295.00002, 3; MS 599.RR40), 1850-1890.

Piaget, J. [*Language and thought of the child*] (M. Gabain, Trans.) Cleveland: Meridian Books, 1955. (Originally published, 1926.)

Searle, J.R. *Speech acts: An essay in the philosophy of language*. Cambridge, England: Cambridge University Press, 1969.

Sinclair-de Zwart, H. Language acquisition and cognitive development. In T.E. Moore (Ed.), *Cognitive development and the acquisition of language*. New York: Academic Press, 1973.

Strand, F.L. *Physiology*. New York: Macmillan, 1978.

Vygotsky, L.S. [*Thought and language*] (E. Hanfmann, G. Vakar, Trans.) Cambridge, Mass.: M.I.T. Press, 1962. (Originally published, 1934.)

Yoder, D. A linguistic workshop. Lubbock, Tex., January 1983.

## Chapter 4

# Phase One: Prelanguage Development

*The silent reach, the silent face,*
*The beautiful sounds of silence*
*Whispered the infant.*

## Chapter Objectives

1. Describe the operational processes of the prelanguage child.
2. Explain the relationship between semantics and preparation for language skills.
3. Explain the relationship between semantics and the sociocognitive development of the pre-language child.
4. Explain why this phase is referred to as the prelanguage phase of semantic development.
5. Explain what is meant by the term ''semantic feature.''
6. Explain what is meant by the term ''spontaneous imitation.''
7. Explain the production changes during the prelanguage phase in terms of motor development.
8. Explain the relationship between knowledge and semantic development in this phase.
9. Explain the signs or characteristics of the transition between Phase One and Phase Two.

## INTRODUCTION

The purpose of this chapter is to integrate the information provided in Chapters 1, 2, and 3 about communication into the first phase of development referred to as Phase One—The Prelanguage System. The term "prelanguage" is used to denote the fact that at this stage of development the child does not yet have a language system. In fact, this child has very few language skills so that most of the communication is done through nonverbal markers or indices. Take the example of a cup. A nonverbal marker is an object, action, or an event indicating that the hearer is looking at the cup. The child's pointing marks a shared referent of the "speaker" (the nonverbal, prelanguage child) and the hearer.

An index does not share a referent but marks the communication that the hearer interprets or assumes. For example, an adult is playing with an infant who raises his shoulders slightly when the activity ceases. The adult recognizes the relationship between the activity ceasing and the child's body movements and assumes that the body movement is a way to get the adult to begin play. This assumption or interpretation of the child's activity makes the child's body movement act as an index. In other words, the adult assumes that this movement indicates a specific desire, need, or want, and in some way the index changes the environment. The main difference between the nonverbal marker and the index has to do with the clarity of the message. With the marker, the speaker and hearer share a referent, whereas with the index, the hearer assumes a need or want for the child. The burden of the message is with the hearer and is not shared between the speaker and the hearer.

### Developing Indices and Markers

At some point in a child's existence, there is some nonverbal movement or vocalization that can be assumed by the hearer so that the child can directly or unknowingly (indirectly) indicate a need, desire, or want. Sometimes the indicator is so unconventional or insignificant in nature that it goes unnoticed and the child does not affect someone. As suggested in the preceding chapters, if another person is not affected, the child will show even fewer behaviors that could be considered indicators. Under typical conditions and in typical learning environments, the indicators appear to be part of the child's growth pattern and so little concern is spent trying to decide what might be considered an index or indicator. Only after the child produces a significant number of indicators that are interpreted and acted upon by caregiving adults does a child show any sort of marking in an exchange between the caregivers and the child.

**Indicator Development**

Since communication comes before the language skills necessary to formulate or develop a linguistic system, the earliest forms of communication must be considered. The indicator is one of the first forms of communication. The indicator is considered a form of communication because a message is assumed on the part of the hearer and the hearer acts as if the indicator had changed the hearer's behavior in some desired manner. There is an incredible number of natural indicators that are acted upon by the adult hearers in any child's environment. These natural indicators include the motor developmental patterns, the child's change in facial expression according to changes in the environment, the child's daily activity patterns.

The change in motor developmental patterns is as important if not more significant in affecting a child's communication patterns as the change in vocalization. The literature primarily groups the newborn child's motor patterns into a gradual change from jerky, arrhythmical to unjerky, rhythmical movements sometime during the first year. This change in patterns can be seen in the following description: A two-month-old baby exhibits jerky movements in all extremities. The arms and legs constantly wiggle even when the infant is feeding or asleep. As the central nervous system develops, the infant's jerky movements begin to show some rounded kicking of the feet and some extension of the arms. A child who is four months old will usually show some kicks of both feet that are rounded in movement rather than jerky and show some rounded extension of the arms toward a caregiver. The child's motor development is still progressing so that the child no longer feels floppy. There is some development of the trunk and neck and the child begins to hold his or her head up, getting ready for trunk control that will be sufficient for the child to sit supported.

By six months of age many babies can sit, resting against an arm or a person's chest so that there is just a little extra support of the trunk. The child is learning how to separate the arms and legs from the rest of the body so that each extremity may be moved independently. By eight months, the child can sit independently. This means the child has freed trunk control from movement of the legs and arms. Sitting unsupported, the child may be able to lean against one side and reach for something, take it with a sufficient grasp, and bring it to his or her mouth. The child can look while sitting unsupported in all directions and the tracking of the eyes that was fairly well developed by three months now becomes a tool to get people to get specific objects and not just to attend to needs.

Prior to this time, the child could look at an object or indicate through crying or some other vocalization a change in basic needs. By eight months, the child is demonstrating a change in the environment through the use of the eyes. By ten months the child has enough independence between the extremities and the trunk that the child can pull his or her body up so that legs and trunk may act separately.

By twelve months the child moves only one foot, separate from the rest of the body, to indicate motor readiness for walking. It's not long before the child is walking.

The changes in the first year of motor development are constantly interpreted by perceptive caregivers. The child reaches for an object and the parent puts a bottle, rattle, toy, or whatever is nearby in the child's hand. If the child drops the object, the caregiver usually picks up the object and tries to continue, under the assumption that the child wants the object. If the child kicks rhythmically during the changing of a diaper, the parent usually interprets this movement as a sign of relief and assigns a positive feeling to the act for the child. With this assumption, the parent talks pleasantly to the child, using a higher-pitched intonation pattern and shorter utterances while smiling. The child looks at the change in the adult's face and the parent assigns the notion of understanding and recognition to the child. The parent might say, "Oh, you like to play!" This becomes a start signal for the parent to play a finger or toe game with the infant. The more the child changes with each of the parent changes, the more likely it is for the adult to assign some meaning to the change and to perpetuate more change by using the assigned meaning as a signal to change.

It's not difficult to see why the infant becomes such a joy for the caregivers. The more the child wiggles, reaches, watches, and responds to the caregivers' watching, reaching, playing, and changing, the more complex the infant's use of signs. This early relationship between the child and significant others in the environment is a speaker-hearer shared relationship that cannot be underestimated in its sociocognitive effect on the child's development.

The early behavioral changes act as sociocognitive indicators of communication. The term "sociocognitive" is used to denote the interplay between cognitive development and social interaction described in Chapter 3. The child's response to the caregiver's changes records information about the environment in the child's brain. The caregiver's input or changes are also recorded in some fashion so that the child's cortical region is being stimulated for further physiological development. These cognitive changes, which are really recorded information for further organization and use, are perpetuated through the interaction of the caregiver and the child. The interaction is social in nature so that the cognitive changes continue to occur; that is, learning continues to occur because the child has some social interaction with the caregiver.

These changes that the parent or caregiver uses to promote more changes in the context allow for learning to progress. More and more information about the sensory input of the changes and about the caregiver's responses continues to be encoded by the child. Each time the child's behavior is interpreted as an indicator of some need, the adult has added information to the child about relationships in the environment. For example, the child wiggles his or her feet and the parent says, "Oh, you want to play wiggles!" Then the parent begins to wiggle each of the child's toes, laughing, tickling, and talking to the child. The child may have innocently wiggled his or her feet; the parent assumed the indicator of wanting to play; and then the parent acted as if the child had changed the environment through wiggling his or her feet. The parent verbally marked the event with language as well as with hand movements, smiles, tickles, etc.

Since most children are social in nature, this type of adult-to-child interaction sets the stage for the child's acquisition of certain relationships in the environment—relationships that describe the acts between actions, agents, objects, and events. The basic indicators that are developmental changes allow the child to communicate via the adult's interpretation. Bates (1979) described some of the child's first interactive behaviors as prototype communicative acts. In a sense, these indicators are prototypes since the burden for an act to be communicative is always with the hearer.

Bruner (1975) describes the relationship between the child's activity and the caregiver according to action. He calls the interaction between the parent's activity and the child's activity "joint action" (1974). This is an excellent term for the process that is shared between the wiggles of the child and the interpretations of the caregiver. If either of the participants would cease his or her activity, the interaction would also cease. Therefore, the motion between the two participants is really a "joint activity." The result or product of the "joint attention" to a referent of action, object, or event is shared through the child's and adult's joint activity.

These early indicating behaviors are also interpreted in terms of perlocutionary acts (Bates, Camaioni, & Volterra, 1975). It is true that the act is not locutionary in the sense that there is an intended meaning, but the infant's motor acts may also not be perlocutionary. The child may not have an intended meaning but may perform an act that carries assumed meaning by the adult. If the child's meaning were clearly obvious to the child and the hearer, the child would have no reason for refining and beginning to show specification through vocal acts. It would seem that the first acts of the child are communicative to the hearer only in the sense of an assumed indicator that is interpreted by the adult. Later, these indicators take on more meaning by the child and actually become markers for specific referents by the deliberate use of gestures.

## Development of Markers

The indicators that are assumed by the adult or caregiver allow for information to be coded representing sociocognitive development. Such social acts necessitate a refinement of the system so that communication may become intentional and purposive in semantics and meaning is apparently shared by both the speaker and hearer. As the indicators are used by the adult, the adult assigns meaning to specific actions, objects, and events through primarily linguistic means. For example, the child reaches and the adult says, "Oh, you want your cup!" The adult has assumed the child wanted the cup and turned the child's arm extension into a purposeful act of indicating a want. The adult then identifies the desired object as a ''cup.'' This identification by the adult is a marking skill that allows the child to receive more information about the context and store it with his or her previous experiential information. Basically, the adult's marking allows for a refinement or narrowing of information about a situation.

The narrowing or refinement of information is not the result of limiting information but the result of adding information so that the child can develop organized units. Since there are probably some physiological restrictions, the increase in information requires the child to do more organization. This organization is based solely on the physiological properties of the child in combination with the child's past experiences. During the prelanguage phase the child is able to nonverbally indicate all of the various relationships of the environment and begin to demonstrate some mutual conventions with adults or others. This shows that the child has acquired the necessary information through previous experiences and that the child is capable of receiving or encoding the marking of the environment by the speakers (adults) and can put it with past information for use as a joint referent.

For example, information from previous experiences has been encoded in terms of basic intonation patterns referring to specific states. The child begins using these intonation patterns coupled with the sounds that have been coded. The closer the patterns are to the conventions of the adult, the closer the information appears to represent what the adult might interpret.

The child produces those sound patterns that are physiologically the easiest coupled with those sound patterns that are in the child's environment. A pattern might be ''mama'' and the parent immediately interprets the sound pattern as an indicator that the child wants the mother. If the mother is present, referring to mother might make this vocalization more of a marker. In both cases, the communication form is no longer just a motoric act but the child is now into vocalization and the vocalization can be either as an icon or a sign of an index.

**Developing Signs**

The ability of the child to develop a sign during this prelanguage phase depends not only on the interpretation of adults but also on the child's ability to physiologically develop. The central nervous system is still developing, as is the positioning of the larynx in relation to the pharynx. There is also learning taking place that is probably an active change in the physiological makeup of the cortex. The sociocognitive indicators contribute to the first necessary process in the later acquisition of language skills. This process is a result of the indicators increasing in frequency until some of the indicators actually become markers through nonverbal modes of communication. When these nonverbal markers become more complex, there appears the use of vocalization that also pairs the nonverbal markers. For example, the child points to the cup and says, "cup." The caregiver immediately responds to the nonverbal and vocal communication by giving the cup to the child. The act of giving the cup to the child is now recorded by the child as an experience with information similar to other experiences.

At this time, the child is probably using a sign to represent an index. The message is dependent on the hearer, but the child has vocally added something more than would have been expected in an automatic act meaningful only as interpreted by the adult. There are many prelanguage subcomponents that could be analyzed according to the psycholinguistic, static methods described in Chapters 1 and 2. However, the most important aspect of development at any phase is that nothing is discrete. During the prelanguage phase there is a process taking place between the child and the significant people in the child's environment. This process is a form of deixis in which the individuals share a portion of the environment and through this sharing an interaction can be maintained.

The maintenance of interaction (McLean & Snyder-McLean, 1978) can be described in terms of the nonverbal, vocal, or both nonverbal and vocal interaction on the part of the child as well as the nonverbal, vocal, or both nonverbal and vocal interaction on the part of the adult. For any type of interaction to be maintained, there must be some sort of communication that has meaning to one of the speakers.

When the one speaker gets tired of assuming the meaning for both speakers, the situation will break down. For example, the adult initiates interaction with a child by saying "Do you want your cup?" The adult says this with a higher than usual pitch, a smile, and while extending the cup toward the child. The child pays no attention to the interaction attempt. The parent will probably go ahead and put the cup within the child's space and perhaps even in the child's hand. If the child still does not gaze at the cup, manipulate the cup, throw the cup, or attend to the adult with some indicator, the communication attempt stops. Since "normal" children will respond to all sorts of stimuli from the environment, the parent usually maintains the interaction.

Once the child vocalizes, the parent or caregiver begins to allow the child more responsibility in the relationship. Before the first vocalization the parent might pause at the end of a nonverbal exchange but now the parent pauses and waits for more of an exchange from the child. Children who have the sociocognitive requisites to become more verbal may not show verbal skills until there is the social expectation on the part of the hearer for the child to respond or to initiate the basic requests for needs and wants from the environment. Therefore, the beginning of the child's use of signs as icons or indices in the environment depends not only on the child's own physiological readiness, and the cognitive contextual readiness, but also on social effects. Note that the basic human desire to be social can be fulfilled by nonverbal maintenance of interaction without acquiring verbal skills. However, without the social desire, nothing appears to be developing as expected.

As described in Chapter 3, the readiness of the context with both the speaker and the hearer as part of the context is considered the preparatory set. Once the child becomes part of the adult's preparatory set, the child is in a position to acquire significant amounts of information through the process of *deixis*. Deixis requires the preparatory set and all of the components of that set to function. Prior to the establishment of a deixis, the child is developing the prerequisites necessary to establish an interactive relationship with the significant people in his or her environment. However, the deixis process is a complete interaction in which the burden of the communication task rests not only with the hearer. By the time the child is capable of using signs, the deixis is close to being established. During the prelanguage phase the deixis process provides the child with the prerequisites for more complex semantic development.

## SEMANTIC NOTIONS

Leonard (1976) described the relationship of certain semantic concepts in the child. These semantic notions are organized around the child's interaction with the objects, actions, people, and events in the child's environment. Although the child may have nonverbally expressed various relationships, as described in the previous two sections of this chapter, the child does not verbally express these relationships without indicating how more than one object, action, or event is contextually bound to another object, action, or event. Until the child can verbally express these relationships, the adult assumes the relationship for the child. For example, the child says, "Doggie!" The adult says, "The dog is eating!" Because the child pointed to the dog at the same time that the child performed an utterance act while the dog was eating, the adult might interpret the child's utterance as showing a relationship between the dog and the act of eating. Much of the literature appears to make these assumptions for the child. There is no problem with these assumptions except for the purposes of research. In other words, it is the adult's assumption that promotes the information acquisition process of the child for further learning of how to communicate. But to say that the child has used a vocalization such as "doggie" to represent a specific semantic notion is not necessarily an accurate description of the way a child develops.

Note the characteristics of the process:

1. The child is developing a deixis with the caregivers and significant others in the environment.
2. The speakers linguistically mark the acts that the child participates in as part of the preparatory set.
3. As the child participates in these relationships between acts and adult linguistic marking, the child acquires more information about the situation organizing the information.

4. The adult also nonverbally marks these relationships for the child so that the child's acts also become relationships.

These relationships have been described in the literature with terminology that originally came from the case grammar of researchers such as Fillmore (1968) and Chafe (1970). The relationships that exist in the child's environment are very different from the relationships between words in a grammatical construction. It should be noted that although many of the semantic notion terms are from case grammar, to describe the child's usage from the viewpoint of adult grammatical construction may be an error. The child's own vocabulary set (lexicon) reflects meaningful relationships with the context and not necessarily with adult grammar. The basic difference is that case grammar describes how words are used within a construction, whereas the child's use of these semantic relationships describes *how* the child is functioning in the environment.

Semantic relationships that represent concepts such as agent-action or action-object are grammatical notions that are adult definitions *not* representative of the child's relationships. Such relationships or semantic notions could be expressed nonverbally as well as verbally.

These semantic notions include relationships that represent by marking each of the following situations: agent performing an action, an action being performed on an object, an agent in relationship to an action receiving an object, an action of position, an object being placed in a position, an object being given to a person as a similar indirect recipient. These semantic notions may also be in a relationship that describes the function of the child's utterance act (Lucas, 1980). This function is different from the relationship and so should be discussed separately.

## SEMANTIC FUNCTIONS

The way an utterance is intended to function or the way an adult assumes an utterance functions is known as the semantic function of the relationship. For example, an utterance act may relate an agent with the performance of an action and that may also serve as the function. In other words, it is assumed that the child wanted to perform an utterance act that indicates what the agent is doing. If that is the case, this would be a simple assertion of "X is Y," as described in Chapters 2 and 3. However, the utterance may indicate that something is to occur again and so the literature describes this as the semantic function of recurrence. In terms of a semantic relationship the utterance might have been "more juice" and based on the context that the adult assumed the child wanted more juice. This utterance act would describe the recurrence of juice, which is the function of the juice to the qualifier "more." However, it is slightly misleading to assume that the entire utterance functions as a recurrence. The entire utterance within a preparatory set and the given appropriate essential elements functions as a request to obtain juice. Therefore, a distinction between the function of the lexical items within the utterance act as compared to the function of the overall utterance is necessary.

The semantic functions described in the literature include recurrence, possession, location, existence, etc. These semantic functions indicate what the relationship between the words should indicate. However, the function of the entire utterance might be more appropriately described in terms of what the purpose is assumed to be by the hearer. For example, in recurrence, the utterance act shows a semantic relationship between a qualifier or quantifier and the object, action, or event. The semantic function is to get something to occur again. When the utterance act is produced, there is usually a request for an object, action, or event. With possession, there again is a qualifier in relationship to the speaker. When the utterance act is performed, the child indicates this relationship usually through a simple X or Y assertion.

Even though these first utterances might be described in terms of semantic relationships to the child and the child's environment, in terms of semantic functions and the overall utterance, the prelanguage child produces few if any complete speech acts.

## DEVELOPMENT OF SPEECH ACTS

A classic study by Dore (1973) is repeatedly used in the literature to show what early children's utterances represent. However, it should be noted that these early utterances as described by the context represent the adult's interpretation in far too many instances. Dore manages to circumvent this problem by calling his list of speech acts "primitive speech acts." Unfortunately, the reason for calling these utterances primitive speech acts is seldom addressed in the literature. Individuals continue to include these acts as part of a child's early development.

The list that Dore provides for speech acts really can be divided into those that become speech acts with all of the required linguistic properties and those that do not. The acts that will meet the requirements of an adult semantic system except for linguistic form include: requests for actions and possibly answers; protesting, which is similar to some demands (Lucas, 1977); and calling. Those acts not included in the requirements of an adult semantic system include: labeling, greeting, practicing, repeating, and answering. To see the difference, each group will be examined separately.

### Primitive Speech Acts

The term "primitive" denotes an immature or crude form. The term "primitive speech acts" (PSAs) includes those acts that would meet all requirements of a speech act (preparatory set, propositional content, sincerity, and essential elements) with the use of primitive or rudimentary language skills not yet a part of a linguistic system. These primitive speech acts continue to develop through the child's ability to be more specific with use of advanced skills until the linguistic system consists of a series of speech acts in speech events.

The requests (Dore, 1973) include all of the semantic components, except that the child cannot meet the requirements of a language/linguistic system.

Protesting (Dore, 1973) is almost the same as "denial" (Lucas, 1980) and other forms of rejecting an object, action, or event of a hearer. The specifications for this act include all of the semantic properties except the ability to use language in a linguistic system for the essential elements. Callings (Dore, 1973) do act to get someone's attention and do meet all the semantic requirements, with the language component of the essential element improving with acquisition of the conventions.

### Interpretations of Speech Acts

Because Dore used an adult interpretation as part of the criteria to determine what the intent of the utterance might be, the methodology led him to include several nonspeech act categories that do not represent even a primitive attempt at a speech act by the child. For example, if a speech act must have a preparatory set that includes a hearer, then practicing cannot be a speech act. Practicing has no intended effect on any hearer. It would not be included as a speech act. The vocalizations would be considered nonpurposeful. This does not mean that the utterances of a child when not directed at a hearer are not part of a developmental pattern. But it does mean that the utterances will not continue to occur unless the child is disordered in development. If the utterances were to continue, they would represent nonprocessed, nonmeaningful productions.

Labeling also could not be considered a speech act. "Labeling" is a term used to represent the adult's interpretation of the child's purpose in producing an utterance. Since children do not continue to label, the purpose as interpreted by the adult is not real. In other words, the child would continue to have this social need to label if it were real; since the child does not continue to label, the adult's interpretation must be the adult's intent or purpose, not the child's intent. Again, this does not mean that the child who exhibits this type of behavior does not have another need. But it does mean that the act of labeling does not meet the semantic properties of a speech act and therefore is not part of a child's sociocognitive development for more advanced language skills. Another implication is that labeling from an adult perspective is probably a worthless task to teach a child since all of the meaning rests with the hearer, not the child or the speaker. From clinical work, it is apparent that children may be taught to attach a label to a variety of things upon cue but still not be able to increase language skills. This lack of increase is a result of the failure to meet the requirements of the semantic properties of the speech act (preparatory set, propositional, sincerity, essential elements).

Greeting, repeating, and answering are like practicing and labeling. The adult assumes an interpretation of the intent, but the child is not really capable of specifying the intent for the utterance to have the social purpose of affecting the hearer in some way. These latter PSAs really do not meet even the most primitive or rudimentary components of the speech act.

Thus, those acts that meet the speech act requirements meet the semantic requisites of language development, whereas those acts such as labeling, practicing, and answering do not meet the semantic requirements and therefore do not act as a learning device for facilitating language through the sociocognitive processes.

## COMMUNICATIVE ACT

If the child produces very few true speech act types during the prelanguage phase, what do the vocalizations and nonverbal behaviors represent? As previously described, the vocalizations represent relationships between the child and his or her environment as first interpreted by the adult. These relationships have functions within their form, and they are *attempts* at speech acts. The child is capable, by the end of the prelanguage phase, to meet all the necessary components of a speech act except for language skills representative of a more complex system.

The communication of a child capable during the prelanguage phase of producing utterance acts that have the semantic representation of various relationships and functions to act upon the environment is quite complicated. However, this period of development is still referred to as prelanguage, because the child does not have higher language skills.

The establishment of a deixis demonstrates the majority of sociocognitive prerequisites of language skills. The ability to perform these sophisticated communication acts according to the interpretation of the environment assists the child in learning further about the environment. When enough information has been acquired, the child can represent signs through icons or indices. Symbols are not really acquired during the prelanguage phase because the child has not acquired enough information to directly refer and represent through displacement principles. However, the deixis ability soon necessitates a refinement process. Most of the children in the first phase of development use the process of spontaneous imitation to develop lexical symbolization.

### Spontaneous Imitation

The term ''spontaneous imitation'' refers to a prelanguage process of lexicalization. The child imitates conventions heard just before his or her utterance or quite some time before. In order for the child to be able to imitate these conventions, the child has to process the sign well enough to code and retrieve. However, with most spontaneous imitations the child may demonstrate little knowledge of what is being said. When the child uses spontaneous imitation, the environment usually accepts or rejects it and the child acquires more information. This rapid process of assimilating information by the use of previously heard conventions allows the child to access a variety of new terms that have some limited amounts of information.

The ability to acquire a number of lexical terms for one's use is called the acquisition of lexical terms or "lexicalization"—the child's development of a lexicon. The child stops using nonverbal means of communication as the primary mode at about 12 to 14 months, when he or she has developed the ability to represent adult-interpreted relationships. When the child can use personally based relationships to modify the environment, the need to be able to expand the way in which the environment can be changed is created and new lexical items may be necessary. The child's newly created need requires skill to be able to refer to a variety of actions, objects, and events so that others can act correspondingly. Thus spontaneous imitation allows the child to act on the environment by conventional means, but not necessarily with all the adult meanings. The effects on the hearer provide more feedback so that new terms may be accessed. Thus the child's lexicalization, semantic in nature and cognitively based, requires social interaction. One of the ways this intervention occurs is through spontaneous imitation.

Spontaneous imitation also allows the child to differentiate one form from another. For example, the present progressive form "-ing" will represent an ongoing activity as compared to "-ed," which represents a completed action. These morphological inflections are also part of the lexical term and only through the child's interactive use does the inflection show differentiation. Thus, the child acquires information from his or her own use as well as from the adult's use.

Since spontaneous imitation represents the child's processing, it has the intonation of the child's voice, not the patterns of the adult who is being imitated. This makes spontaneous imitation very different from the echolalia that is a disorder in communication—a disorder that probably exists because it lacks a semantic basis (Lucas, 1980).

Spontaneous imitation is different from direct or elicited imitation. Children do not do direct imitation. It is not a process but a methodology that is used to see what children can do. It has no purpose in development and, moreover, later direct imitation would violate the sincerity rule when it would appear that the speaker is socially mocking the person imitated. Direct imitation is different in form from spontaneous imitation in that the child tries to use the exact structures of the adult. In spontaneous imitation the child uses the structures that are within his or her competence. Elicited imitation is also different from spontaneous imitation. It refers to a methodology that tries to get a child to imitate at the child's level of competence. Whether or not the elicited imitation of the child is truly the child's level of competence cannot be guaranteed.

Children typically do some spontaneous imitation at the critical phase of change between prelanguage (Phase One) and language skills (Phase Two). The amount of spontaneous imitation that individual children do varies considerably. It is also at this point of phase transition that some children stop, reflecting the child's inability to progress into a higher semantic or conceptual development.

The child who spontaneously imitates is demonstrating a sociocognitive process that encourages advanced lexicalization and, of course, the development of corresponding conventions. This spontaneous imitation, unlike direct or elicited imitation, facilitates semantic development. However, a child who imitates for a period of time without the corresponding meaning shows a lack of semantic (sociocognitive) development that is necessary for further language development. Out of the differentiation and development of semantics through the communication acts of the prelanguage phase will come later language skills. From this development the child will begin to alter meaning through a process of modulation (Brown, 1973).

**Semantic Features**

The theoretical literature regarding semantic features considers how certain words relate to each other in terms of characteristics or properties. It also considers how children might acquire certain dimensional concepts that are similar to each other except for one characteristic. For example, the semantic interpretists consider the dictionary of a speaker to include all of those entries that might fit into a definition. The word "table" might have several characteristics that fit into the dictionary entry of "table." On the other hand, several researchers (e.g., Clark & Clark, 1977; Donaldson & Wales, 1970; Hart & Moore, 1973; Nelson, 1974; Palermo, 1973; Wales & Campbell, 1970) have considered how children acquire concepts such as "big" and "little" or dimensional terms such as "up" and "down" according to the relationship between the two terms. Some research considers how certain words relate to each other within a given set, for example, in the set of kinship terms, how "aunt" and "uncle" are related to the semantic field. The three areas of study, interpretive semantics, semantic fields, and acquisition of dimensional terms, consider the similarities and differences between lexical items. These bits of information that distinguish one lexical item from another may be considered semantic features.

Semantic features are those characteristics or properties that are coded about a child's or speaker's environment. Given a sufficient number of features that are related, another lexical term becomes the coded information. In other words, a child receives sensory information that becomes coded and then as more experiences occur, the organized information begins to be grouped into larger units.

When a sufficient number of these units are organized, the next step of organization is to refer to this grouping with one lexical term. For example, the perceptual features or configuration plus the functional feature "eating" become grouped so that the item is referred to as "table."

The child's ability to group these features for referring allows for a significant amount of specification to occur within a language. During the prelanguage phase the child uses sociocognitive skills to acquire semantic features about basic objects, actions, and events in his or her environment. The child's ability to organize the features determines the rate at which the child is able to further advance in language development. Thus, semantic features are the bits of information forming the semantic basis of language. It is also during this prelanguage phase that the basic semantic features increase through the processes of deixis and spontaneous imitation.

### Semantic Feature Types

Basic learning may be viewed as an acquisition of semantic features. The semantic feature is the basic unit of knowledge that a child or adult might acquire. The way in which these units of knowledge become acquired depends on the child's neurological integrity and the means of organizing the features into a system for use.

Some researchers suggest that there are probably two basic types of features—perceptual and functional. The perceptual features refer to those basic bits of information that pertain to an object's, action's, or event's perceptual characteristics, such as visual configuration, smell, touch, taste, etc. On the other hand, the functional semantic features refer more to the way in which something is used. As suggested in Chapter 3, the functional features require the greatest amount of displacement and thus are probably coded more by hearing than by any other sensory information. Perceptual features may be coded in any mode and much of the information probably is coded through vision.

Once the basic semantic features are acquired, they may be organized into larger units that may be referred to as a lexical term, as in the example "table" above. However, if more features are acquired about the tables in the child's environment, there may come a need to increase the number of lexical terms to cover all of the knowledge about tables. Soon the child calls one table a desk, another table is called the coffee table, a third table is the kitchen table, and another the dining room table. During the prelanguage phase of development, this type of differentiation does not take place. In fact, this phase is characterized by the opposite. During the prelanguage phase, the child shows a lack of specification and may actually call anything that someone eats from a "table." It is during the second phase that the child's differentiation begins to result in overextension. In overextension the child overextends the use of a term because of the child's semantic feature knowledge. The process of overextension (see Chapter 5) in the second phase also facilitates lexicalization in much the same way that spontaneous imitation does in the prelanguage phase.

During the prelanguage phase, many words that are distinctive units to an adult are considered as one unit. The child may consistently say "books" believing that the referring marker is "books" and not "book." The child may run words together thinking that the marker is one unit. For example, the child might say, "ride-a-horse" for the name of the object, horse. When enough information has been acquired, the child is ready to move on to the next phase of development.

## PRELANGUAGE REQUISITES

During the prelanguage phase it is apparent that the process of deixis and the process of spontaneous imitation provide a sociocognitive need and a tool for acquiring semantic features for the basis of language skills to be developed in the second phase. There are also some quality requirements, which include sufficient frequency, sufficient variety, and sufficient opportunity. Chapter 7 describes the result of breakdowns during this phase if these quality indicators are not met. For the purpose of this chapter it is important to recognize that chronological age is not as important as which processes are engaged. For example, once a social purpose through mutual interaction is established, language skills quickly develop (Lucas, 1977). If the spontaneous imitation begins to utilize the child's system as perceived by the adult's system, the child will rapidly have a need for moving to the next phase. Therefore, the rapidity that is encountered once certain processes occur really dictates the prognosis and thus the timeline, rather than chronological development. Chapters 8 and 9 provide an assessment of these levels of development.

"What is sufficient frequency, sufficient variety, and sufficient opportunity?" There are no exact answers to these questions at this time, but some general guidelines might be used until research can determine the percentage of each. In any given situation in which a potential speaker and hearer are present, every time there is an obvious opportunity for a child to initiate communicative acts, a child should do so unless he or she is not comfortable with the situation for some reason.

The comfortability of the situation must be judged by the adult examiner. If a child does not initiate communicative acts when given an obvious opportunity, then the child does not have the social requisites for language skills to continue to develop. If the frequency of initiation is sufficient, then the majority of the utterances should be novel. It is estimated that 70 to 80 percent of a prelanguage child's communicative acts are novel once the child has sufficient frequency of basic semantic relations. At this point the child will begin to use spontaneous imitation or may go into the next process of the next phase of development.

One of the most crucial but often overlooked quality requirements is the amount of opportunity provided a prelanguage child for initiating communicative acts. If a communicative situation is to be established, there must be shared time allotted between the speaker and hearer. If the amount of time the child spends in the initiator role is disproportionate to the amount of time the significant adults spend, the child is probably not given enough time or sufficient adult effects. The caregivers may be doing most of the communicating for the child, thus accepting the major responsibility in the communication. If the child does not have the opportunity to engage in communication, the acquisition of more advanced skills cannot be expected.

## SUMMARY

The prelanguage phase of development is characterized by the acquisition of the prerequisites for adultlike speech acts through semantic development in interactions between the child as a speaker or hearer and significant others in the child's environment. The adult and child together utilize the child's nonverbal development as interpreted to affect the behaviors of others so that early motor patterns, vocalizations, etc., soon become meaningful to the child and differentiated by meaning into a process of lexicalization. When semantic features are so abundant that new terms are required, the child uses the process of spontaneous imitation for further development of advanced language skills in the second phase.

**REFERENCES**

Bates, E. *The emergence of symbols.* New York: Academic Press, 1979.

Bates, E.; Camaioni, L.; & Volterra, V. The acquisition of performatives prior to speech. *Merrill-Palmer Quarterly,* 1975, *21*(3), 205-225.

Brown, R. *A first language: The early stages.* Cambridge, Mass.: Harvard University Press, 1973.

Bruner, J.S. From communication to language—A psychological perspective. *Cognition,* 1975, *3*(3), 255-287.

Bruner, J.S. The ontogenesis of speech acts. *Journal of Child Language,* 1974, *2*, 1-19.

Chafe, W. Meaning and the structure of language. Chicago: The University of Chicago Press, 1970.

Clark, H.H., & Clark, E.V. *Psychology and language.* New York: Harcourt Brace Jovanovich, 1977.

Donaldson, M., & Wales, R. On the acquisition of some relational terms. In J.R. Hayes (Ed.), *Cognition and the development of language.* New York: John Wiley & Sons, 1970.

Dore, J. The development of speech acts (Doctoral dissertation, City University of New York, 1973). *Dissertation Abstracts International,* 1973, *34* (University Microfilms No. 73-14, 374)

Fillmore, C.J. The case for case. In E. Bach & R.T. Harms (Eds.), *Universals in linguistic theory.* New York: Holt, Rinehart & Winston, 1968.

Hart, R.A., & Moore, G.T. The development of spatial cognition: A review. In R.M. Downs & D. Stea (Eds.), *Image and environment—cognitive mapping and spatial behavior.* Chicago: Aldine, 1973.

Leonard, L.B. *Meaning in child language*. New York: Grune & Stratton, 1976.

Lucas, E.V. The feasibility of speech acts as a language approach for emotionally disturbed children (Doctoral dissertation, University of Georgia, 1977). *Dissertation Abstracts International*, 1978, *38*, 3479B-3967B. (University Microfilms No. 77-30, 488)

Lucas, E.V. *Semantic and pragmatic language disorders: Assessment and remediation*. Rockville, Md.: Aspen Systems, 1980.

McLean, J.E., & Snyder-McLean, L.K. *A transactional approach to early language training*. Columbus, Ohio: Charles E. Merrill, 1978.

Nelson, K. Concept, word and sentence. *Psychological Review*, 1974, *81*(4), 267-285.

Palermo, D.S. More about less: A study of language comprehension. *Journal of Verbal Learning and Verbal Behavior*, 1973, *12*, 211-221.

Wales, R., & Campbell, R. On the development of comparison and the comparison of development. In G.B.Flores d'Arcais & J.M.Levelt (Eds.), *Advances in psycholinguistics*. Amsterdam: North Holland Publishing Co., 1970.

## Chapter 5

# Phase Two: Language Development

*The resounding joys of laughter,*
*The questions time and again,*
*Certainly there isn't a better time*
*than ''When?''*

## Chapter Objectives

1. Explain what is meant by "language development" in Phase Two.
2. Explain the transition between prelanguage and language development.
3. Explain the importance of the speech act to language development.
4. Explain the process of overextension/underextension.
5. Explain the process of overgeneralization.
6. Explain the process of expansion.
7. Explain the process of modulation.
8. Explain the importance of flexibility and productivity in language development.
9. Describe the various speech acts specified for children in this phase.

## INTRODUCTION

Phase One of semantic development was considered a prelanguage phase in which the necessary prerequisites for later language acquisition were developed. Phase Two establishes the basis for developing a linguistic system. Although the prelanguage phase provided the child with advanced communication skills, the child had at best only prerequisites to language skills. By the end of the second phase, the child will have advanced language skills but still will be lacking in some of the linguistic principles that afford an open-ended opportunity for advanced learning.

## WHAT IS THE NATURE OF LANGUAGE?

Language development is characterized by a structural expansion through semantic modulation and overextension processes. Each of these allows for morphology, syntax, and phonology to be used in the child's constructions. The following sections will describe the processes of expansion, modulation, and overextension.

### Expansion

Much of the literature about the caregiver's interaction with a child has been devoted to the types of language used by the adult (e.g., Bateson, 1975; Snow & Ferguson, 1977). One of the techniques seen in maternal usage has been expansion. The child performs an utterance act and the parent assumes the message is a reduction of a grammatical form, which the parent gives back to the child. The form is an expansion of the child's utterance. Although this describes what the parent does with the child, it does not explain why the parent does it or what the expansion does for the child. There has been some research to indicate that expansion alone does not facilitate language skills. Logically speaking, this is probably true. It would seem unreasonable for a speaker to reiterate an expansion of a structure if the expansion did not add anything to the communication act.

Even though the maternal role is probably different from what other individuals might have with a child, the fact that any speaker would only expand on structure seems to violate the communication principles involved in the speech act. Specifically, the sincerity rule would be violated unless the expansion had some other purpose. Children making the transition from spontaneous imitation of semantic relations to more complicated structures seem to employ a semantic process called modulation, which allows the expansion to occur.

## Modulation

Children who are in the transition between Phase One and Phase Two demon-strate modulation, the semantic process that allows semantic notions to be changed to represent more specific concepts. The addition of morphological inflections and functors (nonreferential words) is through a process whereby a meaning is changed. The change in meaning as discussed by Brown (1973) is accomplished by the same semantic feature addition discussed in Chapter 4. The more semantic features that are acquired, the more likely it is that a child would need a new way to express the newly organized information. For example, if a child differentiates between one shoe and two, the child uses some system to mark the change in meaning by the acquisition of information about the differentiation between concepts of one and more than one.

Children do not verbalize these concepts but their productions do represent the change in language skills. This lack of ability to verbalize the principles as they are acquired supports the notion that the child makes the distinction not based on conventional principles but on the underlying meaning. For example, Bloom, Lifter, & Tanouye (1977) have discussed verb changes and what each inflectional suffix may represent in meaning.

Bowerman (1973) has suggested that syntax and morphology are mapped on to the child's underlying semantic base. However, this modulation process that expands the structural complexity of the child's utterances seems more a continua-tion in the acquisition of semantic features. The child has a need to make distinctions between concepts that have similar characteristics or semantic fea-tures, and so changes or modulation occurs. The literature has been so concerned with trying to define *what* a child does in language that researchers have often overlooked the reason *why* these changes occur.

The changing of the child's utterances (modulation) shows rapid progression through the addition of several grammatical morphemes at the beginning of Phase Two. This increase in overall complexity is part of the expansion process. The child's utterances include the distinctions of present active to progressive, "in" to "on," plural to singular, past regular to past irregular, possessive to nonposses-sive, article "a" to "the," contractives to uncontractible copular and auxiliary (see Brown, 1973, for an explanation of these morphemes).

The structure of the child's utterances quickly incorporates more and more functors as the child's language abilities grow. By the time a child is approaching his or her third birthday much of the basic modulation is finished, lexicalization is at its peak, and the child is capable of performing adultlike speech acts even though a complete linguistic system has not been developed.

**Overextension**

Overextension is a normal process that allows a child to use a referent in a situation that might not be quite like one in which an adult would use the same term. As a result of this usage, the child obtains feedback about the meaning and is able to access more information, which results in more usable information. The child's concept based on the child's experiences is of course different from the adult's concept based on the adult's experiences. Therefore, when a child has acquired enough information to organize features and represent the features with a referent, the child may try to symbolize. The sign-to-symbol relationship will represent what the child knows about the sign. For example, the child has information about the ways in which certain things referred to and marked as "tables" might be used. When the child encounters a desk, the purpose of the desk overlaps with the purposes of a table and the child calls the desk a "table." This is an overextension of the word "table."

Overextension as a "normal" sociocognitive process used to learn about common objectives, actions, and referents, should be distinguished from those problems of referent identification and newly created words or semantic neologisms used by adults or older children (Lucas, 1980). In Phase Two, overextension is quite normal, whereas in the linguistic phase of development, the person has enough information to ask specific questions about labels and should have the ability to use a new label without creating one. The adult or older child who uses a lexical tag with overlapping semantic features has a language disorder.

As the child's language increases by modulating meaning and thus expanding structural complexity, there is an increase in semantic complexity. While the structure is increasing, the overextensions allow for a quick development of lexicon. The child at the middle of Phase Two development (about three to four chronological years) has all of the necessary semantic skills to adequately produce a variety of speech acts in a variety of situations. The following section will report on research in this area.

**SPEECH ACTS IN PHASE TWO**

Since a basic proposition when uttered with the appropriate essential elements, such as mood and voice of the verb, stress, and body posture, has an effect on the hearer, a child having a significant amount of language skills should be able to perform basic speech acts. The acts reported by Dore (1973) were primarily communicative in nature, but given the basic semantic components of a speech act and the fact that three-year-old children produce simple and compound sentences that allow for language specificity, the author decided to investigate the types of speech acts that three-year-old children use. Mabel Brown Rostamizadeh (1981) set up the basic research, the data from which were later used in a series of studies by the author. Material from her work is reprinted with permission.

The initial research performed by Rostamizadeh consisted of two dyadic conditions used to provide ample opportunity for six three-year-old children to use speech acts. The unique property of this research was that instead of using adult interpretation to determine the taxonomy for what the child's language usage was to be called, the criteria for speech acts were listed on a data form under the categories of linguistic, paralinguistic, and nonlinguistic. The criteria were employed to identify the type of speech act demonstrated, with no influence from the adult's interpretation of interest, function, or effect.

## Subjects

The children for Rostamizadeh's studies were selected from a nursery school at a western university. The parents were from middle to upper social strata and were often occupationally affiliated with the university.

As part of the Child Find Screening Program, the children were screened prior to the study for possible speech, language, or hearing problems by university students majoring in speech pathology and/or audiology. Those children who did not pass the screening or who had known speech, language, or hearing problems, including bilingual children, were excluded from the study. The parents of all eligible subjects were given a ''permission to participate'' form that met all ''rights of subjects'' regulations. Six children who met the age criteria and were not hesitant to participate were randomly selected from the returned permission slips. Prior to beginning the study, the investigator interacted with each child in the nursery school setting in order to develop a ''positive'' relationship.

## Data Collection

For each data collection Rostamizadeh gave the subject the choice of two manipulative or messy play activities controlled for cognitive development. After the subjects chose the activity with which they wished to play, they were videotaped in two dyadic conditions on two separate days for a maximum of twenty minutes for each condition. Videotaping was through a one-way mirror into the research room at the nursery school. Rostamizadeh transcribed the videotaped linguistic, paralinguistic, and nonlinguistic information onto data collection sheets (for example, see Exhibit 5-1). The speech events were then analyzed according to the semantic criteria of speech acts, that is, according to propositional content, preparatory, sincerity, and essential principles.

The actual conditions for the recording consisted of two dyad types: adult-child and child-peer. During the first session with each child in the adult-child condition, Rostamizadeh followed the language leads of the child in order to minimize

**Exhibit 5-1** Data Collection Sheet for Determining Speech Act Types

VIDEO TAPE NUMBER #1, subject #3  CHILDREN subject #3

SPEECH EVENT

INVESTIGATOR yes_____ no_____

CONTEXT AND MATERIALS playdough, rollers, knives, cookie cutters

| SPEECH ACT | LINGUISTIC CONTENT | PARALINGUISTICS | NONLINGUISTICS |
|---|---|---|---|
| 1. S tells H X is Y | S: Make another one.<br>H: This one is hard to do. | falling contour (ess. 1) | S looks at H, hands H playdough; J rolls it, S reaches for it (ess. 1) |
| 2. S tells H | S: It's bigger! | rising, then falling (ess. 2) | S takes ball, looks at it and pinches off a piece (prep. 2) |
| 3. S tells H | H: It is!?<br>S: Call you roll it up.<br>H: Can I roll it up? | long pause<br>whisper voice, falling contour | S is trying to roll it out (prep. 3)<br>S gives H the ball of dough (ess. 3) |
| 4. S informs H X is Y | S: Now . . . take a gob of it<br>H: What? | S smiles, looks at H falling contour (ess. 4) | H rolls it; S takes it back (prep. 4) |
| 5. S informs H X | S: Gob of . . .<br>H: O.K. | falling contour (ess. 5) | S takes one out demonstrating to H, H takes one too (ess. 5)<br>both pretend to eat |

*Source:* M.B. Rostamizadeh, *A Comparison of Two Dyadic Conditions for Speech Act Types in Three-Year-Old Children.* 1981. Reprinted by permission.

the influence of her language upon the child's type and frequency of speech acts. For the second part of the investigation each of the six subjects interacted with a peer, from the sample, in play contexts to produce a child-peer dyadic condition.

## Data Analysis

For analyzing the transcription of the videotape, five types of criteria were used: (1) The context of the linguistic utterance was specified to provide a detailed description of the particular play setting, the subject(s) involved, and the behaviors preceding and following the act by the persons involved. This contextual information was used to determine the preparatory set, which in turn provided information for propositional content. (2) The referent or topic had to be specified in order to determine the linguistic content of the propositional and the essential rules. (3) The linguistic content of the speaker was augmented by specific paralinguistic and nonlinguistic markers. The significant paralinguistic devices included (a) rising, falling, and level intonation patterns; (b) high versus low voice pitch; (c) long versus short pauses; (d) stressed versus unstressed words; and (e) speeding up versus slowing down speech rate within the utterance. The paralinguistic information was necessary to determine illocutionary force indicating devices that aided in determining the sincerity and essential principles. (The illocutionary force-indicating devices are paralinguistic aspects of the utterance act that in English conventions include the mood, tense, and voice of the verb, and the stress. The term illocutionary comes from the theory of speech acts in which the intent is determined by such linguistic, nonlinguistic, and, of course, paralinguistic essential elements.) (4) Nonlinguistic markers that may have given additional meaning to the speech act included the following types of body language: (a) facial gestures (e.g., level, raised, or furrowed brows, smiles, frowns, or relaxed lip positions); (b) lack of or use of eye contact or observation; (c) nodding or shaking of head; (d) body positions (e.g., body turned toward, turned away from, or touching another person); and (e) hand movements (e.g., gestures). The paralinguistic and nonlinguistic markers aided in determining the essential criteria of the speech act as well as the sincerity principle. From the above criteria of the speech event, the speech act types that the six children used in the two dyadic conditions were identified.

## Results

According to Rostamizadeh, "The description of the speech act types used by three-year-old children was determined by considering the proposition; the effects on the hearer; the preparatory conditions for the proposition; the sincerity of the illocutionary force; and the essential effectiveness of the linguistic, paralinguistic, and nonlinguistic information" (p. 16).

To determine the propositional effects, the child's utterances were analyzed using philosophical notation similar to that of Searle (1969). This type of philosophical notation has also been used by generative semanticists (e.g., Antinucci and Parisi, 1973) to demonstrate the semantic organization underlying a child's utterance act. The utterance act is assumed to have a basic proposition (X) that may or may not be altered by the predication (Y). Table 5-1 illustrates the types of proposition and predicate relationships that were found to be present in the three-year-old children's utterances.

The propositional content alone could not determine the type of speech act since the contextual nonlinguistic and paralinguistic information that provide the intent and hearer effects must be considered. If the illocutionary force or intent was different from the linguistic marking, the sincerity rule was considered to be violated. This violation would be the case for pretending, joking, etc. If the utterance lacked any part of the semantic criteria such as a proposition, either

**Table 5-1** Types of Proposition to Predicate Relationships Used by Three-Year-Old Children

| Propositional Types | Examples |
| --- | --- |
| X | "No!" |
| X is Y | "There's a lot of dough." |
| X(Y) | "I need a roller." |
| $\emptyset$ | "And it's . . ." |
| {X} is Y | "I knew it was." |
| {X} (Y) | "A hole." |
| X ; Y is Y | "Yeah. It almost happens when I do this." |
| X(Y) [X(Y)] | "I'll leave the star there. You can have the star and I'll have the other one." |
| X is Y {;} X is Y | "My Dad is real strong, he can snap these off." |

Notation: X = proposition; Y = predication; ; = that is; $\emptyset$ = optional; ( ) = of. It should be emphasized that multiple propositions and predications can occur such as the following:

| | |
| --- | --- |
| $X_1$ is $Y_1$ ; $X_2$ is $Y_2$ | "If you want to see the biggest backhoe in the whole world just go to the Stadium." |
| $X_1$ is $Y_1$ ($X_2$ is $Y_2$) | "I'm gonna take it off put it on here." |
| $X_1$ is $Y_1$ [$X_2$ is ($Y_2$)] | "She, she . . . she put, she was putting the cups in, in, the bathroom and then they went drop." |

*Source:* M.B. Rostamizadeh, *A Comparison of Two Dyadic Conditions for Speech Act Types in Three-Year-Old Children*, 1981. Reprinted by permission.

assumed or present, a speech act could not be considered complete. Thus, Rostamizadeh states, "these types of incomplete speech acts as well as violations [which are also incomplete speech acts] were not used to determine the types of speech acts used by three-year-old children. Only those utterances that met the propositional content criteria and were used through appropriate paralinguistic and nonlinguistic devices [essential elements] to have a specific effect [illocutionary force] on the hearer were analyzed" (p. 18).

The semantic criteria or felicity conditions (see Chapter 1) were then grouped and each group was therefore a specific speech act type. Table 5-2 illustrates the thirteen speech act types found to be present in the six three-year-old children. Descriptions and operational definitions of the speech act types follow.

**Assertion**

The most common speech act was the assertion, with the criteria the same as described by Searle (1969) and Lucas (1977, 1980). Examples of the linguistic, paralinguistic, and nonlinguistic elements constituting the assertion include:

| Proposition | Utterance | Paralinguistic | Context |
|---|---|---|---|
| S tells H X is Y | "A piece fell off of here." | S laughs | Block falls off and adult picks it up. |
| S tells H X is Y | "That, that's white piece." | falling contour and long pause | Child returns to work after the piece fell off the table. |

**Table 5-2** Speech Act Types Found in Three-Year-Old Children

| Speech Act Types | Adult-Child Dyad | Child-Peer Dyad | Total |
|---|---|---|---|
| Statement of information | 129 | 62 | 191 |
| Pretend statements of information | 86 | 67 | 154 |
| Assertion | 165 | 81 | 146 |
| Requests for information | 45 | 32 | 77 |
| Requests for action | 50 | 18 | 68 |
| Speculation | 17 | 12 | 29 |
| Pretend rule orders | 8 | 5 | 13 |
| Rule order | 5 | 7 | 12 |
| Denial | 2 | 9 | 11 |
| Pretend requests for information | 4 | 5 | 9 |
| Cessation | 7 | 2 | 9 |
| Requests for objects | 0 | 1 | 1 |
| Pretend requests for action | 0 | 1 | 1 |

With the assertion the proposition is identifiable to both the speaker and hearer, but it may not be obvious to the hearer that the speaker has the idea or the speaker may want the hearer to know the speaker also knows. In other words, the piece falling or the piece being white is obvious to both but the speaker wants the hearer to know that the speaker knows too.

## Statement of Information

The linguistic, paralinguistic, and nonlinguistic elements constituting the statement of information are similar to Lucas's description (1980) and can be found in the following examples from Rostamizadeh's research:

| Proposition | Utterance | Paralinguistic | Content |
|---|---|---|---|
| S informs H X is Y | " I have to roll it out again." | stressed, falling | A piece of dough breaks off and both help to roll out the dough. |
| S tells H X is Y | "I played this one before." | falling contour | Adult acknowledges with a question. . |

The primary difference between the statement of information and the assertion has to do with the presence or absence of the shared referent. With the statement of information, it is not known to the speaker that the X is true. Only the speaker is aware or knows of X and so the speaker must be able to inform the hearer.

## Requests for Information, Action, Objects

Requests for information, action, or objects are similar in their preparatory, sincerity, and usually essential elements, with the primary difference being the propositional content criterion. The propositional content is different because the intended effect of the hearer or the illocutionary force is different for each of the three requests. Rostamizadeh states, "The request for information assumes that there is reason to believe that the hearer can provide the speaker with information not obvious to both" (p. 21). The following examples illustrate the request for information:

| Proposition | Utterance | Paralinguistics | Context |
|---|---|---|---|
| S asks H X is Y | "Are there anymore?" | rising contour | S is looking for a specific lego. H helps search for piece. |
| S asks H X is Y | "What are you doing?" | rising contour | S watches H make a design in the dough. H answers S. |

The request for action is an attempt to get the hearer to perform a specific action. Examples of a request for an action include:

| Proposition | Utterance | Paralinguistics | Context |
|---|---|---|---|
| S calls H<br>{X} is Y | "Oh, wow look!" | spoken loudly using a rising then falling contour | S is taking legos apart rapidly. S steps back a little with hands on hips to speak. H answers in agreement. |
| S tells H<br>X(Y) | "Put some away while I pick up." | rising then falling contour | S is putting away play items. While speaking, S heads under table as her hand gives H the box to put items in. H helps clean up. |

The request for objects is similar to the request for action in that the hearer does perform an action, but the intent is not for the act but for receiving the object of the action. An example of the request for objects follows:

| Proposition | Utterance | Paralinguistics | Context |
|---|---|---|---|
| S tells H<br>$X_1$ is $Y_1$<br>{;} $X_2$ is $Y_2$ | "When you're done with the knife . . . that round . . . give it to me." | falling contour | S glances at H to see what utensil he is using on his dough. H responds negatively. |

## Denial

The denial type of speech act was the same as the Lucas and Hoag denial (1976) and is similar to the term "protesting" used by Dore (1973). The denial speech act rejects an act or event, as evidenced in the following example from Rostamizadeh's research:

| Proposition | Utterance | Paralinguistics | Context |
|---|---|---|---|
| S informs H<br>X is Y | "No, no these are babies." | falling contour | H showing S how to put two legos together. S takes piece and holds it up. |
| S informs H<br>X is Y | "Well, I'm not gonna open the door by myself." | spoken with authority and falling contour | S and H are discussing whether to leave the room. S and H creep toward the door. |

## Rule Order

The rule order (Lucas, 1977; 1980) is a way to alter the behavior of the hearer according to predetermined societal rules. The following examples demonstrate rule orders:

| Proposition | Utterance | Paralinguistics | Context |
|---|---|---|---|
| S tells H X is Y | "(*child's name*), share!" | falling contour | S is standing near H's chair. S moves closer to chair after speaker. |
| S tells H X is Y | "Don't look at it." | falling contour | S looking at H, is tearing dough away from cookie cutter. S makes sure H isn't looking. |

## Speculation

Speculation types of speech acts use a performative verb to alter the intent of the proposition. Types of speculation performative verbs include "think" or "guess." These speech acts are different from assertions or statements of information since the performative alters the relationship between the proposition and predication. The following examples illustrate the speculation speech act:

| Proposition | Utterance | Paralinguistics | Context |
|---|---|---|---|
| S tells H X is Y | "Now I think that won't stick on." | falling contour | H has put together two pieces of legos. S observes pieces and then puts second piece where he wants it. (changing position of piece). |
| S informs H X(Y) | "I guess she wants, want to make play, playdough." | falling contour | H and S are discussing why a child out of the room is sad. S looks up and makes statement. H responds. |

## Pretend Statements, Rule Orders, and Requests

Since propositional content is set through preparatory conditions and expressed with language skills, the proposition is usually equal to the preparatory set, with the use of referents being the same. One specific group of criteria did not have a preparatory set equal to the referent. For example, the child would refer to the adult in the adult-child dyad condition as "baby." Even though it is obvious to both the child and adult that the hearer is not a baby, the intent of the utterance, which might be to get the hearer to perform an act (request for action), is not violated so the sincerity conditions exist. These groups of criteria with referents unequal to the preparatory set were termed "pretend," a form of role play. The following examples describe the four types of pretend speech act types: statements of information, rule orderings, requests for action, and requests for information.

| Proposition | Utterance | Paralinguistics | Context |
|---|---|---|---|
| S asks H X is Y | "You know what baby?" | rising contour | Looks at H while cutting playdough. S answers back. |
| S informs H X is Y | "*This* is the bed down there." | stressed and falling contour | S looking at H points to wall behind H. H moves to "bed." |
| S informs H X is Y | "Yeah, Mommy has to feed you." | falling contour | S and H are making a playdough pie. There's an exchange of eye contact. H nods head in agreement. |

## Cessation

A final group did not meet the criteria in the literature for denial so a new speech act type was identified. This group deals with the existence or nonexistence of an agent or object and the ability to stop its action as opposed to denying the existence of an object, action, or event. Examples of cessation follow:

| Proposition | Utterance | Paralinguistics | Context |
|---|---|---|---|
| S tells H X is Y | "Don't . . . throw it." | loud voice said with emphasis | S wants H to give some dough to her. H complies. |
| S tells H {X} is Y | "No, don't . . . I want to carry them." | falling contour | S and H are cleaning up room. H starts to leave room with box of toys. S makes the request. H complies. |

## Summary

These speech acts are real entities that beautifully describe the "nature of language." As observed in the data, there exists an interplay between the speaker's intent to affect a hearer and the actual speaker's use of specific, semantic-based language skills to alter the attitudes, beliefs, or behaviors of the hearer. The ability to perform the utterance act is separate from the final effect on the hearer. The final effect is a product of the interaction between the language skills, as determined by the preparatory set (previous experiences determine the information or semantic features about the situation) and expressed as propositional content through the nonlinguistic, paralinguistic conditions. The paralinguistic and sometimes the nonlinguistic information contributes to the illocutionary force indicating devices that affect the hearer possibly more than the specific language skills.

Rostamizadeh found that the children produced almost twice as many utterances in the adult-child condition as in the child-peer condition. This was due to the greater use of nonverbal communication by the adult. The adult was there to follow the child's lead, whereas in the child-child dyad the two children were interacting equally. Therefore, it was concluded that the adult's nonverbal communication may be more effective in maintaining interaction with children than language skills.

The language skills of the children in Phase Two are rapidly developed from the underlying semantic basis and represent means of specifying the sociocognitive skills but do not represent the end. The language skills represent a means to an end and thus need to be evaluated in those conditions rather than as a separate entity, static in nature.

The Rostamizadeh research was a refreshing and isolated example of pragmaticism methodology in practice. Whereas previous psycholinguists have attempted to interpret children's utterances from adult preparatory sets (contexts), Rostamizadeh used the child's linguistic, nonlinguistic, and paralinguistic performances as criteria for defining differences and similarities in performance. Similar usages and effects were grouped at the same speech act performance rather than according to arbitrary adult interpretations or taxonomies (e.g., Dore, 1973). This type of pragmaticism methodology is critical to determining how and why children develop language tools.

## FURTHER ANALYSIS OF SPEECH ACTS

From the data collected by Rostamizadeh, Lucas and Tatarsky-Taylor (1981) made further analyses of the speech acts. There were 823 successful speech acts used by the three-year-old children, with 519 of the acts produced in the child-adult dyadic condition and 304 produced in the child-peer condition. In order to determine if the difference in the two conditions was significant, an analysis of variance of speech act types was made, which indicated that the children did produce statistically significantly fewer speech acts (total of all speech act types) when in child-peer groups as compared with the child-adult dyadic condition. The effect of the condition was significant at the .05 level. The number of speech acts in the child-child condition should have been greater, since both children's speech acts were added to the total. Since the adult followed the lead of the child, it is apparent that her nonverbal attention increased the child's speech acts, whereas the children taking turns with each other in an activity decreased the overall number for each child as well as the total number produced in the same amount of time.

This result is significant for the purposes of remediation and for working with children. The educational implication is that those nonverbal behaviors that the researcher used could be utilized in education.

The speech act types across dyadic conditions were totaled and compared to determine which speech act types were used significantly more than others. Table 5-3 describes the means for the speech acts rank ordered from the most used to the least used. The Tukey's HSD test (Kirk, 1968) for individual comparisons was applied to determine the speech act types that were used the most. Any difference of 9.95 or more between any two means was considered a statistically significant difference. The following section reports the data that Lucas and Tatarsky-Taylor (1981) found when analyzing the individual speech acts and the individual children who participated as subjects in the study.

**Assertion**

The assertion was the most frequently used speech act both across and within dyadic conditions and it was used significantly more than any other speech act. All subjects used the assertion. The criteria that determined the speech act of assertion were the same as Lucas (1977) had earlier listed using Searle (1969) as a guideline. An example of an assertion along with the other speech acts may be found in Table 5-4.

---

**Table 5-3** Means for Speech Act Types Used by Three-Year-Old Children

| Speech Act Type | Mean |
| --- | --- |
| Assertion | 20.58 |
| Statement of Information | 15.92 |
| Pretend Statement of Information | 12.75 |
| Request for Information | 6.67 |
| Request for Action | 5.58 |
| Speculation | 2.42 |
| Pretend Rule Order | 1.08 |
| Rule Order | .92 |
| Denial | .92 |
| Stopping Action | .75 |
| Pretend Request for Information | .75 |
| Pretend Request for Action | .08 |
| Request for Object | .08 |

*Source:* M.B. Rostamizadeh, *A Comparison of Two Dyadic Conditions for Speech Act Types in Three-Year-Old Children,* 1981. Reprinted by permission.

**Table 5-4** Examples of Speech Act Types

| Speech Act | Utterance Act | Paralinguistics | Nonlinguistic |
|---|---|---|---|
| assertion | Child: Now I put this and now I roll it. Adult: That's good rolling. | falling contour | C looks at adult. C pounds on playdough. C tries to roll playdough. |
| statement of information | Child: I-I saw I saw them building the *biggest* backhoe. | falling contour with stress on "biggest" | Ian looks at play toys he's working—adult following referent by gaze. |
| pretend statement of information | $Child_1$: I'll cook you pie. | $Child_1$—falling contour $Child_2$—laughs for several seconds | $C_1$ gazes at $C_2$. Both observe own play then $C_1$ looks at $C_2$ to see "why she is laughing." |
| request for information | Child: You're going to play with it? | rising contour | Eye contact and resumes cutting playdough before answer is given. |
| pretend request for information | $Child_1$: Where's the pie? | rising contour higher pitch | $C_1$ squishes playdough and looks at adult—gives eye contact. |
| request for action | Child: Now, roll this. | falling contour | C pinches off a piece and hands it to the adult. |
| pretend request for action | $Child_2$: *Just* cook it mama. | high pitch; falling contour with emphasis on "just" | $Child_2$ stands and pushes rolling pin away and then sits down. |
| speculation | Maybe I better put some down here. | falling contour | Takes one lego piece off and moves it to another place. |
| rule order | No! You have to take the cookie cutter . . . here. (One nursery school rule is that only toys at a table may be used in an activity.) | falling contour | S quickly looks up and performs utterance act with eye contact. |
| pretend rule order | $Child_1$: Then I have to cut it all up and then you can *eat* it all up for dinner. | loudly, falling contour with emphasis on "eat" | Hits playdough with knife and then demonstrates cutting on own hand. |

**Table 5-4** continued

| Speech Act | Utterance Act | Paralinguistics | Nonlinguistic |
|---|---|---|---|
| denial | Child$_2$: Nope! (continues from previous example) | emphatically— falling contour | Stops looking at Child$_1$ and then drops playdough in another pan. |
| stopping act (cessation) | Adult: I have a piece right here. Child: Don't! | falling contour— emphatic | Adult picks up playdough to roll it. Adult puts down piece. |
| request for object | When you're done with the knife . . . that round . . . give it to me. | falling contour | Child glances at other child and at objects. The child looks at her own work and utters the request. |

The main consideration about assertion is that the proposition is obvious to both the speaker and the hearer but the speaker wants the hearer to know that the speaker knows too. Evidently, children in this phase of development do a lot of asserting, whether with an adult or with another peer. Since Phase Two development is characterized by increased semantic complexity resulting in increased structural complexity, it is not surprising that the child is using assertion much like a parent uses an expansion (most of the time the expansion is probably functioning like an assertion) to facilitate language skills. Furthermore, the typically developing three-year-old is more likely to use an assertion than a basic request for either an action or an object. In comparison, the language-disordered child (Lucas, 1977) uses few utterances that are not for meeting basic needs, wants, and desires. Using an assertion constitutes a social interaction of letting someone know the speaker knows rather than an attempt to get needs met. Appendix D lists the semantic components of each of the thirteen speech acts.

**Statement of Information**

The statement of information was the second most frequently used speech act across dyadic conditions. The primary difference between an assertion and a statement of information is that the hearer does not know the information that the speaker is providing in the utterance act. The information in the proposition of the statement of information is primarily factual and an example is found in Table 5-4.

**Pretend Statement of Information**

The pretend statement of information ranked third among the most frequently used speech act types. This speech act had to have its own category because even though the criteria are the same as for the statement of information, as previously described, the proposition was not the same as the preparatory set. This particular speech act was used by all children. Two of the female subjects used this act the most (see Table 5-4).

**Request for Information**

The request for information speech act was the fourth most frequently used speech act type and it was used across dyadic conditions and by all children. This type of act was seldom eliminated from the data because of violations of the felicity conditions. Felicity conditions are the semantic constituents of the speech act. The ability to use the request for information without error suggests that the children could quite effectively use this speech act. However, the form of the language did not always meet the adult standard. An example of this type of speech act may be found in Table 5-4.

**Pretend Request for Information**

The conditions for pretend requests for information are the same as for the request for information except that the preparatory set of the pretend is imaginary whereas it is real for the propositional content of the request for information. Only two children, the same females that used numerous pretend statements of information, used this speech act type. Table 5-4 provides an example of these two children using a pretend request for information.

**Request for Action**

Requests for action were used almost as frequently as requests for information by all children across dyadic conditions. Two of the subjects used a significantly larger number of requests for action than did the other children. Table 5-4 provides an example of the request for action. Most of the requests for action were of the imperative form rather than the interrogative form. Approximately one-half of the requests for action were used as indirect requests. Tatarsky-Taylor explained the significance of the indirect requests of three-year-olds. This explanation will be discussed in a later section of this chapter.

### Pretend Request for Action

The pretend request for action had the same semantic rules as the request for action except that the preparatory set made the proposition imaginary. An example of the pretend request for action may be found in Table 5-4. This type of speech act was rarely used and used only by the two girls who used the high number of pretend statements of information and pretend requests for information.

### Speculation

The speculation speech act was used infrequently by all children across the dyadic conditions. Two of the boys used more speculations than any of the other children. An example of a speculation may be found in Table 5-4. Speculations are different from assertions and statements of information in that the speaker does not know for certain that the proposition is a fact. These speech acts are often marked with a verb such as ''think'' or ''guess.''

### Rule Order

Rule orderings were used by four of the six children infrequently but across dyadic conditions. The rule order expresses the conditions of a situation according to some predetermined societal convention. An example of a rule order may be found in Table 5-4. The rule order is different from the assertion, request for information, and the request for action in that it restates a previously determined rule, not a personal request, fact, or common knowledge.

### Pretend Rule Order

Pretend rule orderings are similar to rule orders except that the rules are pretend or imaginary in nature. An example of a pretend order may be found in Table 5-4. Only three of the six children used this pretend speech act, again, the same two who used other pretend forms. This speech act was infrequently used across dyadic conditions by the three children.

### Denial

Few denial speech acts were found across dyadic conditions. The two children who used a lot of pretending were also the only ones to use this type of speech act. Most of the denials were simply ''No'' or ''No + X.'' An example of the denial is found in Table 5-4.

**Stopping Action (Cessation)**

The stopping action speech act was used by four of the children, infrequently but across both dyadic conditions. The stopping action is different from the denial in that the denial could refer to nonexistence or refusal to comply with a request or rule order. However, the cessation was used to get the hearer to stop an action that was already engaged. Table 5-4 provides an example of the stopping action speech act type.

**Request for Object**

Only one child used direct request for an object when interacting with another peer. However, many more indirect requests for objects were used by all children and across the dyadic conditions. Table 5-4 illustrates the request for objects. It was similar to the request for action and request for information speech acts. The felicity conditions may be found in Appendix D for all of the thirteen speech act types. It should be noted that indirect requests represent a higher semantic complexity than direct requests.

**Summary**

Analyzing the different speech act types, it appears that some speech act types were used by all children and that the type of condition really did not make a difference. It should also be apparent that some of the children used one type of speech act more consistently than any other type of speech act.

The interpreter often views these individual differences in speech usage as personality traits. For example, the child who used numerous rule orders was characterized by the teacher as "bossy" in personality.

In order to determine if the differences among the children was a result of the dyadic condition or of individual differences, the numbers and types of speech acts used by each child were ranked and compared across dyadic conditions. It was found that each child consistently used some speech act types more than others, regardless of the situation. These results suggest that the individual differences found in the children remained proportionately constant across dyadic conditions even though the children consistently used more speech acts with the adult than with a peer. If children use specific types of speech acts more often than other speech act types that other children use more consistently, the individual differences must be personal. Children as young as three years of age may have already developed certain styles for interacting with hearers. Each child of the study was carefully analyzed by Lucas and Tatarsky-Taylor in order to determine what the individual differences across dyadic conditions were like.

**Subject One**

Subject One, a three-year-old male, ranked second in the total number of speech acts used. Most of his speech acts were assertions, statements of information, and speculations. Subject One was found to use the most assertions (522) and the most statements of information (40) across dyadic conditions. This child also used the greatest number of assertions (34) and the second greatest number of statements of information (13) across the child-peer dyadic conditions. Subject One rarely used any form of pretend or form of requests. In addition to the most number of speech acts, this child's explanations were lengthy and syntactically more complex. For example, "I-I-I-I think they have to take out that biggest backhoe in the whole world only they have to carry it out together because it *too* big."

Why should Subject One who used the greatest number of assertions and statements of information also have the greatest complexity? As previously stated, the children who have language disorders tend to use few assertions and statements of information and are more likely to use a significant number of requests to meet basic needs. Although interrogative forms can be very complex and can represent a very sophisticated language system, basic needs do not need complex forms because complex semantic notions are not being represented. A child who is beyond the stage of basic semantic needs is much more likely to need complex structures to represent complex semantic ideas in a variety of ways. Assertions and statements of information reflect the child's "here and now" cognitive orientation to his or her learning environment.

This child's play was about what he was doing and he provided a running commentary in a parallel-talk fashion with the other peer as well as in the adult-child dyad condition. His structures built with legos were elaborate both vertically and horizontally. When he attempted semantically complex structures that he could not handle, he would shift the basic idea so as to be able to express himself. This subject had numerous incomplete attempts at speech acts, which, of course, were not counted in the total, and it should be noted that his successful speech acts were significantly greater than the unsuccessful attempts.

Furthermore, Subject One employed the same speech act strategy across the dyadic conditions, using about twice as many of the same speech act types with the peer as with the adult. He interacted with both the adult and the peer in the same way, using the same nonverbal as well as verbal behavior. Because this child was so involved in telling what he had done or was doing and because he primarily used only two types of speech acts, he was followed to see what his advanced learning skills were like. According to the teacher who continued to take data on his language skills over the next 12 months, this child's learning accelerated and complexity both semantically and syntactically escalated.

This child must have been significantly into the expansion part of Phase Two when the original research was begun. It should be noted that the number of speech acts may be important and that although Subject One used primarily only two types (six different in total), he was capable of other speech acts. Therefore, the frequency of all speech acts may not be as important as overall frequency. Furthermore, assertions and statements of information may provide more of an opportunity for increasing complexity, whereas speech acts for requests provide the child with the opportunity to develop a social interaction that can then promote the Phase Two level of development. In summary, this subject was well into Phase Two development and beyond what might be expected of a child just entering Phase Two.

### Subject Two

Subject Two, a three-year-old male, used the least number of speech acts across dyadic conditions and only six of thirteen speech act types. Subject One also used only six of the thirteen speech act types but the advanced variables of frequency and complexity were much greater. Subject One's play was quite elaborate, whereas Subject Two, who also played with legos, used three-year-old tactics while creating much more conventional types of objects.

When Subject Two had difficulty with lego pieces he would request actions and objects, usually in an indirect form. He also used some requests for information. When playing with the adult he remained silent most of the time and when with the other child he would comment on a topic already introduced but never introduce his own topic. He used the same verbal and nonverbal strategies in both dyadic conditions to interact and to receive help with the legos. He not only maintained his individual speech act strategies across dyadic conditions but also used about twice as many of the same speech act types with the adult as with the peer.

The infrequency of speech acts, the lower development of play, and the restricted use of speech act types as illustrated by more requests for basic needs suggest that Subject Two was functioning at a lower level of semantic development than Subject One. An example of Subject Two's most complex type of structure was ''But, I can't take that off.'' This subject is probably just entering the Phase Two of development. He is acquiring structure through expansion by modulation but he is not really ready to refine the structures. After analyzing all the speech events, the teacher was asked what she thought was the cognitive level of development of each child. The teacher indicated that Subject Two ''seemed young'' as he was socially more into himself and cognitively did not engage in more sophisticated levels of play, drawing, or language skills.

### Subject Three

Of the six subjects, Subject Three ranked fifth in the total number of speech acts and he used only seven of the thirteen types. The majority of his speech acts were statements of information, assertions, requests for information, and requests for action. Less frequent use of speculations, rule orderings, stopping action, denial, and pretend statements of information was observed.

Subject Three maintained his individual speech act strategies across dyadic conditions, using nearly the same number and types of speech acts in both conditions even though the two people in the dyads responded to him differently. In the adult-child dyadic condition, this child played silently, occasionally asking for an action. However, in the other situation the peer would ask him for assistance and carried most of the initiation. This change did not affect Subject Three's types of speech acts. In both conditions Subject Three rarely initiated acts. He either responded or played silently, depending on who was with him. He did request action of the peer, just as he did with the adult, except this peer would not comply. The types of requests were primarily indirect and the other three-year-old evidently did not see any reason for responding to them. When the peer would not comply, Subject Three would start to mumble to himself and try to physically complete the request.

Again, based on the play, language, and frequency of speech acts (flexibility), this child is considered not as developed as Subject One but slightly more developed than Subject Two. This child's language skills are typical of the first third of development of Phase Two. This child is expanding and shows significant modulation but the rapid increase in complexity of semantics (refinement) has not begun.

## Subject Four

Subject Four was a three-year-old female who used nine of the thirteen speech act types and ranked fourth in the total number of successful speech acts used across dyadic conditions. Most of her successful speech acts consisted of statements of information, assertions, requests for action, and requests for information. Less often, she used rule orderings, pretend statements of information, speculations, stopping action, and pretend rule orderings.

Not only did Subject Four use a variety of speech act types but she also used more requests for actions and information across dyadic conditions than the rest of the children. She was very persistent in following through with finding out information when with the adult. She totally dominated the play situation with the adult and with the peer. In both conditions she spontaneously provided information, made assertions or speculations about events, and requested actions. Although the majority of this child's speech acts were successful attempts, approximately one-half of the requesting for action or information attempts contained violations primarily of the essential element. The violations were not counted as successful speech acts. Therefore, this child may have had the highest frequency level had she been able to use appropriate or conventional essential elements.

This child maintained her individual speech act strategies across the conditions, using approximately twice as many with the adult as with the peer, even though the peer was quite passive and she could have used as many as with the adult. This child was an aggressor in both situations and showed not only a variety of speech act types but also a significant frequency of speech acts. Her play was as advanced as Subject One's play, which indicates that she was well into Phase Two of development.

## Subject Five

Subject Five was observed to use all thirteen of the speech act types and this three-year-old female was ranked third in the total number of successful speech acts used by the children. The majority of her speech acts consisted of statements of information, assertions, pretend statements of information, and requests for information. All of these four speech act types allow for advanced syntactical and semantic development with expansion of ideas expressed by language skills.

In both conditions, Subject Five used primarily pretend types of speech acts. Playdough was turned into a family meal with the adult told that she was the baby. With the peer, the child had to bargain over the roles. In the child-adult condition, she used a greater number of requests for information than requests for action; however, in the child-child condition, she used the same number of requests for information as requests for action. This is probably due to the fact that the adult responded better nonverbally, reducing the need for requests for action. It also is probably the result of this child recognizing the adult's greater ability as a hearer to answer requests for information.

This child's play was highly imaginative and creative and well directed through language in both conditions. She used the playdough in a number of make-believe activities and she was much more inquisitive, as demonstrated by her making many more successful requests for information than the other children. She directed the activity with the adult but in the peer situation the two children (Subject Five and Subject Six) were in direct conflict over who was going to control. However, Subject Five tended to win most conflict situations. For example, Subject Five: "Uh! I wanna make my *own* pie . . . I have to make *my* pie!" Subject Six: "Noooo!" Subject Five: "Cindy, share! I'm gonna run out and tell the teacher." Subject Six: "Uh, uh" (shakes head in negative fashion). Then Subject Six conceded and said, "I'll share!"

Subject Five not only was victor in these conditions but also used more rule orders. It should be noted that in the child-child dyad there was no adult present. (The adult investigator was videotaping through a one-way mirror. The children were left alone to play. They made their selection of materials and were told that they had to play at the table until the teacher came back. Two of the subjects decided at one point that they had played enough and started to leave. The investigator redirected them and was able to get them back to playing.)

Subject Five used the same strategies across the dyadic conditions and although she used more with the adult, the number was only slightly larger, whereas with the other subjects the number was almost double. This particular subject was probably quite advanced in the Phase Two of development. Her structures were advanced and she used them in a variety of ways including many pretend and imaginative ways. She was closer to being at the end of Phase Two development than were most of the other subjects.

### Subject Six

Like Subject Five, Subject Six was observed using all of the thirteen speech acts in a highly imaginative play setting. The majority of Subject Six's speech acts were pretend statements of information, assertions, requests for information, requests for action, and statements of information. The numerous pretend utterances were used to direct the adult as well as to try to direct the peer. (The peer was Subject Five, who usually ended up being the manipulator.)

Subject Six always involved the adult in the play, showing a higher social development than that of some of the self-centered players.

In lexical development Subject Six showed a wide variety of semantic development in several areas, from being able to name specific ingredients of recipes to determining the purpose of tasks. Whereas Subject Five showed many violations, Subject Six showed few violations, especially with the pretend statements of information. Subject Six maintained the speech act strategies across the two dyadic conditions, using exactly twice as many with the cooperative adult as with the noncompliant peer. She also used many more assertions in the adult situation than in the child situation.

Of the six subjects, Subject Six was probably the most advanced, being slightly more flexible and productive with language skills than Subject Five. Her semantic complexity in terms of variety of lexicon may also have been slightly more varied and thus more advanced than Subject Five. Subject Six had less trouble saying what she wanted to say and thus there were fewer violations. Subject Six had more control of her language skills and appeared to be finishing the Phase Two development. In another six months, this child would probably show the beginning skills of Phase Three.

As previously mentioned, all of the subjects had many violations. The next section discusses the concept of violation and what it means in terms of acquiring the linguistic system.

## VIOLATIONS

The original purpose of collecting the data was to determine the types of speech acts that three-year-old children perform. The methodology was set up so that the speech act types were determined from grouping the semantic criteria. Those utterance acts that were the same for the preparatory set, propositional content, sincerity, and essential criteria (see Appendix D) were grouped as speech acts. If a child's utterance did not meet any one of these semantic criteria, the utterance act was considered incomplete as a speech act. One or more of the criteria not met meant that there was one or more violations.

The children were found to use significantly more successful speech acts than violations. Only 184 were attempts or violations out of 701 in the child-adult dyad. The violation rate was approximately 26.2 percent for this condition. In the child-child condition, there were 457 attempted with 140 violations, which accounted for 30.6 percent. These data mean that in any given communication condition, there will be some attempts at speech acts that for one or more reasons are not completed. For these three-year-old children the rate of unsuccessful attempts was between 26 percent and 30 percent. The rate for adults' conversations may not be any lower and in some situations may be somewhat higher.

The greater the number of unsuccessful speech act attempts, the greater the problem in socially interacting with an individual. If a child faces a high rate of unsuccessful speech acts, there are only a few options available: the child could rely more on gestures and even pantomime to communicate or the child could become more passive, with physical manipulation meeting his or her basic needs. Language-disordered children seldom have a high frequency of attempted speech acts. In fact, some language-disordered children do not attempt any speech acts (Lucas, 1977). Their language skills remain rudimentary and are often replaced by stereotypic utterances or nonpurposeful or automatic utterances such as greetings, countings, and labelings.

What is the role of these violations in language development? The following sections discuss the violations for each of the speech act types.

### Statement of Information

Violations of the statement of information usually involved inadequate semantic and thus syntactic ability to provide sufficient information about the intended proposition. In some cases the violation was a result of the child mumbling to himself or herself. In the child-adult situation, the adult would ask for a clarification such as ''What?'' But in the child-child situation, peers rarely asked for a clarification. Adults tend to take on the burden of communication more often with children, whereas children who are peers aren't really interested in taking on the speaker and hearer responsibility at the same time. Unintelligible utterances were basically ignored by the peers. Most of the children rarely violated a statement of information attempt. Subject One used the most statements of information and consequently most of his violations were with this type of speech act.

It should be noted that the violations are interpreted using the criteria as one or another type of speech act. The fact that the speech act is unsuccessful means that there may have been a different attempt or different intent than is assumed.

### Assertions

A low number of attempts at assertions were unsuccessful. Failures resulted because a child might have turned his or her back on the hearer just as the utterance act occurred or because the child marked the utterance with a rising intonation. For the three-year-old, some assertions were made and asked at the same time, indicating that maybe the information was not so obvious but that the child wanted to let the hearer know that he or she knew the information. In such a case, a tag form might be used. For example, "She went to the classroom, right?" A statement that another child was going back to the classroom had been made in front of this child. The child knew the information and it was obvious that the adult did too. The assertion was a violation of the semantic conditions, particularly the sincerity rule. Therefore, the actual intent cannot be determined.

### Request for Information

The most frequent violation was when a child would ask for information and then continue talking without waiting to receive the information. Thus, the child violated the sincerity criterion that he or she really did want the information. In the child-child dyad, peers constantly ignored requests for information even when the speaker would pause or wait for the information.

In some instances the children did not have the syntactic or semantic skills to request the information in a specific way for the hearer to be affected appropriately. Subject Four made the most attempts at requests for information and also had the most incomplete attempts at requests for information.

### Request for Action

One interesting type of request for action that violated the preparatory set was when only the hearer could perform an action, yet the child would request that he himself do the act. For example, Subject Three was playing with the playdough and said to himself, "Take the ball." This type of requesting action was found across both dyadic conditions.

In the adult-child dyad, one child told an inanimate object, a lego, to perform an action. This is not much different from the situation in which an adult talks to a car to get it started, or to a plant to help it grow. In these instances the criteria for a speech act are unfulfilled since there is no other hearer; however, the speaker may act as the speaker's own hearer and these utterances may serve to affect the speaker-hearer. Some counseling techniques also use this approach.

Subject Four had the most problems with requests for action but she also used a high percentage of the total number of successful speech acts that were requests for action across the dyadic conditions.

## Request for Objects

The sincerity rule or criterion was violated once for the request for objects. Subject Four asked Subject Three for a rolling pin and then proceeded to grab it before Subject Three could hand it to her.

## Speculation

Subjects One and Two were the only ones that violated the speech act of speculation. Most of the attempts that were unsuccessful were semantically incomplete and were used with a verb such as "think" in the form of a tag question. If the utterance was semantically incomplete it means that the hearer was not able to determine what the propositional content was. If the utterance act took the form of a tag question, the hearer was being asked to verify the speculation. Since speculation involves the child's or speaker's own beliefs or attitudes there would be no way that a hearer could verify those speculations. Therefore, the sincerity criterion was violated.

There were few violations of this speech act type but it should be noted that there were very few successful speculations. Subject One had the most speculations across dyadic conditions and he did not violate any of the conditions for this speech act.

## Rule Order

There were very few rule orders and the violations were also few. In two instances, the hearer effect was unknown. Subject One told himself the rule in one instance and Subject Six told an inanimate object the rule in one instance.

Whereas these children with very flexible language skills and with the high frequency of productive utterances occurring used few rule orders, it was found (Lucas, 1977) that children with severe language disorders used a high proportionate number of rule orders. It appears that the language-disordered children were more apt to use utterances that were repeated, such as rule orders, in inappropriate situations. The use of the rule order takes the place of novel utterances that assert, state information, etc. This increase of rule orders by language-disordered children has significant implications for intervention treatment (see Chapter 10).

### Pretend Statement of Information

Subject Five used a large number of unsuccessful attempts in the child-adult dyad. She also used a large number of successful pretend statements of information across dyadic conditions. The other attempts at pretend statements of information that were unsuccessful were the result of problems with the essential elements. For example, many of the children did not use enough intensity for the hearer to respond but, played back on the videotape, the type of speech act attempt could be determined.

### Pretend Request for Action

Subjects Five and Six were the only ones to have unsuccessful pretend requests for action speech acts. These subjects were also the only ones who used a greater number of any type of pretend speech acts that were complete and therefore successful.

### Miscellaneous Violations

There were other types of vocalizations that were verbal in nature but do not fit the speech act criteria. These acts included singing, imitations, interjections, and exclamations. According to speech act semantic criteria, none of these acts are really speech acts, but the two most advanced subjects (Five and Six) used the most of these other types of vocalizations. Since language-disordered children who use a lot of these non-speech act types of verbalizations are replacing productive language development, what are the non-language-impaired children doing? The two most advanced children were also the ones with the greatest variety of speech acts and the most advanced sociocognitive interaction with the adult and the other peer, even though these two subjects had these other types of verbalizations.

Perhaps there are some rules for when it is appropriate to use these other types of verbalizations. It certainly would be appropriate in a highly imaginative play situation that was interspersed with successful speech acts. However, a child who uses these other vocalizations without the appropriate context, that is preparatory set, and without a purpose, such as pretend or play, is a child that lacks the societal conventions for acquiring speech acts. Furthermore, the two subjects who used so many of these other vocalizations were true initiators of activity in both dyadic conditions; however, language-disordered children who use these other vocalizations may do so not only at the expense of speech acts but at the expense of most initiation of activity. Language-disordered children are typically physical manipulators who are passive at engaging in any sort of communication that may lead to a verbal initiation.

In addition to the violations that were observed, there was also a significant amount of indirect speech acts used by these children. The next section describes the indirect speech act.

## INDIRECT SPEECH ACTS

An indirect request acts as a speech act that would be a request except that it is marked as if it were an interrogative. In terms of semantic criteria, the indirect request is an assumption on the part of the speaker that the person will do as requested. The three-year-old subjects were also capable of responding to indirect requests.

Since the hearer is capable of performing as requested and since the speaker assumes that the hearer will do as requested, the speaker can use a "polite" form to request. For example, "Can you give me a roller?" is a request that on the surface indicates a choice of responses for the hearer. But according to the preparatory set, there is only one response—to give the roller. The reason there is only one choice is that the roller is certainly attainable by the hearer and the speaker is capable of seeing that the hearer is capable of getting the roller. The real question is not whether the hearer is capable of getting the roller but is a request for the hearer to hand the roller to the speaker.

The children used requests concerning the hearer's ability to perform a desired action or give a desired object in both dyadic conditions. The adult answered the indirect request as if it were a direct request and so did the children. The children answered the indirect requests more than 50 percent of the time. The remaining time the children either ignored or denied the request. For application to language disorders, it is significant to note that three-year-old children handled these indirect requests, whereas most language-disordered children have difficulty with indirect requests. They tend to respond to any question or request in a literal manner, probably because they are not past the initial semantics of Phase Two developments. They are still operating at a reduced semantic level even though their forms *appear* to be more advanced.

In addition to the ability to perform indirect requests, the children produced a few indirect requests stated as "wishful thinking." For example, Subjects Three and Four were discussing who was going to open the door so they could leave. Subject Three asked Subject Four to open the door. Subject Four said, "I want *you* to."

Another type of indirect request was where the hearer assumed the intent for the speaker. For example, Subject Six said to the adult, "Will you roll this for me?" The adult didn't say she would or wouldn't since that was the surface question. The adult just went ahead and rolled the playdough. A similar type of indirect request may be termed the "proposal" (Searle, 1975), as when a speaker uses a form such as "Let's do X." The "Let's" is really not a choice but a very specific request. Three of the six children used the proposal, although infrequently.

Some of the children would perform an indirect request by using a tag interrogative form. For example, "Pretend that your name is Mary, O.K.?" The first part of the question is a direct request but the tag changes the meaning to that of an indirect request (Searle, 1975). Only one child, Subject Six, was capable of using tag question forms.

One of the most frequent types of indirect request was in the form "I need X." This statement has added meaning in a situation that has a different preparatory set than might be expected for a statement of information or an assertion. In a different preparatory set, the hearer is expected to comply so that the "I need X" is satisfied, turning this into an indirect request (Searle, 1975). These indirect types of requests were observed in both dyadic conditions but only one child offered an indirect form of help: "I can cut it for you." With the "I need X" form there sometimes was a pause and a "please," as in "I need X, please."

Instead of the capability of the hearer being questioned, the children sometimes used a form to question their capability, thus indirectly asking for help. For example, "I can't pull it off by myself." The adult hearer immediately helped the subject pull the lego off.

Although it was obvious that three-year-old children are capable of producing indirect requests as well as responding to indirect requests as predicted, there were not enough indirect forms to determine if the children had any strategy for using a particular type of indirect request. It is obvious that the three-year-old children would make more indirect requests concerned with what they were doing than direct requests. Furthermore, the polite aspects of "please," etc., change the meaning and are used sparingly by these children. This does not mean that there is a developmental difference between children who do or do not use "please," but rather that these children are not used to using that polite form. Instead, indirect requests are considered polite and acceptable to these children.

## LANGUAGE—PHASE TWO

Our analysis of the developmental aspects of six three-year-old children has provided an overview of what language during Phase Two may resemble. The processes of overextension, expansion, and modulation were briefly discussed so that the structural characteristics of language skills could be seen as the products of underlying semantic processes.

Expansion provides the language phase child with a way to increase structural complexity from understanding the environmental experience. As had been reiterated numerous times in the literature, new forms spring from old ideas (e.g., Ferguson & Slobin, 1973). The ability to expand comes from the modulation process of changing meaning through the addition of morphological inflections, functors, etc. Finally, the language phase child's lexicalization develops rapidly and the extension, either over- or under-, of the semantic features allows the child to access new terms. These three processes are characteristic of the Phase Two child.

The Phase Two child is different from the Phase One child because now the child has a more advanced communication system. The Phase Two child has all the characteristics of language: phonology, morphology, syntax, and structural semantics, with the greatest growth occurring in ways to use specific language skills. However, these skills are products of the underlying sociocognitive development of meaning. To analyze the language areas without considering sociocognitive development would not be beneficial for application purposes. As evidenced with the six three-year-old children, several differences and similarities need to be considered. The following section summarizes the use of those language skills by the Phase Two child.

## Speech Act Types

If a child is acquiring language in a systematic and sequential manner that is typical of children in Phase Two (all milestones for syntax, morphology, phonology, and surface semantics are adequate), then the child should evidence the ability to successfully alter the attitudes, behaviors, and beliefs of the hearers in his or her environment. If the child is comfortable, there should be no strong preference shown for either adults or peer children. If a child shows these strong preferences, then the child probably doesn't have the social development necessary to expand his or her language skills through interaction with a variety of speaker-hearers.

None of the three-year-olds produced less than one successful speech act per minute. In fact, they all produced a number greater than one per minute. Being conservative, since this was a small sample, and using one per minute as a guideline, no child in Phase Two should be producing less than one successful speech act per minute, provided that child is with a comfortable hearer and is given the opportunity. Whether the hearer is an adult or a peer should not affect basic output. The number of overall speech acts should be twice as great or at least greater with a good hearer (adult) than with a peer who doesn't respond nonverbally to requests, etc.

From observing the types of speech acts coupled with the semantic processes (based on sociocognitive development) that the children in Phase Two utilize, the following conclusions may be made.

The assertion and statement of information were used by all children; therefore, a child who is typically developing would probably use a large number of these two types of acts. These acts allow the child to expand language skills and to get feedback from the hearer in terms of semantic development. The child can increase structural complexity by using structures about information that is commonly known or shared by both the speaker and the hearer. Any statement or assertion that is not quite complete in semantic skills will be corrected or modified by a good hearer.

The request forms present the most difficulty. These three-year-old children are already capable of using an indirect request but the ability to use advanced interrogative structures would not be observed until the end of Phase Two development when children begin to ask all of their "when" and "where" questions. "Why" questions, begun earlier, allow the child to develop more information, thus supporting previously acquired information as well as adding to the information. These question tactics probably allow the child to increase the lexicalization that occurs so rapidly throughout this entire Phase Two.

It would not be wise to expect a certain type of speech act to be represented by a certain percentage; nor would it be wise to expect a child to produce all thirteen speech act types. As previously stated, the ways in which the speech act types are used tell us something about the development of a child in terms of sociocognitive maturation but they do not tell us anything about language skills. However, language skills should be developed at a pace equal to the sociocognitive development. Therefore in the typical Phase Two child, the ways in which speech acts are used should say something about language development.

For language-disordered children it is easier to determine language ability by looking at the frequency of speech acts, the purpose for using speech acts, and the use of other, less meaningful verbalizations in place of speech acts. For example, a four-year-old child who uses only requests is getting basic needs met, at a developmental level less than the least mature three-year-old child in the study. Unless a child shows an assertion and a statement of information as true speech acts with all of the semantic criteria met (appropriate context, preparatory set, sincerity, and essential element), the child is really not into the Phase Two of development and is probably experiencing a breakdown between Phase One and Phase Two. The child may evidence greater structural skills, i.e., specific language skills, but he or she will not show a language system that is synergistic and capable of progressing into the linguistic phase.

It is important to note that the Phase Two child shows different types of strategies for interacting that are probably part of the sociocognitive development recognized by laymen as "personality." Recall the girl that was consistently aggressive and consistently winning battles who was considered by some of the teacher aides as "bossy." This girl, like the other children, had developed language skills that could be representative of lifelong communication strategies. Furthermore, the children proportionately used the same types of speech acts in both types of dyad conditions, even when the child was put in with another child who was not a good hearer and who did not comply either verbally or nonverbally. Therefore, "pragmatics" research must not consider one child's speech acts and then decide that that is the way all children function. Even when analyzing speech acts, it is apparent that by three years of age children have their individual strategies. Only a pragmaticism methodology will demonstrate such individual differences among children.

The obvious differences in three-year-old children suggest particular caution in applying milestones that have been gathered from one or two children. For example, Halliday's work (1973, 1975), although classical in nature, was originally based on Halliday's own son. If three-year-old children have such different learning strategies, one can speculate that children 9 to 12 months old might also have individual learning strategies.

These data also point out that chronological age is not as important as the ability to use skills. Among the six three-year-old children there were at least three different developmental levels, all within Phase Two. One child was so advanced that she was at the end of Phase Two, a point typical of children around five years of age. Two of the subjects were advanced and right in the middle of the phase (typically about four years of age), and at least one subject was beginning Phase Two, typical of most 30- to 36-month-old children. The fact that all of the children were able to alter hearers' behaviors in desired ways with a reasonably low percentage of violations (26 to 30 percent) meant that they were in Phase Two and learning. The language skills of a child who cannot do that manipulation will not continue to develop adequately and the child is not really in the language phase (Phase Two).

In assessing a child, the diagnostician should be interested in not just where the child is in development but also how the child got there and where the child is going. Later chapters discuss assessment for each phase, but it should be noted that for Phase Two the structural evidence is secondary to the learning strategies. If the processes are developed for the strategies to be evident, the child will progress through Phase Two.

## SUMMARY

The purpose of this chapter was to discuss Phase Two language development. Language is defined as consisting of syntax, morphology, and phonology skills that are used according to a developmental level of sociocognitive skills. The best way to determine whether or not a child is using a language system is to observe his or her language usage. Usage may be assessed by analyzing the speech act development in the child during Phase Two.

## REFERENCES

Antinucci, F., & Parisi, D. Early language acquisition: A model and some data. In C.A. Ferguson & D.I. Slobin (Eds.), *Studies of child language development*. New York: Holt, Rinehart & Winston, 1973.

Bateson, M.C. Mother-infant exchanges: The epigenesis of conversational interaction. In D. Aaronson & R.W. Rieber (Eds.), *Developmental psycholinguistics and communication disorders*. New York: New York Academy of Sciences, Annals of the New York Academy of Science, 1975, *263*, 101-113.

Bloom, L., Lifter, K., & Tanouye, E. *The semantics of verbs and the acquisition of grammatical morphemes*. Paper presented at the meeting of the American Speech and Hearing Association, Chicago, November 1977.

Bowerman, M. *Early syntactic development*. Cambridge, England: Cambridge University Press, 1973.

Brown, R. *A first language: The early stages*. Cambridge, Mass.: Harvard University Press, 1973.

Dore, J. The development of speech acts (Doctoral dissertation, City University of New York, 1973). *Dissertation Abstracts International, 1973, 34*. (University Microfilms No. 73-14, 374.)

Ferguson, C.A., & Slobin, D.I. (Eds.). *Studies of child language development*. New York: Holt, Rinehart & Winston, 1973.

Halliday, M.A.K. *Explorations on the functions of language*. New York: Elsevier North Holland, 1973.

Halliday, M.A.K. *Learning how to mean: Explorations in the development of language*. New York: Elsevier North Holland, 1975.

Kirk, R.E. *Experimental design: Procedure for the behavioral sciences*. Belmont, Calif.: Brooks/ Cole, 1968.

Lucas, E.V., & Hoag, L. Speech acts: A language therapy strategy for emotionally disturbed children. Paper presented at the Interdisciplinary Linguistics Conference: Language Perspectives, Louisville, Kentucky, May 1976.

Lucas, E.V., & Tatarsky-Taylor, L. *The dyadic effects of child-peer and child-adult interactions on speech act types of non-handicapped three-year-old children*. Unpublished research project, Texas Tech University, 1981.

Lucas, E.V. The feasibility of speech acts as a language approach for emotionally disturbed children. (Doctoral dissertation, University of Georgia, 1977). *Dissertation Abstracts International, 1978, 38*, 3479B-3967B. (University Microfilms No. 77-30, 488)

Lucas, E.V. *Semantic and pragmatic language disorders: Assessment and remediation*. Rockville, Md.: Aspen Systems, 1980.

Rostamizadeh, M.B. *A comparison of two dyadic conditions for speech act types in three-year-old children*. Master's thesis, Washington State University, 1981.

Searle, J.R. *Speech acts: An essay in the philosophy of language*. Cambridge, England: Cambridge University Press, 1969.

Searle, J.R. A taxonomy of illocutionary acts. In K. Gunderson (Ed.), *Language, mind, and knowledge: Minnesota studies in the philosophy of science* (Vol. XI). Minneapolis: University of Minnesota Press, 1975.

Snow, C.E., & Ferguson, C.A. *Talking to children*. Cambridge, England: Cambridge University Press, 1977.

## Chapter 6

# Phase Three: The Linguistic System

*A linguistic system: Sweet*
*Melodic, Complex: $E = MC^2$*

## Chapter Objectives

1. Describe the semantic properties of a linguistic system.
2. Explain the transition between Phase Two and Phase Three.
3. List some of the skills a person in Phase Three is capable of performing.
4. Describe the relationship between semanticity and displacement.
5. Describe the significance of a linguistic system as compared to a language system.
6. Describe the displacement properties.
7. Explain what is meant by the "linguistic nature" of a speech act.
8. List a variety of linguistic types of speech acts.

## INTRODUCTION

Chapter 4 described the prelanguage requisites for developing language, and Chapter 5 described the language developments within the speech act. The purpose of this chapter is to describe the transition between Phase Two and Phase Three and to discuss the product, a linguistic system. This linguistic system allows for complex semantic development to be used in a variety of speech acts to alter a hearer's behaviors as well as attitudes and beliefs.

## LANGUAGE TRANSITION

Once the basic language structures are acquired in Phase Two, the child has a need to refine those structures so as to be able to affect the hearer in the most efficient way. The process of refining the semantics includes the deletion of redundant meaning through ellipsis so that dependent and independent clauses may become more complex as the creation of new symbols is facilitated. For example, if the utterance "The girl threw the ball" would be combined with "The ball is a beach ball," the final utterance would be "The girl threw the beach ball." This could be made more complex by conjoining the two utterances about the girl to form "The girl who threw the beach ball is my sister."

To be able to combine these simple ideas into more complex structures suggests that the speaker has acquired semantic relationships not only between the basic ideas (Phase One) but also among the ideas (Phase Two), and is also able to express the ideas from various points of reference (Phase Three). The ability to deal with multiple factors indicates a transition not only cognitively but also socially. The linguistic phase speaker who is making the transition is able to relate sophisticated stories and conjoin the relationships within the story with the appropriate language skills from Phase Two. For language-disordered children, this transition is a site of major disruption that interferes with the acquisition of a linguistic system. Recall that the first place of possible disruption was between Phase One and Phase Two. A child who does not make this second transition between Phase Two and Phase Three would have acquired a sophisticated language system but not a linguistic system governed by the linguistic principles of semanticity, redundancy, displacement, flexibility, and productivity.

## LINGUISTIC PRINCIPLES

The linguistic principles that were discussed in Chapter 2 as part of the semantic, synergistic system provide the necessary skills for the child to make the transition between Phase Two and Phase Three development. These semantic principles or processes of semanticity, displacement, redundancy, flexibility, and productivity are at their maximum level of formulation in the transition period between Phase Two and Phase Three. It is the development of these linguistic processes for use in speech act productions that makes the difference between a child who has advanced language skills and a child who has advanced language skill functioning within a linguistic system.

Semanticity, the rapid acquisition of semantic features for organization into attached lexical tags, becomes a useful tool in Phase Two, but this tool acts in Phase Three to facilitate other learning in the child speaker. The semantic features in Phase Three accumulate to become concepts that can act to develop other concepts. The term "table" uttered by the Phase One child to represent a relationship communicated a need as interpreted by the hearer. In Phase Two the child said something about the table in a proposition-predication relationship such as "That is our table." In Phase Three the child is able to take the information about the concept of "table" and apply it to the next situation to create new ideas. "Hey, that rock is like an old table that does not have any legs, only a top." By the time this principle of semanticity has been used for a period of time, the ideas become novel and not just forms of past representations. The adolescent might say, "The cloud raced by the players, tabling all hopes of rain for a game cancellation." It should be noted that only the adolescent who has acquired the maximum ability to use semantic principles will be able to say this type of utterance in a novel situation.

Through semanticity, lexicalization has become concept development at the linguistic level, rather than the building of bits of information (semantic features), as in Phase One and Phase Two. Thus, during the linguistic phase the signs are what Peirce would call "pure symbols." The child who is in the elementary grades or beyond should be able to take a symbol and create other symbols—true symbolization that takes the form of analogies, metaphors, indirect speech acts, and so forth. From the symbols, definitions are created so that the child is now capable of learning beyond the here and now through definitions—definitions that employ symbolic use of symbols. In Phase Three, redundancy is at its maximum so that there are new terms developed to define the newly constructed concepts, just as a scientist creates a word for a new invention or discovery—a word that better defines through symbols what has occurred in the past development of an idea.

This adult level of language usage, the use of a linguistic system, is quite efficient for adults who are able to use the system, but quite inappropriate for the child who is having trouble. In other words, definitions or broad categorization for the adult learner is quite appropriate, but for the child, it is quite complex, as previously indicated by the explanation of Phase One and Phase Two requirements. What is appropriate for the child with learning problems is the level of semanticity at which the child is functioning, such as Phase One semantic relationships or Phase Two semantic feature acquisition from the here and now (see Chapters 9, 10, and 11 for intervention). It is probably easier for an educator or clinician to understand the synergistics of semanticity at the linguistic level than at the other two phases, just because the educator or clinician is more likely operating at the semanticity level of definitions than at either of the other two phases of development.

Semanticity at the linguistic phase provides the speaker with a variety of ways to perform in the learning situation of everyday life. The speaker can produce a joke and understand the meaning of a joke, whereas the language learner may repeat a joke and even laugh without an understanding of the meaning. Whether or not the linguistic user finds a joke to be funny depends on the person's own meaning for the joke based on past experiences. The semanticity of the linguistic system allows the person to create new jokes that are funny to the hearer because words or signs are true symbols and thus have multiple meanings to the hearer. This is the case with puns.

A linguistic system allows the speaker to perform speech acts that have advanced performative and nonperformative verbs, such as "promise," "vow," "pledge," "encourage," "marry," "baptize," "unite," "swear," "condemn," "ridicule," "approve," "feel," "praise," "appreciate," "evaluate," "revise," "ponder," "think," "guess," "believe," "suffer," "acquaint," "critique," "suspend," "blind," "enrich," "empower," and so forth. Although many of the aforementioned words are not true performatives, they are truly symbolic, since the utterance of the word is an act beyond the surface form. For example, a person does not promise until the word "promise" is uttered with the speech act semantic conditions being met and the effects are as intended on the hearer. Therefore, a promise cannot be made nonverbally—it is only through the verbal utterance that such an act can be understood.

Most children who have made the language to linguistic transition are able to produce and understand the minimum level of meaningfulness of the previously mentioned verbs. Children who do not understand these types of utterances will encounter learning and possibly societal problems in life. From observation of adolescents who have been habitual violators of society's laws, it is apparent that these individuals have not been able to understand the synergistic value of certain types of utterances with strong performative or linguistic value. To these individuals "promise" is a word much like "tell" or "say."

## Research in Semanticity

To gain a better understanding of the importance of semanticity in Phase Three, let us examine some recent research involving children between the ages of seven and fourteen who had been screened or "tested" by the speech and language pathologist and who were diagnosed as having a reading or learning problem but not a language problem. Upon listening to such a child and analyzing the child's language sample, it was apparent that the child had a fair language system but not a linguistic system. (Chapters 8 and 11 will discuss assessment and intervention for the linguistic system.) The primary characteristic of the language system that did not function for academic learning was that it lacked the semanticity for developing concepts related to displacement of space and time.

A project was begun in 1982 aimed at collecting a battery of information on every child who was referred to the Texas Tech University Clinic as having reading and learning problems but no proven language therapy.

The collected data (Arwood & Swanson, 1982) included qualitative analyses of the language samples according to Lucas's rules (1980), reading test scores, samples of writing, academic achievement scores, and records from school. Within six months, data on ten subjects between the ages of 7 and 11 had been collected. Each of these children was found to have language systems that were deficient in semantic properties for displacement commensurate with a linguistic system. Thus, each of these children had not demonstrated the progression between Phase Two and Phase Three. Some had been asked to repeat grades, some had been put in a resource room to get assistance with reading, and some had been given tutoring in class or by the parent out of school. All had very poor achievement records, with test scores reflecting a maximum of first grade or low second grade work even though many of the children should have been in the third or fourth grade.

After the data were collected, all of the children were put into therapy for specific remediation of the *language* breakdown rather than for assistance with the symptom—poor reading. Although the results of the intervention have not yet been formally reported, there have been consistent reports of the children making progress in school. One child has gone from failing grades to all A's. One child has gone from C's and D's to A's and B's and will be dismissed from therapy after this semester. He has been re-enrolled in therapy to ensure that all of the problems with semantic displacement have been remediated. One child quit trying and the parents took him out of private school and put him into public school with language intervention as the primary support service. The parents last reported that the child was beginning to try again. Why did these children fail at reading and other academic subjects when their basic language system was intact? The answer has to do with the synergistic quality of the system.

In order to read, a child has to be able to understand the relationships of all the symbols used and to allow one symbol to represent another symbol. If a child has acquired the basic language skills of Phase Two, he or she might be able to read some words by sight configuration but not understand the relationship among symbols until he or she is verbally able to manipulate symbols. This is why some children who are not verbal learn how to read at a minimum visual level. However, without some verbal form substitute either through language boards, computers, etc., the child will not demonstrate the ability to make symbols stand for other symbols in a perfect symbolic fashion. Writing is the same type of function. Any reading or writing task beyond the basic visual configuration that requires comprehension of sounded out symbols, for example, will put too much stress on a system that cannot manipulate symbols effectively.

When semanticity is at its maximum, a child can learn any task that requires the manipulation of symbols to stand for other ideas or signs. The child not only reads the word "table" but understands its relationship to other words in the sentence, paragraph, and more important, the story. In fact, one assessment guideline for working with these children is to determine whether or not they can tell a story that demonstrates all of the relationships a real story illustrates.

Most children between the ages of five and seven are able to tell incredible stories in the appropriate sequenced detail. However, children who are not able to manipulate symbols at the linguistic level are not able to tell stories with the same appropriate detail related to sequence. If these children cannot tell a story, how can they be expected to sequence the symbols on a page that represent someone else's story into a meaningful task called reading? (Chapter 11 will provide examples of such children's stories and language abilities.) Remember, this text is about the synergistics of the language system, not the products. If only the products were considered, these children would demonstrate adequate syntax, morphology, and surface semantics in an adequate phonological system. However, synergistically speaking, they will not have reached the linguistic phase of development.

Earlier in this chapter, several characteristics of the linguistic system were related to the principles of semanticity. These characteristics included telling jokes, creating multiple meanings for humor as in the use of puns, and the ability to use performatives. To this list should be added the ability to learn other symbolic manipulations including advanced mathematical and computational skills, the ability to tell stories with the appropriate detail and sequencing, and the ability to do verbal reasoning. This last item, verbal reasoning, requires not only semanticity but also displacement to be developed at an advanced symbolic level. It should be noted that displacement is needed for the academic tasks of reading, writing, following directions, telling stories, doing advanced verbal mathematical problems, computations, and so forth.

As described in Chapter 2, displacement refers to the child's ability to refer to an object, action, or event as it relates to other objects, actions, and events. The degree to which the referent is removed in space and time reflects the extent of displacement used. For example, the child sees a cup, points to the cup, and says "cup." The object "cup" is a shared referent with the hearer, who picks up the cup and hands it to the child. The child has developed the ability to refer to something away from his or her own body. Later the cup is not in sight and the child says "cup" with a rising intonation. The hearer says, "Oh, you want your cup again." The hearer is making an assumption that this is what the child intended so the hearer goes into the other room and gets the cup. If this is what the child intended, the child is indeed able to refer to something that is not in sight.

With semantic development the child is able to ask about specifics related to the cup that are not visible or tangible. For example, in the utterance "Mommy, why is the cup full?" the word "full" has an arbitrary point of reference that may or may not be shared by the two participants. To the mother, the cup is full because the juice is about a half inch from the top. To the child, the cup can only be full if the juice is all the way to the top—to the rim of the cup. The child's ability to manipulate the term "full" indicates some ability to refer to something that is not specifically tangible such as a table or to something that describes a perceptual feature such as shape. However, these nontangible, nonspecific referents require that the child be able to manipulate certain points of reference, as in the example where "full" can refer to the whole cup or to the amount the cup can hold.

Points of reference include the child in relation to other objects, actions, or events; the objects, actions, and events in relation to other objects, actions, and events; and other persons in relation to persons, objects, actions, and events. For example, most children who have good language but who do not have linguistic systems think that a person's lap is lost when the person stands up. Although a native speaker does not usually refer to "lap" when someone is standing, the adult speaker could say, "I spilled sauce on my lap," and point to the stains. However, the child might say, "Where is your lap?" The ability to displace oneself in the environment in relation to other reference points is gradually acquired through the development of semantic features related to these displacement concepts. The child's semantic ability continues to grow through the relationships expressed by space, time, quality, and quantity concepts such as "big," "down," "up," "short," "full," "deep," "some," "larger," and so forth.

These spatiotemporal, quality, and quantity concepts describe the relationships of objects, actions, people, and events as they are moved or as they move through space. A story is connected by these types of relational words that refer to displacement properties and not necessarily to specific referents. For example, a child says, "I had to do two problems in math this morning that the rest of the class didn't know how to do. One of the problems was about a man who sold some cows at the market. The other problem was about a woman who drove to visit her friend. I had to find out how much gas the lady used." The adult says, "How did you do the problems?" The child says, "Well, I forget the numbers, but they were division problems." This child may be only in the third or fourth grade, but has obviously developed a very nice linguistic system for learning.

Reconsider the sentence "I had to do two problems in math this morning that the rest of the class didn't know how to do." What are the linguistic concepts beyond language skills that are being expressed? The child has acquired enough semantic features for semanticity to occur requiring that more than one idea be put into the same sentence. These multiple ideas include: one as compared to more than one problem, math versus some other types of problem solving, "do" versus "read" the problems, the concept of when the problems were done, and, embedded in the previous ideas, the concept that the other people in the class could not do the problems. If this child did not have the spatiotemporal concepts to specify when or why, the child's utterance would not have conveyed the necessary information. Furthermore, the child described the types of problems he solved. Such problems are performances of advanced speech acts based on displacement of time, distance, amount, quantity, cost, etc. A child who had not made the transition into the linguistic system would not be able to perform speech acts based on these concepts.

Given the semanticity of the language system and the ability to displace the semantic concepts, the child should have the flexibility and productivity to deal with the types of things that have been mentioned: jokes, multiple meanings, analogies, telling stories, reasoning, performing and understanding the acts of promising, etc.

It is through the manipulation of the linguistic system that other symbol systems may be created. In fact, the extent to which verbal abilities may control or manipulate a speaker as his or her own hearer may be based on the linguistic system. For example, to reason why someone committed a transgression may prevent a person from retaliating with a thoughtless killing. Once the circumstances are verbalized, the speaker who is his or her own hearer recognizes the reason for the transgression and shrugs off the act. The justice system and performance within the justice system are based on a linguistic code that possibly some, if not many, of those who violate the code cannot understand. Chapter 13 will discuss some of the implications and ramifications of understanding the linguistic, synergistic system.

## THE LINGUISTIC SPEECH ACT

The rest of this chapter will discuss the relationship of the linguistic system to language skills and to early communication in terms of the semantic properties of the speech act.

A child who has acquired some basic communication skills has also acquired some of the semantic conditions of the speech act. These conditions include the nonverbal and some paralinguistic skills for the essential elements while incorporating information in semantic features about the shared reference of the preparatory set. The concept or propositional content is continuously built and the sincerity is acquired through the expected conventions of meaning.

In addition to these semantic conditions, the child is able to use syntactic, morphological, and phonological conventions by the age of three or somewhere in the second phase to perform a variety of speech acts to alter the attitudes, beliefs, and behaviors of a hearer in a variety of specified ways. In the early part of Phase

Two, the child used speech acts that mainly communicated a basic need. As the child's knowledge grew in semantic complexity, the child began to manipulate the semantic conditions so as to pretend or speculate. By the end of Phase Two, the child was able to perform speech acts that would manipulate attitudes as well as actions of the hearer.

In the linguistic phase, speech acts serve as problem solvers beyond basic needs and beyond basic assertions and statements of information. The linguistic system acts to organize previously gained information into new concepts. For example, the judge says, "I now pronounce you man and wife." The judge who is using the linguistic system is performing a speech act that has the ultimate semantic complexity. The symbols (words or utterance acts) perform a function that cannot by legal convention occur without the symbols. In other words, the performance of the judge in marrying two individuals cannot occur without the use of a symbolic sign. In this case the performance of a linguistic speech act is the highest form of symbolic function, a perfect symbol. Remember that the words are not the symbols, but the performance is the symbolic function. The words are symbolic signs. The complete performance of the speech act is the pure symbolic act.

Perhaps another example will help illustrate the linguistic function of a speech act. The teacher says, "Sally is your best friend." Until the teacher said this, the child may not have thought of Sally as anything but a person who hits and kicks. The teacher's utterance may act as a speech act with language referents or it may serve a linguistic speech act function. If the utterance act is accepted for its language value, the child says, "She isn't my friend." If the speech act has linguistic value, the child might say, "I don't think she wants to be my friend because she hit me." Or the child might say, "Oh, I guess she is my best friend." For the teacher's utterance to have the desired speech act effect on the child, the child as the hearer must accept the utterance's linguistic (semantic) effect. This effect is a change in attitudes and/or beliefs, and not just in behaviors.

Whether or not something is accepted with linguistic speech act value depends on the hearer's own semantic level regarding the act. The more semantically complex, that is, the more the idea has been verbally acted upon by the hearer, the more likely that the utterance act will develop the linguistic value. However, if the utterance act is intended to change behavior in the immediate situation, the linguistic value is not intended or acted upon by the hearer. Only the behavioral change from the verbal language specification is completed.

Another example of linguistic speech act performance might be as follows: A policeman says, "You are under arrest for breaking the law." The person cannot act appropriately nor can the person who broke the law adjust his or her beliefs or attitudes about breaking the law until the policeman has placed the person under arrest. If the policeman puts handcuffs on the hearer, the hearer might assume that something out of the usual range of behaviors is occurring. If the hearer verbalizes the idea "Oh, I guess I'm being arrested," he or she is arrested.

It is not until either the policeman or the hearer states the condition of being arrested that this act exists. Again the language alone, that is, the syntax, morphology, and word meanings, does not convey the linguistic value. The linguistic value is in the performance of the speech act under semantic conditions (preparatory, propositional, sincerity, and essential) with the intended illocutionary force of specifying the changes expected of the hearer.

If the person breaking the law had been told to do specific things indicative of being arrested, such as raising the hands, he or she might do them when the policeman uttered, "You are under arrest for breaking the law." However, if the person had never been arrested before, he or she might not have the appropriate preparatory set and would have to be told by the speaker what behaviors were to take place.

## SUMMARY

The child who communicates is developing a set of semantic features for use in language development. However, the goal of language development is not the ability to produce psycholinguistic structures as identified by the observing researchers. Syntax, morphology, and phonology express the form that is expanded through the acquisition of more complex semantics by the process of semanticity so that displacement, flexibility, and productivity may occur. The child or adult with a linguistic system is a person who can not only produce a wide variety of settings but also act on the covert attitudes and beliefs of a wide variety of hearers as well as on their overt behaviors.

This person with a linguistic system is capable of learning through use of the system and is capable of manipulating symbols to represent newly created symbols. All manipulation occurs through the performance of effective speech acts that increase in semantic complexity. Whether or not the content of the speech act is meaningful to the hearer depends on the hearer's past experiences as well as on the interpretant's mental set of semantic features. This mental set could be influenced by the emotional and psychological as well as physiological well-being of the individual.

Anything that disrupts the process of semanticity will disrupt the linguistic functioning of the individual. Whether or not the content is "abstract" to the hearer depends on what level the hearer has reached in manipulating symbols. An utterance such as "Justice for all" can be interpreted according to the hearer's understanding of the meaning. The more easily understood the semantics, the more easily understood is the speech act performance and the more likely is the hearer affected in the way the speaker intended. This suggests that the semantic complexity is a shared level between the speaker and the hearer and that the concreteness depends on the semantic displacement level shared by the two participants of the speech event. Only with a linguistic system can the speaker perform at the maximum level of effectiveness. The next chapter describes what may happen when there is a breakdown in the system and the types of problems that may occur.

**REFERENCES**

Arwood, E., & Swanson, B. *Learning, language disorders*. Master's project, Texas Tech University, 1982.

Lucas, E.V. *Semantic and pragmatic language disorders: Assessment and remediation*. Rockville, Md.: Aspen Systems, 1980.

## Chapter 7

# The Semantic Model

*Constancy has no change,*
*Movement has no will—*
*Speech acts have will but no constancy.*

## Chapter Objectives

1. Describe the semantic model according to the characteristics of a synergistic system.
2. Explain how the linguistic principles fit into the development of the model.
3. Explain the speech act criteria for the synergistic model.
4. Explain the relationship between the meaning and the tool.
5. Explain the relationship between language use and language acquisition.
6. Describe the difference between normal language acquisition and language disorders.
7. Explain the relationship between the phases of semantic development discussed in the preceding chapters and the model described in this chapter.
8. Explain the various critical developmental periods for semantic acquisition.
9. Describe the processes of the three phases of semantic development and their relationship to language disorders.

## INTRODUCTION

The purpose of this chapter is to integrate the principles, philosophy, and theory described in the preceding chapters into an operational model. The design of the model must be able to include the dynamics of a linguistic system, the skills of language, and the cognitive and social processes for development of any kind of communication.

To account for the dynamics, the model by necessity is synergistic or semantic in nature, cognitive in origin, and pragmatic when linguistically developed. The model must be able to account for observable behavior in language-disordered as well as nonhandicapped individuals. Therefore, the model must account for language processes of acquisition as well as for disordered language products.

Although theoretical in nature, the model must allow for experimentation, research, and evaluation of its components. The proposed semantic model is presented in tentative form so that all of these criteria may be considered.

## THE PARADIGM

A model is usually thought of as a representation and a standard for comparison. In this case, the model represents what may occur as a child acquires language skills. The data found in the speaker's utterances are used as the comparison. This model is a paradigm, the basis of which is semantics. Cases are tested against the characteristics of speakers to determine its workability. Table 7-1 provides an overall picture of the model.

There are four levels of internal semantic complexity. Each of these four levels may be impaired: (1) sensation may or may not be received; (2) sensation may or may not be organized into features; (3) features may or may not be organized by attachment to novel experiences; and (4) features may or may not be organized into concepts. As shown in Table 7-1 there are also three levels of development: Phase One—Prelanguage Communication Development, Phase Two—Language Development, and Phase Three—Linguistic Development. At each phase, a child could have difficulty and a semantic disorder in the acquisition of language skills for linguistic use would occur.

Table 7-2 illustrates the same paradigm but demonstrates that at the three phases there will be different types of resulting language disorders. To explain the disorders, the remainder of the chapter will be spent demonstrating the different kinds of problems that occur at the three phases of semantic development. These problems will be highlighted by use of case studies.

**Table 7-1** The Arwood Synergistic Model of Semantic Development

| Semantic Levels | Communication Phase One | Language Phase Two | Linguistics Phase Three |
|---|---|---|---|
| Sensation (thought object) | ******** ******** ******** ******** | ******** ******** ******** ******** | ******** ******** ******** ******** |
| Feature Perception (icon) | **** **** **** **** | ******** ******** ******** ******** | ******** ******** ******** ******** |
| Feature Organization (index) | **** **** **** **** | ******** ******** ******** ******** | ******** ******** ******** ******** |
| Concept Manipulation (true symbols) | | **** **** **** **** | ******** ******** ******** ******** |

**Table 7-2** The Breakdown of Semantic Development According to Levels of Usage

| Level | Communication Phase One | Language Phase Two | Linguistics Phase Three |
|---|---|---|---|
| Receiving Sensation (auditory only) | Visual compensation | With intervention: Development of language forms | With intervention: Deficits in maximum displacement (space, time, quality, quantity) |
| Feature Perception | If severe, alters interaction | Without intervention: Range in deficits from organized conventions to lack of any language | Without intervention: Severe deficits in displacements to no displacement |
| Feature Organization | Minimal, nonverbal usually adequate | Without intervention: Elaborate pantomime, difficulty acquiring conventions | Without intervention: no displacements without intervention |
| Concept Manipulation | | Without intervention: No development | |

## PHASE ONE—PRELANGUAGE COMMUNICATION DEVELOPMENT

A child who would be operating at the prelanguage level could demonstrate a breakdown in the communication acquisition level of semantic development. Therefore, the prelanguage child would have difficulty establishing an interactive situation for later language development to occur, as illustrated in Table 7-3. In Table 7-3, the various processes that have been discussed in preceding chapters are listed across from the phase of development that depends on the process for further development. During prelanguage development, it is critical that the deixis that established the preparatory set and the propositional content for the speech act be established. As indicated by the stars, the Phase One child needs to begin to use spontaneous imitation and to a lesser extent also expansion, extension, and modulation.

The breakdown during Phase One is going to result in the sensation not being received and processed well enough for one of the aforementioned processes to be facilitated. Facilitation of this process is an all-or-none ability; either the child demonstrates the ability to perform according to the laws of the semantic process or the child does not. Therefore, a language-disordered child would demonstrate behaviors consistent with the breakdown. The child who is functioning at the prelanguage phase of semantic development will show minimal, if any, social interaction and will demonstrate minimal, if any, use of modulation and spontaneous imitation. The result of this minimal demonstration is some characteristic patterns of language disorder or more appropriately, in this case, communication deficits.

For example, if a child minimally interacts with a person, the child will also show utterances restricted in both variety and frequency. As defined in Chapter 4, spontaneous imitation is a process only when there is a variety of utterances in a variety of unrestricted contexts. Therefore, a child with minimal interaction will also demonstrate minimal, if any, spontaneous imitation as well as having problems with the flexibility and variety of utterances.

From the previous explanation and the illustrations, it should be apparent that the prelanguage child's system is restricted by either sensory and/or perceptual development. Either sensory or perceptual deficits will affect the way in which the child can interact. The communication product then is also deficient. The sensory and/or perceptual deficiencies may occur for a number of reasons, including early separation trauma, prolonged intensive care without appropriate stimulation, punitive communication situations, physiological differences, physical or anatomical differences, and so forth. All of these factors influence the development of the sociocognitive semantics described in Chapters 2 and 3.

Any of the aforementioned reasons may affect the child's ability to initiate and maintain an interaction so that stimulation and perceptual organization of that interaction may occur. In such a case, semantic features do not become organized

**Table 7-3** Processes Found during the Three Phases of Semantic Development

| Sociocognitive Processes | Communication Phase One | Language Phase Two | Linguistics Phase Three |
|---|---|---|---|
| Deixis | **************** **************** ************** | | |
| Spontaneous Imitation | ********** ********* ********* ********** | | |
| Modulation | ************ ************** ************ | | |
| Overextension Underextension | | ************************ ************************ ************************ ************************ ************************ ************************ | |
| Expansion | | ********************** ********************** ********************** | |
| Over-generalization | | ****************** ****************** ****************** ****************** | |
| Redundancy | | ****************** ****************** ****************** | |
| Semanticity | | | ********************** ********************** ********************** |
| Displacement (maximum) | | | ************** ************** ************** ************** |

semantic notions or relations and functions. The following case study illustrates the type of child who may be functioning at the first phase of semantic development, that is, as a primary communicator at best, utilizing the basic sign-to-symbol relationship for communicative acts.

Albert, a four-year-old male, was brought to a university speech, language, and hearing clinic for an evaluation as part of a multidisciplinary pediatric team appraisal. From observation of the child with the primary caregiver, in this case, his mother, little purposeful interaction was seen. The mother did not verbally or nonverbally address the child at any time, nor did she verbally redirect the child. All interaction, as such, was by physical manipulation without gaze or eye contact establishing a joint reference between the mother and the child.

If the examiners had only been concerned with the child's verbal products, the evaluation would have been very short and would have revealed very little about this child's learning. Since it was imperative that the learning abilities be evaluated in order to determine how to help this child, the child's prelanguage sociocognitive abilities were also considered.

Since the child showed no maintenance or initiation of interaction, how was he learning and what was causing the deviance in development? There would be three combinations of possibilities as to why the child did not interact with people: (1) The child did not have the cognitive skills; that is, he showed an inability to learn semantic features through environmental experience; (2) The child did not have the social requisites to demonstrate what semantic features were being acquired; and (3) The child had a physiological problem that prevented the processing of sensory information.

The cognitive explanation was immediately ruled out since Albert did show the ability to manipulate objects through nonverbal means, indicating semantic notions such as recurrence, possession, denial, and the objective. However, Albert did not demonstrate action or agency. All nonverbal demonstrations were done after a considerable "warm-up" time with a cousin playing next to Albert.

Even though his cognitive ability seemed to be adequate for supporting a basic icon-to-index development for communication, Albert did not initiate or maintain any action. For example, Albert would push a ball to the cousin but would not request the act to be continued or retrieve the ball if it rolled across the room. This inability to maintain an interaction or to begin an act suggests that Albert's problem was in the acquisition of the social need or purpose for communication.

To Albert, the incoming sensory stimuli need not have purpose since he had no reason for using them. Therefore, he had no preference for mode of stimulus. If a child shows no purpose for communicating and no preference for mode, the child must not have a major sensory deficit such as a hearing loss that is preventing him from receiving stimuli.

Any other physiological problem was not obvious. The decision that Albert's problem was primarily social in nature resulting in a failure of features regarding people or agents to be coded was further supported by the social worker's report that there was a high risk of parental abuse, a history of child abandonment, and a mother who had no desire for children. Furthermore, the mother's social interaction with the examiners was inappropriate. She minimally answered the examiners' questions but never asked questions, commented, shared a gaze, or established eye contact.

It is important to determine the primary reason for a problem with language development so that remediation may be planned accordingly. The intervention for a prelanguage child of four years would vary according to whether the child had social, cognitive, or physical deficits. Remediation for Albert would be centered around arranging for ''meaningful'' interaction so that features are coded. Once a purpose for interaction could be established with Albert, the next step of semantic development or semantic relationships would be to begin to include verbal expressions of a variety of notions including agency.

Not all children fail to code semantic features just because of social disruptions. Corey, age two years, was brought by his parents for a speech and language evaluation since he was ''not saying any words yet.'' The mother said she knew that he wasn't ''just slow'' like the doctor and family kept telling her because he was ''different'' from her older son. Corey could dismantle a stereo set and put it back together without any help. Upon observation, Corey demonstrated many of the behaviors often associated with peripheral deafness. He did not attend to his name or to any verbal utterance so it appeared that he could not hear auditory stimulation.

A conflicting piece of information was also observed. Even though Corey did not respond to verbal stimulation, he did respond to footsteps in the hall and he ran to the window when he heard an airplane go past. Therefore, a hearing test was warranted but the possibility of an acuity problem affecting language development seemed unlikely. Furthermore, a cognitive deficit had to be immediately ruled out since the child was able to dismantle the workings of a record player much like mom had reported.

Corey also demonstrated the semantic notions of underlying cognitive development through the manipulation of toys and objects. The manipulation of these objects was separate from the acts of people. Though he visually attended, Corey never responded to gestures or verbal symbols.

Corey acted upon his environment according to his system of learning but there was little evidence of visual or auditory organization of features into anything more communicative than a basic icon or sometimes a minimal index. Some researchers would have described Corey as exhibiting childhood aphasia. Although this may be diagnostically appropriate, for many reasons, the term ''childhood aphasia'' does not tell the educator how Corey is learning so that effective remediation may be determined.

Since Corey did not respond to verbal input, it was concluded that auditory symbols were meaningless to him. Since his hearing acuity was sensitive enough for language input as determined by observation, the stimuli were being received but obviously were not processed or organized. A complete audiological evaluation was attempted but due to Corey's age and the fact that he did not attend to directions or his mother's verbal management, the results were questionable. The audiologist did conclude that Corey's hearing sensitivity could be no worse than a mild loss and that Corey would be able to receive stimulation sufficient enough for at least responding to his name.

Since cognitive skills were adequate and sensation was probably adequate, Corey was put in a junior language group to promote social development. It was believed that given the opportunity and facilitation to use symbols to meet his needs, Corey would begin to demonstrate some nonverbal semantic relations. Corey remained in the language group for one week. He was then put into individual therapy. In the therapy group, Corey could not follow either the nonverbal or verbal messages. He did not try to pantomime or follow other two- and three-year-old children. He would wear a puzzled look and act on the environment but adult's attempts to interact were met with behavior suggesting noncompliance. For example, during free play, Corey tried to operate a record player but found that the record slots were missing one record. He tried desperately to find the record for the slot. It didn't matter what the adults did verbally or nonverbally to redirect Corey, to hide the record player, to visually and verbally explain that one of the records was gone; Corey would not leave the task. Finally, the record player was removed and the adults left him. Corey sobbed quietly to himself.

Referring again to Table 7-2, it is apparent that the breakdown is in the coding of sensation into organized features for meaningful representation at the perceptual level. A program was begun employing sign language to tangibly connect sensory input with lexical tags. If the problem had been only in coding auditory input, Corey should have developed quickly since his sociocognitive skills were impaired only in terms of inability to code the information. However, Corey did *not* progress quickly with sign language.

Two years from the time that Corey was originally evaluated, Corey has been able to demonstrate semantic relations by manual communication. Occasionally, with the use of a Fonator (tactile, auditory trainer), Corey can produce verbalizations that are truly meaningful as opposed to his previous self-stimulating vocalization. The family uses total communication as much as possible with Corey and he now maintains and initiates acts with the semantic relationships being expressed. Although he can follow signed directions in a group and can therefore work with other children, he is able to follow a task better when by himself.

The frequency of the signed semantic relations has increased to the point where he has begun to spontaneously imitate others' signing and others' vocalizations. These spontaneous imitations suggest that Corey may be getting ready for the next phase. It should be noted that Corey has shown no modulation primarily because the use of signs is still too infrequent.

Since the original evaluation, Corey's hearing sensitivity has been tested six times in order to establish some reliability. It was concluded that Corey could have a very marginal, mild hearing loss (sensorineural). A very low gain aid was fitted to see if there were any behavioral changes with amplification since the Fonator had been so enthusiastically received by Corey. The mother and clinicians took daily data on behavior and no one could detect any behavioral changes except that Corey wanted the aid. He will not now take the aid off and he goes to get the aid when it is not on. The importance of audition and Corey's lack of symbolization is further discussed in Chapter 8. For the purpose of this chapter, it should be noted that Corey could not develop meaning or organize features. Even visual, tangible features were difficult for Corey to organize and represent through the use of a symbolic sign either visually or verbally.

In summary, Corey was not able to code features from sensory input into meaningful representations at the symbolic level. Consequently, interpersonal relationships did not develop into communicative acts of any type and only paired environmental situations produced any consistent response. Corey was a pre-language child because he was not physiologically capable of processing stimuli into information for attachment to lexical tags either visually or manually. Corey's ability to cognitively or socially act on the environment was impaired by his inability to organize the semantic features. Verbal and nonverbal acts held little meaning for Corey.

Albert failed to develop prelanguage processes because social prerequisites were not accessed; Corey failed to develop prelanguage processes because his internal system for processing features or meaning was impaired. There are also children who do not progress because cognitive prerequisites have not been met. This may be the case with severely multihandicapped children with what is often called a mental handicap or mental retardation. In Chapter 8 a description of the application of this paradigm of semantic development and corresponding break-down is described in detail. For the present discussion, it should be noted that unless a child demonstrates the minimal processes of Phase One in sequential order, communication remains passive.

Passive communication refers to the child's inability to actively use the sign to learn more about the environment. For icons to develop into an index, the child has to demonstrate certain semantic relationships nonverbally. Eventually, the verbal relationships are demonstrated and the child will actively construct the first verbal symbols. Many intervention programs for severely profoundly handicapped children attempt to facilitate speech sounds in these children without consideration for the underlying social and cognitive requisites. Some programs attempt to use repetitive sounds to facilitate babbling with the anticipation that speech will develop. However, babbling is not a prerequisite for communication in the prelanguage child, nor is it a prerequisite for language in the Phase Two child. Babbling is not a sociocognitive process and thus is not a prerequisite to communication development.

Whereas Albert had social deficits affecting cognitive development and Corey had processing deficits affecting social interaction and cognitive representation, the child with the cognitive deficit will also demonstrate problems with processing and social skills. Such children at the prelanguage phase of development require a situation in which all of these factors may be considered interdependently. The purpose of the pragmaticism methodology is to consider the child as part of a system for functional development. Therefore, assessment as well as remediation for the prelanguage child is based on providing a system of communication that will function for the child's development as well as for his or her environmental learning.

The opportunity for the child to use basic semantic development for further learning is based on a number of variables related to the quality of demonstration of the skills. These skills can be checked by asking the following questions:

1. Does the child's nonverbal behavior demonstrate a *number* of objects, actions, and events in a *variety* of relationships?
2. Does the child use a variety of indicators to represent the aforementioned relationships?
3. Does the child demonstrate a variety of indicators that are differential in nature?
4. Does the child initiate or create new contexts by nonverbal means?
5. Does the child demonstrate self-stimulatory behaviors that suggest a lack of ability to represent during that time?

The first question suggests that the child should be able to demonstrate a number of relationships through nonverbal behavior. The ways in which prelanguage children demonstrate these behaviors include eye gaze, visual tracking, motor movements of the body, gestures, blinking, etc. The relationships should also be expressed through a variety of indicators. For example, if a child has only one way to indicate, then he or she will miss opportunities to socially interact with others in other situations. By missing an opportunity, the child loses the chance to alter or change his or her environment. This lost opportunity results in the child not being able to learn from the action. Remember that the basis of the synergistic system is that the act is the performance. Even if the child wanted to perform, the inability to perform results in a loss of information about the act.

The child should demonstrate a variety of indicators that are differential in nature. The ability to differentiate represents active learning. For example, if a child is not able to differentiate between one adult's voice and another adult's voice, the child will not be able to indicate changes and/or a need for change in his or her environment. This inability to indicate a differential means of communication is synonymous with the child not being able to learn from incoming stimuli. If the system is not activated the synergistic property is soon lost. One of the most characteristic symptoms of a child who is not progressing is the lack of differential means to indicate. Programs of intervention that do not provide for alternate ways to communicate hinder the child's active development.

If a child is able to demonstrate a variety of relationships in a variety of ways, he or she is also probably differentiating among various incoming forms of stimuli and is also able to create new contexts. In other words, if a child is able to respond to the environment in a way that demonstrates active learning, he or she will also demonstrate a way to change the environment. Every time the child responds to the incoming stimuli, the child performs a behavior that in turn affects the environment. Therefore, the more opportunity the child has to act on the environment in appropriate ways, the more likely the child is going to affect the environment or people in the environment in some determined way.

If a child does not perform according to expected contextual information, the corresponding behaviors are not interpreted as representations. If such a child is not able to represent or if the behaviors are not interpreted as representations, the child is not developing according to the sociocognitive processes. This lack of development suggests that the child is not actively learning as expected. The child with inappropriate behaviors, often referred to as self-stimulatory behaviors, is not functioning in a synergistic capacity. The loss of the synergistic quality results in many deviations from the typical system.

A child who is not functioning synergistically at the prelanguage phase is having trouble receiving stimuli, coding the stimuli for semantic organization, and/or coding enough information so that the semantic features may be attached to appropriate lexical tags or markers.

If the previous five questions are answered in relation to the child's functioning within the synergistic system, an appropriate plan of intervention may be developed. When educators and parents begin to understand the system rather than seek milestone information about development, remediation will become much more practical and suitable for these children. Expectations will also be more realistic and prognosis can be better understood. For example, many parents and clinicians or teachers are thrilled when they hear a prelanguage child say his or her first word. However, they quickly become disillusioned when the child fails to progress on to the expected two-word utterances. If these individuals had understood the quality aspect of the synergistic system, they would have realized that one-word units are not representative of functioning. Only the child's means of using signs as icons, indices, or symbols to represent a variety of relationships in a variety of created contexts represents a synergistic system capable of progressing to the next phase of development.

The child who is in the prelanguage phase of development because of a breakdown in the acquisition of the semantic system will demonstrate many of the following atypical behaviors. Since motor development is a key to the prelanguage child's ability to perform behavior typical of a synergistic system, many children who are in the prelanguage phase demonstrate atypical motor patterns. The pediatrician may report that the child is "a fine, healthy two-year-old." The developmental specialist might report that the child was able to "put the cow in the barn.'' However, unless a pragmaticism methodology is considered when observing the child, the evaluator may not recognize atypical motor patterns suggesting that the child was unable to utilize incoming stimuli. In the case of Corey, although he was a healthy child according to the physician and although he was able to perform certain tasks, he did not demonstrate motor patterns typical of a child his age. He would perseverate on a task or work with the detail of a task for extended periods of time beyond what would be expected of most children functioning at the prelanguage age.

A realistic picture of a child cannot be obtained without considering the child's total functioning. The purpose of the synergistic model is to provide a paradigm relating sociocognitive processes with semantic development according to the level of acquisition. Whenever a child exhibits behavior that is atypical, a breakdown in the system may be traced by examining the model as pictured in Tables 7-1, 7-2, and 7-3.

In summary, the child in the prelanguage phase of semantic development may evidence many different types of problems. The main characteristic is that the child is functioning in the first processes of sociocognitive development and that the child is limited to basic communication skills with an icon followed by an index without true symbolic representation. Even children who are not yet ''speaking'' and who may have serious multiple handicaps are testable and there are prognostic indicators as to what the examiner might expect from the child over time (see assessment chapters). The child who is in the prelanguage phase of development will move on to the next phase of development only when the sociocognitive processes have been sufficiently advanced.

## PHASE TWO—LANGUAGE DEVELOPMENT

Phase Two is primarily characterized by expansion, extension, overgeneralization, and the beginnings of the linguistic principles of Phase Three. With the completion of this phase comes the beginning of Phase Three of linguistic development, which includes minimum redundancy, maximum displacement and semanticity for a flexible, productive system. As is true for the third phase, Phase Two may be interrupted at any of the points of development: sensory reception, feature perception, feature organization, and concept manipulation. The child in Phase Two will be acquiring information through the senses and will be able to organize the information into features. However, the quality of reception and organization could be impaired. The result of the impairment is that the child in Phase Two may not acquire adequate semantic development for the expansion and extension to occur at high enough frequency. If the frequency is not sufficient for continued development, the child begins to show a nonsynergistic system.

Nonsynergistic systems result in rigid structures and stereotyped utterances. The speech acts are few and so are the resulting environmental types of changes.

The child cannot acquire rapid lexicalization as in a synergistic system. The more splinter skills that are taught and the more information that this child acquires, the more likely that the language product will represent unconventional ways of functioning in a sign system. For example, many children in Phase Two of development have some conventional skills of phonology, morphology, syntax, and semantics. Even though such a child does have some of the conventional ways to order words or to modulate words, he or she is unable to organize the features into concepts that can be appropriately manipulated. The acquisition of some of the language suggests that the child is able to function with the environment until linguistic demands are made.

Linguistic demands usually do not occur until the child is in the academic situation that requires manipulation of symbols for reading and writing. Then the child who does not progress beyond the second phase of semantic development will evidence serious academic deficiencies. As more academic demands are placed on this Phase Two child, failure is experienced. Resource help, tutoring, extra long nights at homework, therapy, and escape systems become part of the child's existence. Although the prelanguage child remains dependent on the environment for basic needs, the child who acquires some basic language skills is cognitively capable of interacting with the environment for basic needs. The Phase Two child functions for self-help and activities of daily living but has a tremendous job trying to deal with the academic setting. The Phase Two child will not advance past the third grade in academic subjects without language intervention to assist in compensating for a system that is not meeting all of the requirements of being synergistic.

Although the language phase child is typically somewhere between two and seven years of age, most of the necessary language skills for moving into Phase Three of linguistic semantic development are completed between five and seven years of age. There are a number of productive individuals who do not progress beyond the second phase of semantic development. Among these individuals are those with congenital, severe, profound hearing impairments, the mentally retarded population, and some learning/language-disordered individuals.

These people hold laborer types of jobs that do not require much manipulation of concepts through maximum displacement or semanticity. Many intervention programs attempt to assist these individuals with the products of the system—syntax, morphology, reading, writing, phonology, etc., without much success. Unless the system can be developed into more of a synergistic system that can function for learning, these individuals remain at the language phase of development.

The breakdown in semantic development of children in Phase Two may be related to the following: (1) whether or not the features are being coded after being received, (2) whether or not the child is adequately organizing the features, and (3) whether or or not the child is able to attach a lexical tag to the experience. If the child is unable to code the features, it usually means that through some adequate facilitation the child has acquired the basic skills to visually learn enough information about environmental relationships without the ability to either sensorily receive the information or record the information at the appropriate cortical areas. For example, a child who reaches Phase Two but cannot code information will show some preferences for objects over people, will use a minimal number of agents when speaking, will show a rate of learning that is slowed by automatic and stereotyped utterances, will show faster learning visually than auditorily, will show more echoic types of utterances than true spontaneous or elicited imitation, will demonstrate simple constructions only under spontaneous conditions, and may or may not show phonological deviations.

If a child reaches Phase Two of semantic development but has difficulty in processing information, the child's language skills will be qualitatively confused in content or meaning and very often too literal in interpretation. This type of child may look at a picture in a story book and tell the adult that "This mama is taking out the clothes." The child looks at the next picture about the same mama and says, "Here is another mama hanging the clothes." The child thought that the second picture was of a different person because the child who remains at the language phase is unable to manipulate features into other concepts. Thus, the child also shows an inability to understand all relationships.

If the problem in processing is severe, the child who makes it to Phase Two of semantic development will demonstrate severe perceptual and functional confusions. For example, the child may look at a picture of two children sitting on stools at a table and ask, "Why are they standing on their knees?" This child thought that since the children's legs did not show under the table the children had to be standing on their knees. Although the children with these problems in organizing information may have "perceptual problems," the language may be worked on to help organize the child's perception of the content into concepts consisting of semantic features. This organization alleviates the academic failure problems faster than work on reading and other symptomatic problems.

The following section provides two case studies of children who have problems with the development of language past Phase Two.

Jane was a four-year-old female who was referred by her mother, a high-school English teacher. The mother was concerned that Jane's language was not developing appropriately.

At the time of the evaluation, Jane was pantomiming all semantic relationships, with a primary emphasis on objects, actions, and events rather than on agents. Her facial expressions suggested confusion and yet interest in the environment, as did her other means of indicating. Although she could spontaneously imitate, the frequency was too low to move her into an active process of expansion and extension. Jane was minimally functioning at the beginning of Phase Two.

Harmon, on the other hand, was a six-year-old male who had begun expanding surface form to reflect his increased underlying semantic development. His use of utterances reflected basic problems in the organization of perceptual features into concepts that could eventually be manipulated. For example, a picture of two people walking down the street swinging their arms was interpreted by Harmon as "The lady is picking the flowers." Physically, a person could not be walking and also picking flowers but the child saw the flowers along the walkway and thought that the swinging arm was picking the flowers. Harmon could not perceptually alter the points of reference so that he could visualize the spatial difference between the hand and the flowers along the walkway.

Harmon's semantic development had been restricted by an inability to displace semantic features into more semantic acquisition. Semanticity was restricted and Harmon was not making the transition from Phase Two into Phase Three.

The next section will describe the breakdown in linguistic acquisition. It should be noted that the majority of public school language-disordered children in regular academic classrooms are similar to Harmon in that they do not progress into the linguistic system. The breakdown occurs in the processes that assist the child in developing a linguistic system. Children who experience difficulty in acquiring semantic skills for the linguistic system will present several different or atypical types of language disorders, as described by Lucas (1980). The prelanguage child may demonstrate atypical motor and indicating nonverbal devices and the language child may demonstrate atypical verbal devices. The child who does not progress past the language phase does not develop a linguistic system.

## PHASE THREE—LINGUISTIC DEVELOPMENT

Since the semantic system is proposed as a synergistic operation, it is not surprising to find that children with language tools operating by linguistic processes do well academically. To reiterate previous principles, the breakdown in semantic development usually occurs in the transitions between the phases— either between Phase One and Phase Two or between Phase Two and Phase Three. In other words, if a child can demonstrate an intact communication system, he or she should start to show behaviors suggesting a change from one phase to another without any remediation. If the transition occurs, the child should demonstrate behavior typical of the next phase. Therefore, a child who makes the transition into Phase Three should demonstrate no learning problems.

## SUMMARY

To summarize the concepts presented in this chapter: (1) The synergistic system breaks down at times of maximum operation—between phases; (2) The breakdown problems correspond to the various semantic levels of processing; that is, sensory reception, feature perception, feature organization, and concept manipulation; (3) The prognosis for intervention is contingent upon whether or not the sociocognitive processes can be facilitated; and (4) A child with an interruption could experience encoding, processing, and/or problems with attaching the lexical code.

## Chapter 8

# A Pragmaticism Methodology for the Assessment of Language Disorders

*The mind is but a mystery;*
*It ebbs and flows from moment to moment.*
*But the tide carries an array of treasures.*

# Chapter Objectives

1. Explain the assessment procedures developed from a pragmaticism methodology.
2. Describe the various types of problems discussed in this chapter.
3. Explain the purpose of a differential diagnosis.
4. Explain the significance of assessment as it relates to theoretical models.
5. Explain assessment as it relates to the planning of intervention.
6. Explain the relationship of the speech act to assessment.
7. Explain why individuals produce different symptoms in language disorders.
8. Explain the relationship between type of breakdown and the corresponding disorders.
9. Explain the relationship between a pragmaticism methodology and a synergistic system.

## INTRODUCTION

Chapter 7 described the types of breakdown and corresponding problems that may be found in the development of the semantic system. This chapter will describe the assessment procedures used to determine the semantic problems that a child may be experiencing.

The first decision an educator must make is whether or not a child's behavior warrants testing for a language problem. Most evaluators use screening instruments based on tasks that typical children at certain ages are able to complete. In other words, the basic criterion for determining whether or not to test a child for a language problem is based on milestones from typical development. The use of a screening instrument may or may not be appropriate. If the screening test samples the area of deficit, the child's behavior will be adequately surveyed. However, if the screening instrument does not sample the problem area, the child may pass the test even though a severe language problem is present. Screening instruments can only measure the products and not the processes. The assessment procedures described in this chapter are based on the pragmaticism philosophy that examines the consequences of signs and not the signs or specific products per se.

Since screening instruments can only sample products, it is important to recognize that if language disorders are to be determined, a child must be given appropriate measures of the total system—akin to a diagnostic battery. Diagnostic tools are based on the assumption that a deviant performance on a given measure will set the child apart from other children. This conclusion is primarily true. A child who does poorly on a given normative measure will be different from the kinds of children who were used to standardize the measure. The problem with the conclusion is that the difference found on the normative measure does not explain why the difference occurred. These measures of static performances cannot determine how a child is functioning. They can only indicate whether or not the child is different. The only significant conclusion is that the "standardized" measures that are available, especially to speech and language clinicians, do not really give information about how the child is learning.

Because the "standard" measures are incomplete, there has been a move in the field to use criterion-referenced assessment. If administrators will accept these types of tools, the clinician has assessment choices for all children. Most of the criterion-referenced measures have been based on language sample collections. However, if the language sample analyses are based on the psycholinguistic limitations discussed in Chapter 1, they may not give any more information than the standard measures provided. In other words, even though a criterion-referenced measure assists in getting away from the age limit problems that plague language clinicians, the measure does not provide any more information than the standardized battery of tests if the criteria are not content valid. For example, the language clinicians in one district may be able to use a grammatical analysis of language samples as the main criterion for admittance to a language intervention program, but what does the grammatical analysis tell the clinician? Even though the child has not acquired certain structures or uses restricted forms, what does this tell the clinician or the educator? It does not tell the clinician how the child is functioning or why the child is functioning that way. It is even worse when children with severe language problems pass the screening tests of schools and perform adequately on more in-depth testing because the whole basis of the tests is on psycholinguistic grammatical development. The synergistic system described in this text cannot be assessed by screening, standard, or criterion-referenced units pertaining to structure or a grammar.

Appropriate assessment intervention services cannot be provided without a logical and systematic approach to the total child, that is, to the child's synergistic system. Furthermore, the assessment and intervention can only be logical and effective if the clinical content corresponds to the theoretical basis, that is, the approach must be content valid. Content validity rests on the question "Is the examiner really testing what the examiner wants to test?" If the examiner cares only about the products, a psycholinguistic analysis of the product would be appropriate. However, if the examiner wants to know how the child is learning, then another approach that examines the semantic, synergistic system must be used.

In summary, current standardized tests cannot look at the individual child because they are normed on other types of children, children with different systems. Using a standardized measure is almost like trying to compare two totally different objects, in this case two different types of people. The grammatical, psycholinguistic sample analyses utilize the product of the system without any consideration for why the system is the way it is, and tests that look at commodities that do not fit into a theoretical framework are also noninformative. For example, a test might tell the examiner that a child was a reflective thinker. What does this information do in terms of explaining a theoretical framework that accounts for the reason for the language problem as well as for normal development? Unless the testing approach has a theoretical basis that allows for differences in the system or unless the theory can explain differences in the system, the approach is inadequate and too inflexible. It will not provide the necessary information to set up appropriate intervention.

## ASSESSMENT AND INTERVENTION

Prior to beginning an assessment of a child's language system, the examiner should have in mind some questions that will be answered when the testing is complete. These questions should be in a hierarchy so that after all testing is completed, the therapy or service component may be rendered. The following list might serve as a guideline:

1. Does the child's language system differ from what is expected?
2. In what ways does the child's language system differ from the normal?
3. How are the differences manifested in terms of symptoms (products)?
4. How do these differences reflect the child's learning?
5. What can be done to change the system?
6. Will the intervention change the system or just the symptoms?
7. What types of changes can be expected?
8. What is the very first change that can be expected and how much change will be expected?

If these eight questions can be answered, the tester is on the way to having a professional relationship with the client. If these questions are not answered, the testing was merely a service provided by a technician without the professional touch of interpretation and follow-through. Of course, one may add to this minimum set of questions. Note also that although the term "language assessment" may be used, all components of semantic development, that is, prelanguage, language, and linguistic, are included.

Each of these eight questions will be examined in relation to the three phases of development in order to develop appropriate assessment strategies.

## Is the System Different?

As previously described, the system of the child who is having difficulty in acquiring a good communication system is functioning differently from the typical system. Therefore the question "Is the child's system different?" can be answered affirmatively if the child's behavior exhibits deviations from the typical child's developmental milestones. This statement refers to the overall system so that the total system may be assessed. If only part of the system, such as the product, is considered, the diagnostician cannot know if the child's system is functioning differently. However, the converse is true if the system is assessed to the exclusion of the product. The product could then be predicted from the functioning of the system. Likewise, a three-year-old child may not exhibit the expected grammatical development, but this child's system might be intact. In this case the child does not have a language disorder. When given the opportunity to have a need for the acquisition of language tools, the child would exhibit typical development.

A child is language disordered only if his or her system is functioning differently from what might be expected of a typical child. The system includes the sociocognitive processes that have been discussed as they relate to the three phases of development from prelanguage communication through language acquisition into the refinement of a linguistic system. Evidence of the system's functioning may be observed in the behavior of the child in dealing with people, objects, and events of a context situation according to the semantic requirements of a speech act. If the child does not perform as expected, his system may be seen as functioning differently. Further discussion regarding techniques for assessment may be found in later sections of this chapter.

### How Does the System Differ?

In the preceding chapter, the various types of breakdowns according to the three phases of development were examined. The child's system may be differing in the way that information is brought into the system for use, the way in which the information is processed once in the system, or the way in which the information is attached to the experience through lexicalization. These three differences will result in different products at the different transition points.

### What Are the Symptoms?

How are the differences in the system manifested in terms of products or symptoms? The previous chapter described the various types of problems that occur when there is a breakdown at various semantic levels. The differences reflect the changes in how the child is learning. These changes can be assessed by observing a child's behavior in the execution of speech acts for a speech event. Observation of the components includes an analysis of verbal and nonverbal behavior. All areas of language are affected if the underlying semantic basis consisting of sociocognitive processes is interrupted or altered. If communication is a problem, language tools are incomplete, and if the language acquisition is a problem, the linguistic system remains ineffective.

### How Is the Child Learning?

There is probably no way to determine the physiological changes taking place during learning; however, the way in which the child is receiving the information for meaning, processing the information, and attaching tags can be determined by a qualitative analysis of the child's verbal and nonverbal behavior.

The child might rely heavily on visual stimuli for information and not attend to auditory stimuli. This observation could be broken down into an analysis of the types of auditory information as well as visual information that changes the child's behavior. The processing of information is then reflected in how the child talks (if the child is verbal). For example, if a child calls a "ditch" a "rise-in-the-ground," that is how the ditch is being perceived. The differences between a "rise-in-the-ground" and a "ditch" are not recognized by the child.

In summary, learning represents a change in behavior. A child who demonstrates certain preferences for types of stimuli will learn more through use of these media at the expense of other types of input. This information not only tells the clinician about preferences but also about what environmental stimuli will or will not be processed. Conversely, the product reflects the process; so an analysis of how the child uses any of the tools to change attitudes, beliefs, and behaviors should agree with the diagnostician's observations of learning preferences. Determination of how the child is learning is important in order to understand what materials, methods, and procedures will be most appropriate in intervention.

**What Can Be Done?**

There is some uncertainty as to whether or not a system can be changed. It appears that with some children certain etiological limitations cannot be changed; thus, the system will continue to function within those limitations. If the system cannot be changed and the child's communication will reflect the system, what is the prognosis?

This last question is critical to the implementation of intervention. Because the amount of expected change rests on the kind of system limitation as well as on the extent or severity of limitation, once the kind of limitation and severity are determined the examiner should be able to predict in a general way, what types of changes might be expected. For example, a child who has a breakdown between Phase Two and Phase Three is having difficulty with acquiring the higher semantic concepts. It is probably realistic to believe that this child who is operating with a learning, language disorder affecting academic skills has sufficient language skills to learn to compensate. Through intervention this child will acquire significant concept manipulation of space, time, quality, and quantity. Furthermore, it can be expected that the child will do better academically if semantic development is improved and all other factors remain constant.

It is not appropriate to promise changes that cannot be predicted. Nor is it appropriate to leave guardians, parents, and families wondering what the next developmental step might be. Based on the theoretical framework provided in this book, an examiner should be able to tell responsible parties what the next process should be in order to be able to observe any change in the child's behavior. For example, if a child is using some semantic relations with limited variety and with limited effect on the environment, the examiner should be able to predict that unless the frequency of these semantic relations increases, the child will probably not show much more semantic progress. Furthermore, unless the child can use those semantic relations in some very specific ways to alter a person's behavior, the child will probably not have much reason for increasing the frequency.

From some assessments, the examiner has numbers and evaluation data but nothing to tell people who deal with the child on a daily basis what might be expected. Explaining expectations is the same as describing the future goals and objectives of any intervention services that might be provided. For the public school clinician, the expectations are the objectives of the Individualized Educational Plan (IEP) that will be discussed with the parents. When the evaluator has only test scores and numbers, the discussion with the parents can be very frustrating.

A recent evaluation with a multidisciplinary team resulted in the physician telling the well-educated parents of a Down's Syndrome child and adopted Down's Syndrome child that their children were healthy. The developmentalist reported age equivalencies in months for five different standardized scales measuring communication, motor, social/emotional skills, self-help, and self-readiness skills. The report of the developmentalist was very detailed and ages were given for all tasks performed by the two children. When this author was given an opportunity to explain the results of the language evaluation, instead of reporting numbers and tasks the parents were told that both children were learning better by visual rather than by auditory input, that the children evidenced specific problems with the acquisition of further language skills (the five-year-old, for example, was still labeling and labeling was a restricted use of language thus hindering further progress of expansion, modulation, and extension), and that the children each showed signs of being able to move on to the next phase of development provided certain changes were facilitated through intervention. The parents were told what the changes were. In this case, both children needed a greater variety of semantic relations and a greater variety of speech act performances in order for any expansion, modulation, or extension to occur. The older child was too restricted by the environment, for the child and the younger child, who had been adopted because of being abandoned, had not had the opportunity for social reasons.

Although a person who is keen on numbers might have been impressed with the developmentalist's report and unimpressed with the language report, the parents were the opposite. They placed the children in the hands of the language specialists and were enthusiastic about finding what was important in the treatment of their children.

Parents such as these don't really care about the numbers of the tests, or about how the test results measure up to other children's performances on the same measure. They don't even care if the tester has found differences between their child and other children on certain measures. Furthermore, they don't want to know how normal children develop or what normal children should be doing at this point in terms of task responses. Most parents want to know what the next step in remediation is going to be and what can be expected in terms of change.

A pragmaticism methodology not only tells the parent what can be expected but also what needs to be done before such a change can be observed. Perhaps nothing can be done about the system but intervention may allow for changes in how the system functions based on compensatory development. In some cases, facilitating the next sociocognitive processes such as spontaneous imitation through intervention might facilitate the child's growth and possibly put the child into the next phase of development (Phase Two).

It is important to recognize that facilitating this process might actually facilitate a change in the system's functioning. The system uses the process to continue development. As explained in Chapter 2, a child's cognition may be affected by the ability to use language as a tool for further learning. Thus, a system could possibly be changed if certain processes could be facilitated that would change the way in which language directed cognition. The opportunity to evoke such a change in the system is probably governed by physiological maturation time.

### Will the Symptoms Change?

Will the child's system change with intervention or will just the symptoms change? Again, the system could be changed or the limitations might be such that the system could not be changed by external variations; however, the symptoms will predictably change with appropriate intervention. The problem with the symptoms so readily changing is that the child may show changes that are not reflective of effective intervention. For example, if a person works on a child's verb tense usage, changes will occur in the tasks of the therapy setting. However, outside the therapy room, the child may show no change in tenses. Therapy spent on tasks that are symptom related without sufficient time on the language-disordered child's sociocognitive processes is ineffective in changing the system so that it will function synergistically.

If a process is facilitated by intervention, the process won't be automatically shut down when the child leaves a particular context. The process continues to work for the child in whatever context the child may be participating. Therefore, symptomatic changes are not important unless the processes to produce the changes in symptoms are also considered.

### What Types of Changes Can Be Expected?

The changes that can be expected are related to the level of semantic interruption in the child's system as well as the point of transition breakdown in the phase of development. The rate of change is related to how fast the child can learn as evidenced by observation during the assessment. For example, if the examiner tries a few techniques with the child to see if the child could be worked through a logical verbal sequence or if the child could be easily stimulated to spontaneously imitate, the child will therapeutically benefit from those facilitation techniques tried during assessment and later used during intervention. However, if the child shows relatively little change upon stimulation, then therapy on the qualitative aspect of the child's present development will need to be considered before change could be predicted. Severely mentally retarded children usually require significant amounts of stimulation to get any change of behavior. The learning rate would be so slow that one could not expect immediate, rapid changes.

It should be noted that the learning rate is also a measure of sociocognitive integrity. The greater the extent of sociocognitive process deficit, the slower the rate of learning. The slower rate of learning suggests fewer predicted changes.

### What Is the First Change and How Soon Can It Be Expected?

The first predicted change is determined from what is known about the three phases of semantic development presented in Chapters 4, 5, and 6. The rate at which the change would take place would depend on the limitations of the system, the stimulability to facilitate processes, and the rate of sociocognitive learning. The quality of change that can be expected would also be determined by manipulating variables during the assessment.

### Summary

After these eight questions have been answered, the clinician should be ready to start the therapeutic intervention. The following sections describe the assessment strategy for determining a child's phase of development and the corresponding problems.

## THE TOTAL COMMUNICATION SYSTEM

The most difficult task to be accomplished by the examiner is learning how to look at the total child and not at the child's tools. Most diagnosticians have been trained to administer certain tests or tasks and if the diagnostician had a good teacher, the diagnostician was also taught to interpret the child's responses. Instead of examining test scores, the diagnostician is now expected to look at a child and interpret the child's behaviors. In order to do any type of interpretation, a diagnostician has to have some sort of criteria for comparing the child's behaviors against some standard. The criteria should be what is known about typical development and, more important, what is known about atypical development. As with most evaluations, the diagnostician might want to start with the complaint of the referral source such as the parent, teacher, resource room aide, etc. If there is no referral source, the diagnostician may want to begin testing.

### Referral Source

The referral source usually tells the tester what general area is a problem. It is the diagnostician's job to determine to what extent the problem exists, what is causing the symptoms of the problem, and what can be done to improve the child's present functioning. For example, the referral source says, "The child doesn't talk very well." If the diagnostician reports back that the child has a language problem, nothing new has been added to the referral source's knowledge. The referral source already said that the child didn't talk well.

There are some typical kinds of referral complaints that help the clinician zero in on possible problems. The person who says that the child isn't talking well means that the child's utterance frequently is low and that the utterances are not well formed, suggesting a possible impairment in Phase Two development of language skills.

If a child is said to be slow in developing language, his or her language is probably no more advanced than the end of Phase One or the beginning of Phase Two. If the referral source says the child is not understandable, the child has probably developed quite a few skills in Phase Two of semantic development but not enough modulation has taken place to expand the utterances so that the child's phonological system is intact. Most children who are more than 75 percent unintelligible to a stranger are in need of modulation for increasing the number of functors (nonreferential words) and morphological inflections. These improve the relationship between morphemes and the morphophonemic system and result in better phonology. After the basic modulation is developed, the child may still exhibit some errors with phonemes but many of these will be articulatory and not language in nature.

Too many children considered as articulation cases really possess phonological or language problems. With traditional articulation therapy, these language problems obviously are not remediated as rapidly as possible. In Chapter 10, an example of one such child will be provided.

If the complaint of the referral source is that the child has problems in school, the problem probably exists in the transition between Phase Two and Phase Three. If the child has a language problem, it will manifest itself with the acquisition of advanced semantic skills so that more complex semantic concepts such as those used in displacement of space and time are not acquired. The child then has problems in the classroom trying to follow directions or in learning how to read or write.

If the referral source says the child doesn't talk much and might be retarded, the child's skills are probably prelanguage and no more than into the beginning of Phase Two. The child also will probably show other symptoms of a slow learning rate.

Sometimes these referral source complaints are misleading and sometimes they are not available. But they can be used to get a diagnostician thinking in a certain direction that may speed up the assessment process. If the referral source complaints are not available or if the source does not seem to be reliable, it is best to go ahead with the testing.

## Assessment

There is some discussion in the literature as to what constitutes a diagnostic evaluation, an appraisal, or an assessment. For purposes of this text, an assessment refers to tasks necessary not only to appraise the skills but also to diagnose the problems in communication and linguistic language acquisition. There is another way in addition to the referral source information to rapidly determine the child's level of functioning. Listen to the child talk!

Listening to a child talk seems almost ludicrous to suggest since the purpose of a language assessment is to determine how well a child uses language to talk. However, too many assessments collect every standardized measure for every possible way of looking at psycholinguistic units or language but never find out what the child sounds like.

## Listen to the Child

Listening is an art that requires very little talking. As discussed in Chapter 5, many young children will respond better to nonverbal supportive behavior than to verbal behavior. Therefore, the first rule in listening is to be silent. This is so hard for educators and language clinicians who have been taught to always be in control. Somehow keeping silent makes a person feel insecure, as if by not talking the person is losing control. However, nonverbal behavior probably is a better control for many language-disordered children. The silent pauses give the child, who infrequently says anything, a chance to actually be a participant. Many language-disordered children have not been given opportunities to participate or have not taken the opportunity to participate.

## Nonverbal Behavior

If the adult examiner is quiet there has to be something happening in the diagnostic setting or the child and examiner will both feel uncomfortable. A variety of toys that are creative and allow for role playing are the best types of materials for children between three and maybe as old as five or six years. Children between two and three will want some messy types of activity, such as being able to dump beads, scatter blocks, knead playdough, shovel sand, dump water, etc. Children between birth and two can probably be observed and physically manipulated by interacting with a caregiver. Children around four to five years of age and beyond do well with pictures and conversation.

If the child is attending to the materials, the adult has to provide some nonverbal support. There are three types of nonverbal support: (1) vocalizations that confirm the child's behavior, (2) gestures or other facial and bodily actions that alter the child's behavior, and (3) actions that provide the child with immediate needs. Each of these will be discussed separately.

Vocalizations that are supportive include "ums" and "uh, huhs," or even "ohs." Sometimes the adult might go so far as to comment but vocalizations will work quite well with most children.

The child's behavior can also be supported by adult gestures that point to an object, a smile that expresses approval (open posture), or by the adult showing surprise. These nonverbal adult behaviors encourage the child to continue the task. The adult might also want to play parallel to the child's play. The most important point about nonverbal support is that the adult does not focus on the child's face but gazes in the direction of the child while attending to the activity. The adult only supports the child, without directing attention in any way that might be a request for the child to perform. Direct eye contact will quiet a child who is not sure about being with a stranger. While focus quiets children, some don't want too much space and would rather engage in messy types of activities at a table while the adult parallel plays. This is more suitable for public schools. The adult is always nonverbally acting on the activity but not on the child.

Nonverbal support may also be offered by acting as a hearer in the context. The adult who is the hearer responds to the child's nonverbal and verbal needs. If the child appears to be reaching for a toy, the adult can take the toy and start to use it without looking at the child. This type of communication attempt tells the examiner a lot about the child. If the child is fairly comfortable in the setting and does not continue to get the toy, the social basis for the child's language system has to be immediately questioned. If the child had had adequate social basis, he or she would have tried to communicate the need for the object. Many language-disordered children do not verbally carry through with speech acts if they cannot physically meet the specific needs.

In addition to the nonverbal support the adult can offer, verbal support may also be used while assessing the child's system. Verbalizations should be as short as possible and should not be directed toward the child. Any inquiries about the situation must be to the adult or to the context and not directly to the child. For example, the adult might say, "I wonder what I could do with a tractor." The adult could also comment through an indirect question such as "I guess I should put this here?" This sort of speculative question asks for a response but not specifically of the child. Direct questions should be avoided during the listening portion of the assessment. If the adult rarely talks but only comments and adds nonverbal support, the child will feel more comfortable playing *with* the adult. The play is always directed so that the child or adult can model. The play is never directed at getting responses from a child.

**Opportunity for Assessment**

Once a play situation is developed, a context has been provided for the child to perform speech acts or communicative acts. With older children this opportunity may also be provided by using pictures. With pictures a model of what is expected is given to the child first and then the child follows the adult lead. For example, the adult says, "I'm going to tell you about the first picture and then you tell me about the next one." The adult proceeds to tell a very detailed and exaggerated story about one picture. The purpose of an exaggerated story is to give the child the idea of what constitutes a story. This storytelling strategy gives the child a model for mentioning several ideas about one picture. The way the child connects these ideas or the way the child communicates the ideas will tell the examiner about the child's semantic development.

Without a storytelling model, many language-disordered children will label objects or people in the picture. Since labeling does not meet the speech act criteria, the examiner wants to try to avoid this tactic with the child.

Even though storytelling strategies are used, some language-disordered children will string propositions together without any connecting predications. For example, one string might be: "The boy jump. The girl walk. The ball over there." This stringing of propositions is really not very semantically complex because the relationships within the picture are not expressed. Although the child may exhibit structures that might be more sophisticated than labeling, the structures are not as important as the semantics, the way in which the child organizes perceptions of the environment. The stringing of unrelated propositions that do not show relationships is really nothing more than expanded labeling. The child who does this type of expanded labeling does not meet the semantic requirements of quality necessary to show further growth without intervention.

Conversation about the materials along with the verbal and nonverbal supportive behavior of the adult should provide sufficient opportunity for the child to produce speech acts. If such an opportunity is not provided, the diagnostician is only sampling psycholinguistic tasks that require certain skills for completion not necessarily based on semantic development.

If conversation is used to stimulate language, comments rather than questions are more supportive. For example, a comment about a picture might start a conversation with a school-age child, such as "I have never had a pet." A child might also be encouraged to explain a game. A game consists of rules that are connected by the relationships of the play act with the utterance act. School-age children with semantic problems will often show the greatest problems with this type of task (Lucas, 1980).

Questions about what the child says will also provide the examiner with an idea of the extent of the problem. For example, a school-age child was describing how to play basketball. The child never mentioned what to do with the orange ball. Upon questioning, the child told the adult that the ball is thrown "into a net." When asked if this net was like a soccer goal net, the child said, "Yes!" but the net "was on a pole." The adult asked about the size of the pole. The child said it was about as "big" as the room (8 feet by 6 feet). The adult then asked, "How big is that?'' The child said, ''Oh, about a foot.'' The adult said, ''A foot? What if I told you that a foot was about this big?'' (hands were used to demonstrate the dimension of a foot horizontally). The child said, ''I would freak out!''

After much conversation, the child never could change spatial dimensions to indicate that a pole was high and not big. Furthermore, the child never understood the extent of the height. This child was not able to change reference points from horizontal to vertical even though he was well beyond the age at which most children are able to do this.

Any game or activity will provide an opportunity for a child to explain what he or she likes to do. The adult hearer pretends to know nothing about the activity. The reason for pretending to be naïve is that the sincerity rule would otherwise be violated, thus inhibiting the child's willingness to talk about the activity. If the sincerity rule were violated, the child would believe that the adult already knew everything and that there was direct pressure to test to see if the child knew these things.

Once an opportunity is provided, the examiner is ready to begin collecting data. The data-gathering process must be systematic and include all aspects of the communication act.

## DATA GATHERING

The process of data gathering should be systematic and include all of the quality checks as well as consider the characteristics of the child's system of products and learning. The following section will discuss each of the items that should be checked in a language assessment.

### Observation

At the time of the evaluation, the diagnostician should record the type of situation, context, and materials used to provide an opportunity for the child to perform speech acts. The place of the context and the amount of time used to gather the information about the child's communication behaviors should also be noted.

During the opportunity for speech acts to be performed, the diagnostician should record whether or not the child initiated communicative acts or whether the acts were always initiated by the adults or by others in the context. The type of nonverbal and verbal strategies used to initiate a communicative act should also be recorded. At this point, interpretation is not as important as recording the behaviors of the child accurately for later interpretation.

Assessment of the child's nonverbal behaviors should include observations about the child's mode of communication—gestures, eye contact, gaze, body orientation, and vocalizations, either differentiated or undifferentiated. These general categories also need to be broken down so that the specific behavior may be recorded. The gestures should be described and the context of a gesture should be noted. When recording information about eye contact or gaze, the diagnostician should consider how these behaviors were used to establish communication. Does the child indicate topics or follow topics by either looking at the speaker or hearer or at the activity or object being referred to? The child's body orientation will also indicate referents that are jointly established by the speaker's and hearer's body orientation and these should be noted.

Any vocalizations that appear to be nonmeaningful need to be reported in order to determine their communication value. Exhibit 8-1 illustrates the use of a simple data sheet to record this type of information for later interpretation.

In addition to the basic nonverbal behavior, the diagnostician should record the ways in which these nonverbal behaviors are used to communicate to the hearer. Nonverbal behaviors may represent icon and index signs; they should be recorded at the time of the evaluation or immediately after the observation period. This immediate recording protects the evaluator from making inappropriate judgments.

Any type of semantic relationships indicated by nonverbal behavior should also be recorded. For example, the child might indicate a relationship between the caregiver and what the caregiver is doing by using certain gaze, pointing, and vocalizing signs. The relationship might be interpreted by the hearer as an agent and action relationship. The diagnostician needs to be cautioned about interpreting the context from a normal developmental model. Many children with severe language problems do not show relationships as much as preferences. For example, language-disordered children might show the same nonverbal behaviors as nonlanguage handicapped children, but the pointing, gazing, and vocalizing of the language-disordered children might not be demonstrated in relationship to any object, action, event. They may simply indicate nonmeaningful preferences.

Preferences do indicate that the child is learning but the presence of extreme preferences suggests that these exist at the exclusion of other learning. The use of nonverbal behavior should semantically represent the same typical development of verbal behavior. When the nonverbal behavior does not represent semantic development, the child has certain learning problems that will result in a language disorder if the child develops language skills within this same system.

In summary, the first part of data gathering is for observation of all nonverbal behavior in order to determine the consistencies and inconsistencies between the nonverbal behavior and verbal behavior. As these inconsistencies are observed, the evaluator records the behaviors so as to later interpret the relationship between what is observed and what would be expected under these conditions.

**Exhibit 8-1** Data Sheet for Recording Nonverbal and Verbal Behaviors

Video tape number _____
Speech event number _____
Context and materials _____    Children _____

| Speech Act | Linguistic Content | Paralinguistics | Nonlinguistics |
|---|---|---|---|
| | | | |

## Prelanguage Observation

A few minutes of providing an opportunity for the child to communicate by whatever means the child can use will immediately tell the diagnostician the semantic level of the child's functioning. For example, in the last section it was suggested that the diagnostician initially record all nonverbal and verbal data in order to determine how the child communicates. A few minutes of recording should show that the child primarily uses either prelanguage, language, or linguistic methods of communication. The diagnostician can now explore the level of development.

The prelanguage child's assessment will be almost all nonverbal. The nonverbal behaviors will indicate which semantic relations the child can utilize and *how* the child is utilizing these skills. McLean and Snyder-McLean (1978) present some materials for providing an opportunity to assess the prelanguage child's semantic relational use. Appendix A provides a prelanguage assessment tool (Arwood, 1983).

In interpreting the results a distinction should be made between meaningful behaviors and those behaviors that do not represent anything meaningful. Many severely handicapped children who are operating at the prelanguage phase of semantic development will demonstrate many nonfunctional types of behavior that are not typical and are not found in most children's development. It is critical that these atypical, nonmeaningful behaviors are also reported.

Nonmeaningful behaviors include any self-stimulatory acts. The children who are not capable of utilizing external stimuli will produce as much self-stimulatory behavior as their system will allow, to the exclusion of the external stimuli being processed. For many of these children self-stimulatory acts are not only present but tend to dominate the total behavior pattern. The result is little functional or purposeful behavior. Nonmeaningful behavior has often been misinterpreted as purposeful because in normal development a child's behavior can usually be interpreted according to typical patterns.

The language-disordered or self-stimulatory behavior of many children reflects the inability to organize external stimuli into a pattern that can be attached to experiential learning. Consequently, the self-stimulatory behavior represents what the child's internal system is doing. The only way to determine if a behavior suggests or indicates anything purposeful and intentionally communicative is to evaluate it according to the context. For example, a child might take an object and immediately put it in his or her mouth. The mouthing behavior in a normal developmental scale would be appropriate for children up to and around two years of age. Therefore, it is sometimes assumed that when a severely handicapped child takes an object and puts it to the mouth, the child is functioning at around the two-year-old level or less. This conclusion is inappropriate unless the way or means of mouthing is considered.

Typical two-year-old children may mouth an object but a two-year-old also shows both an incredible number of semantic notions through nonverbal behavior and some vocalizations that are beginning to take on verbal meaning. In fact, the typical child may put an object in the mouth while doing something else that is purposeful. There are also many two-year-old children who do no mouthing of objects. The fifteen-year-old severely handicapped child that immediately puts something in his or her mouth is not the same child as the two-year-old child and is not functioning with a two-year-old semantic system of development.

The fifteen-year-old child will probably demonstrate little purpose in mouthing the object and there will be no pattern of development representative of learning by mouthing. The objects routinely go to the mouth with little other behavior demonstrating the acquisition of semantic relationships either verbally or nonverbally. Furthermore, an adult usually has to intervene to get this severely handicapped child to alter mouthing of the object. The social types of expected interaction to get the adult to share the object or the event after routine mouthing and whether or not anyone picks the object up and gives it back usually do not alter the fifteen-year-old severely handicapped child's course of behavior.

The purpose of the behavior needs to be considered not only in context but also in relationship to other expected behaviors. If children automatically stack things placed in front of them, the vertical height does not indicate the same thing as it does with children that seek out various objects to stack. Usually, the height or length of one-to-one stacking or lining up of blocks will indicate another milestone typical of certain developmental ages.

If a behavior is done automatically or is trained to be done by cue without concern for what is being built and why it is being built, the child is not functioning in the same system as a "normal" child. Most children who stack blocks do it as a task requested by an examiner or do it as part of play representing the building of a house, bridge, or road. If the blocks are put in front of a child who immediately stacks them but who does not demonstrate behavior typical of that type of child in other situations, the stacking must be considered a task that has little sign or communicative value.

By now it should be apparent that it is important for the examiner to consider the way the child does a behavior and whether or not a behavior is truly communicative. There is a tendency for educators to take on so much responsibility for a communicative act that the interpretation of behavior is too generous. For example, an adult who is always the initiator may come to the conclusion that the child has the basic cognitive abilities for language development. This adult has taken on too much of the responsibility of communication for the child. The child must be an active participant if development can be expected to continue to progress.

If the child is not an active participant, the child's social processes for facilitating development are not available. Remember, the child progresses through semantic development not because of cognition or because of a need for socialization; the child shows progress in semantic development because of sociocognitive processes.

Appendix A illustrates what factors must be assessed for the child who would be operating at the prelanguage phase of semantic development. The factors listed in the protocol are based not just on the typical development of a child but also on the atypical development of many children. This prelanguage assessment includes the behaviors to be observed for answering the quality checks about how a child is functioning. Some of these quality checks were initially listed by Lucas (1980) and recently applied to the three phases of semantic development described in this text.

The interpretation of the data gathered on the prelanguage child should tell the diagnostician how the child is learning as well as what the child is capable of demonstrating. This information will provide the basis for the intervention program. Chapter 9 will illustrate how to interpret the data for prelanguage children in order to plan appropriate intervention. At the conclusion of gathering data for the prelanguage child, the evaluator should be able to answer the initial questions about *how* a child is functioning and *what* the next step of development might include under what conditions and *when*.

The interpretation is an assimilation of the information on the child as it fits into the theoretical model presented earlier in this text. It is an integration of careful observation and an understanding of how communication develops. The protocol (Appendix A) will assist in collecting the necessary data and the questions will help in determining the value of the child's learning system. The next step is to take this information and interpret the results according to the areas of breakdown explained in Chapter 7.

## Language Observation

If the diagnostician listens to the child and recognizes that the child is using language skills to communicate, the child is probably functioning in the second phase of development—the language phase. Appendix B provides a protocol for use with the language-developing child. The analysis of a language user not only includes observation of the nonverbal behavior as previously described but also an analysis of the child's language skills. Nonverbal behavior must also be included because the speech act is not complete without all of the extralinguistic information. Children with semantic or pragmatic problems may have sophisticated structural skills and not be identified as having ''language'' problems unless the nonverbal information is also utilized.

The language assessment protocol (Arwood, 1983) (Appendix B) provides information about the type of behavioral observation necessary for the language phase child. The observed behaviors might indicate that the person has some problems utilizing nonverbal behavior to ready a hearer or to set a context to follow a speaker's topic, etc. If the problems are recognized, some type of checklist such as the Behavioral Inventory of Speech Act Performances (BISAP, Lucas, 1977; 1980) might be utilized. After collecting nonverbal observational data, the next step is to analyze the language within the context.

Appendix B provides a protocol for analysis of language skills and nonverbal behavior for determining not only the quantity of verbalization but also, and more important, the quality of language. The protocol lists those skills that should be answered upon completion of the data gathered about the child's use of language. Chapter 10 will present a case study of a child analyzed according to the Language Assessment System (Appendix B) for use in planning intervention.

## Linguistic Observation

The assessment of the linguistic phase is probably as difficult as for the prelanguage phase. The second phase, language development, is probably the easiest because people have had more background in analyzing language skills than either prelanguage or linguistic behaviors.

Children who have incomplete linguistic systems and are moving from Phase Two to Phase Three are difficult to assess because they typically have a breakdown in acquiring the more advanced semantic, sociocognitive processes; therefore, an analysis of advanced semantic development is warranted.

Such children's skills may be analyzed by using speech acts within a speech event to determine whether or not certain semantic skills used for refining language development have been acquired. Appendix C (Arwood, 1983) provides the linguistic assessment system protocol used for assessing the child who is trying to make the transition into Phase Three.

For this child, the use of language skills for learning on a day-to-day basis should be assessed to determine how well the child is doing with language for acquiring academic subjects. Notice that the protocol includes some academic types of subjects in the assessment. The diagnostician is encouraged to become familiar with popular methods of assessing reading and then to look at errors of reading in relationship to the oral language system. The same is true for the writing mode. If a child is having difficulty in the semantic system, then difficulty in learning is also evident.

Any task that requires utilization of semantic properties that the child is not developing would result in error. It is important to remember that *the semantic system is the system of learning* and that there is no separation between learning and the semantic system.

When a child demonstrates differences in learning within a normal framework of expectation, the child is demonstrating differences in genetic endowment and physiological makeup. Handicapped children also possess differences, deficiencies, or errors in their processes of learning or semantic processes.

Assessment of the linguistic phase of development utilizes the child's conversation to determine if the child is able to produce the necessary semantic qualities representative of a linguistic system. The protocol (Appendix C) lists the expectations of a linguistic child. As with the other two protocols, there is a list of behaviors representing sociocognitive processes as well as a list of atypical behaviors that might be found at this level of breakdown (but not necessarily restricted to this level) and a list of quality checks. The disorders of space and time peculiar to the transition between Phase Two and Phase Three are explained in Lucas (1980).

Evaluators' ability to explain the linguistic properties of this phase is contingent on their own ability to produce speech acts in a speech event typical of a linguistic system. In other words, it is probably not possible to examine a system that is functioning at a higher level than the evaluator's system. It should be noted that many adults function only at the language phase, usually the very utmost limits, without a full transition into the linguistic phase of synergistic learning.

## INTERPRETATION

After the basic data collecting has been completed and problems are recorded on a sheet, the diagnostician is ready to do some interpreting in the form of explanation and description.

### Prelanguage Phase

If the child is in the prelanguage phase of development, there are certain requisites before the next phase can be expected. The process of spontaneous imitation along with a frequent number of utterances must occur before expansion will develop. The expansion also will not occur unless there is sufficient nonverbal behavior followed by verbal semantic relations expressed to necessitate modulation.

Remediation for a prelanguage child would emphasize the development of semantic relationships through the procedure of imitation. With the opportunity to use semantic relationships through these imitated models, it is expected that the social interaction will facilitate a higher frequency of utterances. This higher frequency will allow not only for spontaneous imitation but, if the child's physiology is capable of a higher frequency, expansion and modulation will follow. These two sociocognitive processes will push the child into Phase Two of semantic development.

Understanding this basic premise will help the diagnostician decide by whom and when a child should receive special services for language development. Furthermore, understanding what has to occur will force the clinician to expect realistic amounts of change. For example, a child who does not even demonstrate a variety of semantic relations or notions through nonverbal means cannot be expected to "talk." And yet, many educators sit down with this type of child and try to elicit babbling sounds, thinking that because babbling is one of the first types of vocalizations a prerequisite for speech is present.

Speech is only a mode and the child's ability to use signs to indicate, represent, and to symbolize will allow speech to occur. With this type of knowledge, the educator or diagnostician should realize what has to be accomplished to be able to have the skills of the next phase of semantic development. Language skills then get treated as part of the child's total learning and communication system and not separate from the sociocognitive processes. Chapter 9 will delineate some of the intervention techniques for the prelanguage child.

**Language Phase**

The child who is beginning to use certain language skills should meet the quality checks of the protocol (Appendix B). If the child's language does not meet the quality checks, the child's language is not the product of a synergistic system. The quality components will need to be facilitated before the child will exhibit an intact synergistic system.

The use of alternate modes in this phase may be critical for facilitating the child's underlying semantic notions. Shifting to an alternate mode should be decided upon when the child exhibits the prelanguage nonverbal prerequisites but is unable to use the speech mode or when the child is not learning enough from an auditory environment to acquire semantic notions. The alternate mode should act as a learning system for facilitating speech in many children such as Down's Syndrome children or children diagnosed as having autistic types of behaviors. For many physically handicapped children, the alternate mode will become more and more semantically advanced as the child increases in semantic development.

As a child exhibits sufficient expansion and overextension processes with modulation, the complexity of the child's language should increase. Chapter 10 will discuss ways to facilitate expansion in children who are plateauing at the beginning of Phase Two without sufficient progress into and through the development of the second phase. When sufficient complexity has occurred, the child will begin to evidence processes typical of a linguistic system, Phase Three.

As noted, children who are functioning in the language phase can be expected to do very well with the academic basis of reading and writing up to about the third grade level, but without further advancement of the semantic system, they cannot be expected to do well in school or to benefit from advanced academic settings. Note that there is a gap between grade level of achievement and the child's chronological age. Most children who function in the language phase are typically between two and seven years of age. The third grade is for children with chronological ages up to eight or even nine. This gap is the gap between success for some children and failure. In other words, the children who fail, fail usually for at least several months before special services might be requested. Children who are typically in the language phase (ages three to seven) really need more and more linguistic tools for higher academic achievement as they approach the classroom setting. If they do not acquire the linguistic principles, the academic setting becomes very frustrating.

**Linguistic Phase**

The linguistic phase is characterized by the refinement of semantic skills. Knowledge increases to the point of being redundant so that semantic abilities can advance for further learning. The ability to use language skills for different kinds of reasoning allows the child to begin building an open learning system of concept manipulation. As previously stated, a person need not have a linguistic system in order to be self-sufficient. Advanced language skills are adequate for most jobs that do not require reading or writing beyond the third grade level. Therefore, the assessment of the linguistic phase is really an academic matter. Without it public education is difficult for teachers and some children.

**SUMMARY**

Semantic assessment of a child is performed according to the expected phase of functioning by observation and listening. The diagnostician can then check those behaviors representative of certain processes at that phase of development. Behaviors that are atypical as well as normal are recorded. From this information, quality checks can then be made and the evaluator can determine how a child is functioning and what behaviors will need to change for the child to progress to the next phase. A semantic analysis does not differentiate problems in terms of etiology but it does differentiate the types of breakdowns from what is typically expected. This type of differential diagnosis is critical to the intervention plan to be developed for the child. From this information, the educator or diagnostician should be able to explain how fast a child is learning. Chapters 10, 11, and 12 suggest the appropriate course of intervention for the three phases of semantic development.

**REFERENCES**

Arwood, E. Lucas. *Prelanguage assessment system.* Unpublished criterion-referenced checklist, 1983.

Arwood, E. Lucas. *Language assessment system.* Unpublished criterion-referenced checklist, 1983.

Arwood, E. Lucas. *Linguistic assessment system.* Unpublished criterion-referenced checklist, 1983.

Lucas, E.V. The feasibility of speech acts as a language approach for emotionally disturbed children. (Doctoral dissertation, University of Georgia, 1977). *Dissertation Abstracts International,* 1978, *38,* 3479B-3967B. (University Microfilms No. 77-30, 488)

Lucas, E.V. *Semantic and pragmatic language disorders: Assessment and remediation.* Rockville, Md.: Aspen Systems, 1980.

McLean, J.E., & Synder-McLean, L.K. *A transactional approach to early language training.* Columbus, Ohio: Charles E. Merrill, 1978.

## Chapter 9

# Intervention for the Prelanguage System

*Meaning exists in the wiggle,*
*The frown, and the extension.*
*Oh no! The spinning, turning, flapping!*

## Chapter Objectives

1. Write appropriate communication goals for the prelanguage child.
2. Write appropriate communication objectives for the prelanguage child.
3. Explain and describe intervention techniques for use with the prelanguage child.
4. Explain the purpose of using alternate or supplemental modes with the prelanguage child.
5. Describe the methods and procedures used to facilitate sociocognitive processes in the prelanguage child.
6. Describe the way to determine when a prelanguage child is ready to move on in the acquisition of semantics.
7. Obtain adequate data from the intervention provided to account for any change due to intervention.
8. Describe the relationship between prelanguage intervention and the pragmaticism methodology.

## INTRODUCTION

The purpose of this chapter is to provide examples of goals, objectives, and intervention planning for children with a prelanguage system of semantic development. These examples will illustrate the relationship of service and theory as it pertains to prelanguage semantic development. The goals, objectives, methods, and procedures used in this chapter have been developed with real children, whose names and identifying information have been changed to protect their identity. Procedures should be used as examples and one is encouraged to expand on intervention ideas from the theoretical premise and not only from the methods.

## GOALS AND OBJECTIVES

The purpose of dealing with children who are at the prelanguage phase of semantic development is to establish those communication skills that exist as requisites to the later use of speech acts. For three-year-old children (see Chapter 5) to possess a wide variety of speech acts, they must develop the early sociocognitive processes of Phase One prior to being able to use language as a tool. Therefore, the goals and objectives for Prelanguage Phase One are based on the child's communicative behavior determined by a means of assessment similar to the one outlined in Chapter 8 (see also Appendix A).

### Case Study One

The following assessment description with subsequent goals is for a microcephalic six-year, eleven-month-old male who was functioning at the prelanguage phase of development. The determination of this phase of functioning was made by observing that the child's communication was primarily nonverbal, certainly not characteristic of a Phase Two language user. Furthermore, the referral source reported, "He gestures for whatever he wants and [he] says a few words."

The following sections are taken from the prelanguage assessment of this child. From observation and from completing the Prelanguage Assessment System protocol (Appendix A), the following data were obtained.

Case One used some two-term utterances representative of three types of semantic relations: agent with an action, action with an object, and an object with a denial. Under spontaneous imitation he produced one three-term and one four-term utterance representative of the relationships previously mentioned. The variety of semantic relations was limited, as was the number of verbalizations (46 for a two-hour play period). The mother and grandmother watched from an observation room and reported that this frequency was the most that either had ever seen the child produce, suggesting that the number of utterances was actually more than would usually be expected of this child.

Nonverbally, the child demonstrated other types of semantic development, including the functions of existence, rejection, recurrence, and possession. These semantic notions were primarily represented by facial expression, pointing, gesturing, and body orientation. Although he demonstrated preferences for certain people over objects in the environment, most of this boy's interactions were either responses to adult initiations or initiations to get the adult to act as an instrument for him. The lack of frequency of utterances, the limited demonstration of semantic development by verbalization and to some extent by nonverbal means, and the rigid physical commanding behavior to get others to act as instruments suggests that this prelanguage child, who should be functioning as a language child, has very restricted sociocognitive processes for further language development.

It should be noted that the last conclusion comes from the theoretical basis described in the first three chapters. The child's interaction was socially limited. He did not attempt a personal exchange of messages but tried to use the two clinicians involved. Furthermore, theoretically it is assumed that the limited social interaction will restrict the amount of cognitive development that the child exhibited. In fact, this last statement was supported by the data obtained during the evaluation. The fact that the mother and grandmother had never heard as much said by this child suggests that the environment with the family is very different from the environment for testing. In the testing situation the two clinicians responded nonverbally to the child's messages. They would only comment on an activity or play parallel but they did not direct questions or play to the child. Therefore, the child was given the opportunity in the testing situation to interact equally by taking the lead at times. This situation also gave the child the opportunity to demonstrate his maximum level of verbalization. In contrast to this open setting, it was observed that the family tended to protect him by telling him what to do. For example, the child had been running up and down the stairs, yet when they came to get him, the family wanted to hold his hand and help him walk down the stairs.

There was another piece of evidence that the child's semantic development was being limited by a lack of social skills; this child did begin to spontaneously imitate when given the opportunity by the clinician through models presented with rising intonation patterns. Again, other testers and the family indicated that the child, as far as they knew, had not previously performed any type of verbal imitation. This suggests that given the opportunity, the child has the cognitive ability to spontaneously imitate. Even though the frequency of this spontaneous imitation was low, the fact that the child could do it at all considering his age level and the obvious limit in social expectations placed on him suggests that he could perform more advanced communication skills if given the opportunity. The lack of social development was obviously limiting his demonstration of cognitive ability.

For intervention to show success, communication opportunities would have to increase sufficiently to provide a variety of social purposes to express a variety of semantic notions. It was apparent that spontaneous imitation might act as a technique for the intervention. One of the reasons this child may not have been effective verbally was poor intelligibility. Since semantic development depends on auditory abilities, it is not uncommon for severe articulatory problems to exist with these children at the prelanguage level. For this child, verbalizations were only approximations but they were sufficiently consistent so as to be interpreted by a hearer as a sign icon or a sign index. Since any interaction between the clinicians and this child relied heavily on visual interpretation and presentation, the child was assumed to be learning primarily through the visual input.

This visual system was demonstrated by the child's use of a gestural system to communicate, as interpreted by the hearer, basic needs. However, it should also be noted that the child never waited to receive approval of a request for a need but physically acted on the request, getting the water, or the toy, or any other material that he wanted. If he could not physically respond immediately to the task, he manipulated the adult by pulling or pushing to use the adult as an instrument to the solution. Since he so visually and physically interacted with the clinicians, whether or not he might learn quicker with a visual system such as a manual sign system was explored during the evaluation.

In one situation the child gestured and went to get a drink of water. The adult turned off the fountain and directed the child's eyes to the clinician's face and said "water" with a manual sign. The child went to get the water and the clinician immediately shaped the child's hand into the sign and said "water." The child was held from getting the water while these steps were repeated. The child said the word with better intelligibility while attempting the sign. After this one instance, the child's spontaneous imitation of manual and verbal representations increased.

The child's change in behavior, given visual stimulation and the opportunity to affect others' behaviors by verbal means, suggested that his development, although prelanguage in nature, had the potential for further learning of more advanced communication. The intervention goal for this child's program might be written as follows: "Given the opportunity to represent semantic relations by sign or by verbalization, Johnny will affect the hearer through requests, assertions, and denials." Specific objectives would narrow the goal in terms of number of opportunities given to the child as well as types of methods. Spontaneous imitation is significant in this child's case and would be incorporated into the objectives. For example, "Given five opportunities in play to represent semantic relations in requests, assertions, and denials, the child will verbally or manually imitate four of the clinician's models."

By examining this child's behavior and comparing it with the theoretical premise presented earlier in the text, it is possible to determine what might be expected for this child.

According to the theoretical model, the child's functioning is presently at Phase One with some indications that the child is capable of increasing skills *up to* Phase Two. At the present time, there is no indication that the child will ever move completely into Phase Two with expansion, extension, and modulation.

The child's spontaneous imitation is infrequent and will need to be improved before language skills could be greatly increased for modulation and expansion processes to occur. It is apparent that the child can improve in frequency and that articulation can improve given a visual stimulus. Since learning is primarily visual, it appears that the child's ability to utilize auditory information is greatly reduced, also suggesting, especially at this age, a reduced ability to acquire more advanced oral language skills. However, a visual communication system would enhance the child's ability to interact in the environment.

The child's interaction with people was not suitable for establishing a sociocognitive system of communication as suggested in the earlier chapters of this text. Therefore, the opportunity to become a speaker who is capable of altering others' attitudes, beliefs, and behaviors by oral or manual sign is critical to the development of the child's system. Remember that the child's total system is synergistic. Therefore, if the social aspect is impaired then the ability to represent cognitive development is also impaired and this decreases the overall effectiveness of learning. From the limited ability to use nonverbal and verbal means of communication, it is apparent that this child's breakdown has occurred during the first phase of semantic development resulting in a nonsynergistic, nonproductive system without intervention to change the functioning of the system. The child's age suggests that such a synergistic system is not going to be possible but that rudimentary communication skills for interaction in the environment is a realistic goal.

## Case Study Two

The first child lacked sufficient development in sociocognitive functioning and was therefore performing at a disordered phase lower than would be expected for his age. Some diagnosticians would have also reported that the first child was mentally retarded. Whatever the diagnosis based on the overall depressed functioning, the first child is very different from the second case. Case Two was a three year, ten-month-old female who was referred by her mother because the child's speech was "delayed . . . she mainly says vowel sounds."

The parents, who had college educations, had realized that at the age of two their child was not developing speech like other children. It should be noted that it would be at this age that most children would have finished the prelanguage phase and shown signs of moving into the next phase of semantic development. If the parents realized that the child was not developing speech, it would have been worthwhile to check the child's language not her speech. Prior to the evaluation, the child's early childhood program had been providing articulation therapy twice a week but the child's "speech" had not improved. Work on speech when poor language development is probably responsible would not help and in this case it didn't.

The child was given some normative tests for comprehension to get an impression of her use compared to her learning, but it was not really necessary. Observation would have accomplished the same purpose. A language sample was obtained through play and picture stimuli and the clinicians wrote the following *summary* about the sample:

A language sample consisting of seventy-three single term vocalizations was obtained during free play. Less than 50% of the sample was intelligible since most of her utterances consisted only of vowel sounds. Annie communicated primarily through actions, gestures, and noises. For example, instead of saying "airplane," she held out her arms like wings and imitated the sound that is produced by airplanes. When asked to identify a picture of a rabbit, she hopped instead of saying the referent and when asked to identify a picture of a duck she said an approximation of "yellow" and "quack quack."

This type of communication behavior indicates that Annie has visually acquired the functional and perceptual attributes of her environment (what the animal looks like and what the animal does) but has been unable to attach these features to the appropriate lexical items or tags. In other words, she recognizes the characteristics and functions of an object but does not have the appropriate referential concept for it. Therefore, she is unable to describe the environmental relationships. Annie's inability to attach the lexical tags to the features suggests a disorder in the acquisition of language. As evidenced by the way she communicates, the disorder is related to a problem in the auditory system. For example, the fact that she lay down on the floor and closed her eyes when asked to tell what a child in a picture was doing (sleeping) suggests that she has not appropriately processed the lexical tag for that action which has been verbally (auditorily) provided by her adults.

Audiological testing indicated that the child had adequate hearing acuity for receiving speech stimuli from the environment. The conclusion stated the following:

Annie exhibited a severe language disorder due to her inability to attach functional and perceptual features to the appropriate lexical tag. Her auditory processing deficit also manifested itself in her inadequate phonological system and in her inability to sequence syllables for modulation and in her lack of semantic relationships being verbally expressed.

Because Annie's system has a different auditory component than would be typical, Annie had not progressed beyond the prelanguage phase of semantic development. Her utterances were single tags and were accompanied by an atypical, abnormal pantomime system suggesting that her cognitive ability to deal with the environment was much higher than her prelanguage development indicated.

From using the Prelanguage Assessment System protocol (Appendix A), it was important to note that the child was able to initiate interaction and to maintain interaction. However, the means by which this was accomplished consisted of an unusual communication style. There was little nonverbal or verbal evidence that the child had acquired true semantic relationships. Even though pantomime was used to represent an index, the activity appeared to represent single tags much like labels of the situation. The child did not link tags or pantomimes together. Furthermore, all vocalizations, whether of a perceptual or functional attribute, were used like a label rather than for relating events, actions, and objects. Therefore, the first therapy goal was to establish these semantic relationships through as many visual cues as possible to compensate for the auditory deficits. Remember that a deficient system is not synergistic and cannot be assumed to develop in a normal or typical pattern; therefore, the therapy is aimed at compensating for those deficits rather than remediating the system.

The long-term goal was written by the beginning clinician this way: "Annie will represent semantic relations of agents, actions, objects and events in purposeful communicative acts." This goal was also given to the school clinician so that the child would receive language, not speech, therapy four times a week. The therapy at school and at the clinic would concentrate on attaching lexical tags to visually presented relationships. The child would then represent these relationships through a verbal imitation at first followed later by spontaneous production.

Gestures and pantomime were discouraged. Because the child did not use any two-term utterances representative of semantic relations, it was assumed that the first utterances would have to be by imitation. Therefore, the objectives were written: "Given the opportunity, Annie will imitate an utterance representative of either an agent with action or object with action relationship." Data was taken in terms of percentages of imitated to provided utterances. The results were written: "At the beginning of the therapy period, approximately 65% of Annie's utterances representative of semantic relations were imitated with only 25% of her utterances being spontaneous and of a labeling nature. By the last session, Annie's utterances were 80% spontaneous and representative of the agent with action relationship."

It should be noted that Annie was still not producing a *variety* of semantic relations. Therefore, the next step of the therapy emphasized more variety.

Since Annie was receiving help in school and from the university clinic, progress was made within three to four weeks. At that time the child was beginning to show signs of progress toward the next step in semantic development, that is, to use spontaneously imitated semantic relations in the expansion of an idea to include more complexity by modulation. The objectives and goals were updated and the child continued to progress. At one point the child was put into a group session and the progress was reduced because of her specific auditory problems. Furthermore, the group activities consisted primarily of play. Children like Annie have not acquired the lexical tags for a language system through play with caregivers in their environment so the possibility that the child would learn it through play situations in therapy is unlikely. Like many others, Annie needs concentrated work on compensatory visual development in order to acquire more semantic skills for language development. Group situations are best for children who have not had experiences rich with language or who need the social, preparatory set for language opportunities.

The reason for Annie's lack of progress in play is theoretical. The play situation is primarily the same type of situation that the child and many others have in the home environment where good models are present. In this type of good environment, the parents or caregivers provide auditory stimulation that is attached to the experience. The child or adult performs an act and the parent is constantly attaching the verbal representation that the child is to receive auditorily. The fact that this child was assessed as having a problem in utilizing the auditory signal should have been sufficient for clinicians to realize that the child would have to have visual cues or additional semantic features through the visual channel, such as pointing out relationships represented in pictures in order for her to acquire lexical attachments. This child, like many other children with severe language problems, showed a good deal of visual awareness of the environment and very little response to auditory stimuli even though her acuity level was adequate.

It should be noted that the individuals who were responsible for this child's group therapy ignored the initial therapy and evaluation reports even though significant improvement had been documented, and they proceeded to do a complete evaluation of their own that emphasized the standardized measuring of splinter skills. At the end of this second evaluation it was concluded that the child had a severe language disorder and needed help in the "linguistic domain." This conclusion was already well documented by the fact that the child had been enrolled in therapy and that the child had little, if any, true language skills. In fact, the initial assessment described not only what characterized the child's language problem, but also the area of breakdown and the potential auditory problem with learning.

It seems a waste that the wheel is often reinvented with children when a new educator, clinician, or diagnostician sees a child because the new person's familiarity with not only normal but atypical development is weak. New assessments should be completed only when new information can be added to what is already known and not because of test administration biases. Furthermore, the natural group setting, although very good for children who are beginning to function at the Phase Two level of semantic development, will not help the prelanguage child who has sociocognitive needs related to processes of interaction and representing the meaning of those interactions.

If a child is not progressing as expected, techniques used in the group need to be more of an intervention type rather than facilitative in nature. Facilitation refers to the use of naturalistic models (Lucas, 1980), whereas intervention refers to the imposition of change on the child's system from outside models or techniques (Lucas, 1980).

**Additional Cases**

The following case studies of children functioning in the prelanguage phase of semantic development were obtained from a school for severely handicapped children with ages from infancy to adult. These examples of goals and objectives with other prelanguage children should provide some ideas of how to get the goals and objectives from the assessment interpretation or summary:

*Case One: Three years, three months*

> Goal: To develop the following prelanguage communication skills: recurrence and rejection.
> Objectives:
>> 1. Given a 15-minute session, Case One will maintain interaction for a total of 10 minutes using visual line of regard, 8 out of 10 opportunities.
>> 2. Given tactile stimulation, Case One will express rejection or recurrence by pulling away or turning toward the stimulation or by eye blinks, 8 out of 10 opportunities.

The 15-minute sessions provide the child with opportunities to select objects, such as a wind-up toy, or activities, such as the clinician winding up the toy, by means of eye blinks, turning away from the referent or toward the referent. Tactile stimulation would include touching, stroking, and patting of the child. It is apparent from these objectives that the child has some variety of indicators but does not use the nonverbal behavior to represent changes.

*Case Two: Twelve years, three months*

> Goal: To develop prelanguage communication skills of joint reference, object manipulation and exploration, and visual line of regard.
> Objectives:
>> 1. Given food or drink, Case Two will exhibit a joint referent for the food or drink by use of a visually established line of regard during 20 minutes of a 30-minute session.
>> 2. Given a choice of objects, Case Two will choose one object by use of visually establishing a joint referent and then manipulate the object according to the function of the object—with or without the model as needed.

The clinician was trying to get this child to establish a means of communicating so that the child would select food and drink as desired. Manipulation of the objects was used to get the child to maintain an interaction. Many severely handicapped children do not maintain an interaction probably because they do not have an adequate semantic basis.

*Case Three: Four years, four months*

> Goal: To develop prelanguage communication skills of initiating and maintaining interactions, object exploration, and vocally indicating.
> Objectives:
>> 1. Given a 30-minute session, Case Three will maintain interaction for 15 minutes by attending to the referent of an activity through gaze, facial changes such as smiles, and differentiated vocalizations.
>> 2. Given a choice of objects, Case Three will initiate the activity and if the activity should cease, the child will indicate through nonverbal means the desire to maintain the activity.

For this child, the clinician would have a variety of objects, such as wind-up toys, that would be brought to the child and manipulated. The child's gaze and other nonverbal means of communicating an initiation or maintenance of interaction would be reinforced.

*Case Four: Twelve years*

> Goal and Objective: Given a variety of situations, Case Four will request objects and actions for every eight of ten opportunities by manually signing basic semantic relations to be interpreted by the clinician.

This child was higher in semantic development than the previously described four cases. The child was able to use some manual sign language but did so only when asked to respond. Therefore, the emphasis of the therapy was on getting this child to perform the prerequisites to speech acts, with the adult interpreting the semantic relations as if they were complete speech acts.

*Case Five: Four years, one month*

Goal:   To use semantic relations nonverbally and verbally to manipulate objects, actions and events by requesting for objects, requesting for actions, denials, and assertions.

Objectives:

1. Given a 30-minute session, Case Five will initiate and maintain interaction by requesting for objects either vocally or by reaching 8 of every 10 opportunities.
2. Given the same 30-minute session, Case Five will request for actions either vocally or by reaching 8 of every 10 opportunities.
3. Given the same 30-minute session, Case Five will deny or reject an action or activity by turning away from the referent or by pushing it away—the clinician will respond by changing activities.
4. Given the same 30-minute session, Case Five will establish a visual line of regard as a prerequisite to an assertion.

Case Five was more capable of interacting and maintaining an interaction than the previously presented four cases. This child was having difficulty representing semantic development because of severe social deficiencies. The child had spent several weeks in a neonatal intensive care unit that played rock music. The only thing the child wanted to do was listen to rock music undisturbed by people when he was first evaluated. By the end of the first year, the child was moving into the second phase of development.

## INTERVENTION

With examples of goals and objectives having been presented for several different kinds of prelanguage children, the following section will discuss intervention methods and principles for the prelanguage child. Although the purpose of this book is to provide a theoretical framework for dealing with communication, language, and linguistic disorders, unless the connections between theory, assessment, and intervention are provided, application will not always be as effective as predicted.

## Sociocognitive Processes

The intervention used for children who are functioning in the prelanguage (Phase One) phase of semantic development must consider the synergistic aspect of the sociocognitive processes. The child must be able to demonstrate the social interaction process nonverbally in order to demonstrate cognitive (semantic) development. Therefore, the intervention must provide a social context in which the child can change the environment in order to have a social outcome or effect. In addition, the child must have the materials that will provide acquisition of semantic knowledge when acted upon. Finally, the child must be given the opportunity to improve on the actions. Each of these three points will be discussed separately.

A social context for a prelanguage child usually consists of play toys and objects that can be modeled for function, rolled, or manipulated in some way that approaches the daily activities of eating, self-care and so forth. These real types of situations provide a communicative opportunity for the child to get needs met. The adult must not allow the needs to be physically met and must not assume all of the responsibility in the communicative act.

The techniques used for allowing the child to verbally manipulate usually require some initial step of modeling through imitation and some assistance by either an alternate or supplemental mode or by withholding materials, snacks, etc. Lucas (1980) provided some suggestions for therapy with older children who are functioning socially at the prelanguage phase of semantic development. These techniques work the same way for the young child, provided that the prelanguage level is considered in terms of what is modeled and what materials are used.

The majority of children who operate at the prelanguage level do not have the cognitive ability to deal with a picture stimulus, unless the child is like Annie, a case presented earlier in this chapter. Annie had a higher cognitive development that was being limited by her lack of the auditory processing abilities involved in attaching lexical tags to experiences. Annie was close to the end of Phase One development and was not able to use sociocognitive processes to move into Phase Two. Many older children like Annie who are near the end of the first phase in terms of verbally representing semantic relationships but who are not progressing because of problems with the auditory portion of semantic development do well with pictures. For such children with auditory problems, a picture defines relationships and the adult marks this relationship with a paired auditory representation. It should be noted that most prelanguage children are just not at a high enough cognitive level to be able to deal with anything but the activities of daily living such as eating, drinking, changing, etc.

Often children who are severely handicapped are multiply handicapped, which means that they may also demonstrate severe problems with sensory or motor development and be limited in the ability to indicate an icon or index sign. The activities for these children must be taken to them, with emphasis being on their comfort needs. A recent newsletter of The Association for the Severely Handicapped (Lindley and Kershaw, 1982) suggested that too much time is spent on skills that severely handicapped children may never accomplish. Since severely handicapped children do not develop in a systematic order like other children, a child may be able, for example, to communicate about bathroom needs by using a communication board but never be able to babble like a four- or six-month-old child who is not handicapped.

The message of this newsletter article titled ''Mastering Prerequisite Skills: The Readiness Logic'' was quite clear and relates to the pragmaticism methodology of this text: *It is the sociocognitive processes that must be considered, not the tasks or the milestones.* It does no good to sit for hours with a prelanguage child trying to train speech types of sounds or encouraging vegetative vocalizations to form prerequisites of speech. These are splinter skills that do not occur unless the underlying semantic development processes through environmental stimulation as expected. Table 9-1 lists the various levels of prelanguage development and the concomitant expectations.

From the previous discussion some conclusions should be summarized. The context alone does not provide sufficient assistance for this child but the materials when arranged appropriately will provide the prelanguage child with a communicative need. The adult must be ready to accept whatever indicator the child can use to modify the adult's behavior. The use of the indicator acts as an index. In that way, all three aspects of intervention are provided: the environment with the social effect, the appropriate materials for the child's semantic level, and the opportunity to change the adult. Remember that when the child performs an act, the act is encoded so that the child actually learns through the performance. This is the synergistic quality of a semantic system. This learning provides the prelanguage child with a greater need to improve communication, and so the process continues.

An unfortunate aspect of intervention for the prelanguage phase child is that ingenious and sometimes expensive alternatives to speech are often required in order for the child to be able even minimally to represent an index sign. Unfortunately, untrained staff or insufficient funds serve to restrict the child's learning ability so that development remains slow at best. Furthermore, breaks in the learning process such as when school is out for the summer affect the overall functioning of these children since learning is not synergistic. For typically developing children, the summer break is an opportunity to continue to learn in a synergistic fashion.

Sometimes the services even during the school year are costly and the equipment almost impossible to build or finance. For example, the funds for a computer may take years to find and the child is limited until the funds are released. Nevertheless, although limited funds and untrained staff cannot be easily overcome, there is little excuse for a person to work on splinter skills or tasks that are

**Table 9-1** Prelanguage Current Level, Intervention Type, and Subsequent Functioning Level

| Current level | Stimulation type | Subsequent level |
|---|---|---|
| Limited, at best nonverbal response | Establish an index by reinforcing | Establishes social interaction for one mode (e.g., stimulate, child consistently smiles) |
| Child has consistent index (e.g., smile, point, leg kick, eye blink, etc.) | Interact with daily activities for choice by index | Establishes social purpose for communicating—to get needs met |
| Child uses index to get basic needs met | Interact and model (for spontaneous imitation) all semantic relations | Establishes paralinguistic and nonlinguistic principles of speech acts |
| Child uses a variety of semantic relations to meet a variety of functions | Increase frequency for spontaneous imitation to occur or to use imitation for modulation | Phase Two begins |

not going to improve the child's ability to function. The goal for all children at whatever phase of semantic development from the point of view of a pragmaticism methodology is to increase communication—not to make the child talk.

## COMMUNICATION

Since the communication goal is so important for children who are in the prelanguage semantic phase of development, it is probably necessary to review the theoretical rationale of this proposed framework in terms of the intervention goal to improve communication. The following section discusses the importance of communication for certain activities. The adult effects are discussed later in this text.

### Icon Communication

A child who is capable of the semantic level of representing an icon is capable of getting other people to get things or is capable of getting assistance provided that the adult will take the primary responsibility for the message. For example, the child could use the manual sign to represent ''toilet'' and the residential day care worker could take the child to the bathroom. A simple communication board can consist of iconic signs that allow the child to make choices for specific daily needs. It should be noted that although this ability is considered an increase in the child's functioning, unless the staff is willing to accept the primary responsibility for the child's message, the child's communication attempts are basically ignored. What usually happens is that the staff provides a very structured time to try to train the child to make these so-called "functional choices." In reality this type of training is not adequate for the promotion of a sociocognitive basis for the child since the child's need or purpose to communicate is ignored during these structured times. The tasks provided at these times are simply tasks. The staff then gets discouraged and cannot see any improvement except on the data sheets for splinter skills or tasks.

If a child's communication is to become increasingly more complex and thus increasingly more conventional and useful for living, the child's communication must be in context—a natural part of the environment and not just a training session. Daily data on tasks will not tell the educator if the child is a better communicator or not.

Many clinicians and parents have asked about when a visual system should be started to supplement or augment the auditory system. The answer lies with the theoretical framework that was presented earlier: If the child is learning primarily through a visual means as determined by observation during assessment, the child needs as many visual cues as possible to make the processing of communication easier. Another way of saying the same thing: If the child demonstrates an inability to acquire the semantic notions of the environment through conventional marking (auditory in nature), the child needs visual assistance in the marking.

The type of visual assistance depends on the child's need and the child's level of semantic development. At the icon level, the child will do better with a manual sign than with a printed word since the word is a symbolic sign of semantic development. If a child is at the index level, then combined manual signs for representing semantic relationships are better than words that are symbolic. The child who can deal only with icons will only be able to use daily experiences, whereas a child able to deal with an index can work with pictures showing daily activities.

A child who is capable of icons and indices is ready for more symbolic representations. The level of symbolization depends on the child's flexibility and communication productivity. For example, a computer would not be provided for a child who could point to a cup but not indicate a basic need such as drinking. These basic needs require more work with simpler semantic systems such as a communication board before such a symbolic system as the computer would be practical. When communication becomes sophisticated so that the child could handle displacement properties of space and time readily, then the child should be provided with a computer system that functions for maximum displacement and semanticity.

**Index Communication**

The child who can use an index has progressed beyond the iconic sign and is capable of demonstrating a relationship between the sign and the referent. This means that basic semantic relationships could be demonstrated nonverbally and by any other mode of communication. Semantic relationships are necessary for the child to actively function in the workshop type of setting. The demonstration may be nonverbal and the client may never progress into more sophisticated communication acts because of the low frequency and lack of variety of basic relationships, *but* the basic semantic relationship will allow the child to perform a variety of workshop types of activities. A child who is limited to an iconic sign might be trained to do one thing such as lift one piece, but to perform a discrimination task with the one piece so that it is put in the right place would require the ability to perform an index sign. If the child or adult can perform these types of discriminations, then this person can also demonstrate a variety of nonverbal semantic relationships.

If the semantic relationships are expressed verbally, the person has numerous sheltered workshop types of activities that can be performed well. The person cannot be expected to function without some sort of shelter because the relationships are basic only to needs and not to learning directions, etc. For example, these individuals might learn to ride a bus but the learning is through compensatory skills that are primarily visual in nature. If the bus breaks down and the person is left on the street corner, the person limited to an index would have more difficulty getting home than the person capable of using a symbolic sign.

**Symbolic Communication**

An individual capable of symbolic communication has the basics to acquire the language skills that will facilitate the growth and acquisition of a linguistic system with all of the advantages of such a system. This does not preclude the fact that some individuals may begin with some basic symbolization and not be able to progress because of some learning or language disorder. More about the semantic symbol will be discussed in the next two chapters dealing with Phase Two and Phase Three semantic development.

**SUMMARY**

Intervention for persons functioning at Phase One of prelanguage semantic development should be aimed at increasing the necessary sociocognitive functions for better communication, that is, communication that will help the child function in the environment by taking on more of the burden for the communication of the message. The intervention for prelanguage children should never concentrate on the acquisition of developmental milestones or those developmental tasks that some children will never perform. Instead the pragmaticism methodology suggests that the intervention emphasis should always be on the child's synergistic system—as it functions to meet basic communication needs either verbally or nonverbally. These needs may be met by exploiting the child's atypical, non-synergistic system within a given context of communication. The goals of communication for the prelanguage child should emphasize the development of iconic signs to represent an index sign as the semantic information develops. Before the child can progress into Phase Two, some emphasis on the relationship between symbols would also need to be emphasized.

---

**REFERENCES**

Lucas, E.V. *Semantic and pragmatic language disorders: Assessment and intervention.* Rockville, Md.: Aspen Systems, 1980.

Mastering prerequisite skills: The readiness logic. *The Association for Severely Handicapped Newsletter*, 1980.

## Chapter 10

# Intervention for the Language System

*The seeds are sown,*
*The garden plowed—*
*Who should harvest a bountiful mind?*

## Chapter Objectives

1. Describe the relationship between intervention and theory for the language system.
2. Describe how to write intervention goals and objectives for intervention of language disorders.
3. Describe the relationship between the assessment and intervention for the child with language disorders.
4. Explain the purpose of the language intervention techniques presented in this chapter.
5. Explain the relationship between the prelanguage and the language system.
6. Describe the purpose of language intervention for a pragmaticism methodology as opposed to a psycholinguistic methodology.
7. Give examples of certain types of language problems.
8. Provide therapy for a child with language problems based on a pragmaticism theory and methodology.

## INTRODUCTION

The purpose of this chapter is to describe the language intervention process for children who are at the second phase of semantic development, the language phase. Intervention for children with problems in developing language tools emphasizes those processes that allow language to develop for use in altering the attitudes, beliefs and/or behaviors of a hearer. As previously discussed, these processes include expansion, modulation, extension, and overgeneralization. Since these sociocognitive processes are semantic in nature, a pragmaticism methodology is appropriate for developing remediation principles and practices.

From a pragmaticism methodology point of view, the language of the child is a tool—consisting of conventional ways to use a sign (primarily symbolic in nature) to produce consequences in the environment. A psycholinguistic approach that considers language as an entity—or an end-product—cannot have the same consequences expected in an intervention approach. In other words, the pragmaticism methodology considers the synergistic aspect of the tools as they are developed from use and from effects. This methodology recognizes the significance of the speech act semantic constituents as paramount, with the mode—oral language—as the product. Therefore, the methodology of pragmaticism does not deal with milestones per se, unit analyses of tools, or unit relationships. The pragmaticism methodology considers the child in context: What is the child using to manipulate the environment? How is the child altering the communication events of the environment? When can the child be expected to use the environment through manipulation? What are the communication effects of the tools that the child is able to use?

## GOALS AND OBJECTIVES

From the language assessment procedure described in Chapter 8 and the implementation of the protocol on the language assessment system described in Appendix B, sufficient data is gathered to determine the goals and objectives for the child who is functioning in Phase Two of semantic development—the language system phase. The most difficult aspect of planning therapy for the child in the language phase is that it is tempting for the educator or clinician to focus on the child's tools rather than on the effects or consequences of the tools. The development of consequences in the child's environment requires the facilitation of certain sociocognitive processes of modulation, extension, expansion, and overgeneralization. Therefore, the goals emphasize the facilitation of these processes through specific techniques if the child is young enough to use these processes in a synergistic manner. If the child is older than seven or eight years of age, intervention is aimed at helping the child develop compensatory ways of learning to communicate with a nonsynergistic system.

An example of a goal for a child who is young enough to engage in an active process of modulation might be written as follows: "The child will be given the opportunity by pictorial representation to *expand* the basic semantic relations through modulation." The objectives that would be used to meet this goal would include the specific changes expected by modulation, such as the incorporation of functors or the use of grammatical morphemes to represent underlying semantic development. The materials or activities would include the representation of semantic relationships so that the meaning could be presented visually and attached for the child to the auditory code. Goals and objectives emphasizing the opportunity to use modulation through sign representation—that is, by language conventions—may facilitate the process.

The objectives for this type of facilitation might be written as follows: "The child will represent the semantic relations of a three-proposition story by using the proposition to predicate relationship with the functors 'the,' 'a,' and 'an,' the grammatical morphemes 'in' and 'on,' copular variations, and the morphological inflections of plurals and past tenses." A second objective might emphasize the functional and perceptual incorporations of qualifiers and possibly quantifiers into the basic semantic relations. The result of such an emphasis is the development of increased semantic complexity. As described by Lucas (1977), when the semantic complexity affects another person (hearer) in a specified way, the speech act performed is a way to incorporate the semantic system. The final unemphasized product is greater complexity of the system, with semantic refinement observed in the structural complexity.

The converse therapeutic relationship does not exist. The surface form cannot be emphasized with an expected change in the underlying semantics. If the underlying semantics are not increased, the semantic constituents of the child's speech act are not developed. The result of such an inability to perform speech acts is a limitation on the communication system so great that disorders may emerge, with rigid uses of language tools reflecting a lack of cognitive development and social exchange for basic needs to be met.

If the child's language tools may be developed by facilitating sociocognitive processes, the therapy will utilize many natural expansion and expatiation (Muma, 1971) techniques. However, children who are past seven to eight years of age and who have language disorders are not operating with a synergistic system. These children with language disorders (Lucas, 1980) have semantic problems that need direct types of intervention.

Children with language disorders who are in the second phase of development can usually be grouped on the basis of three types of semantic breakdown. The first type of child is quite unintelligible and the hearer assumes that the child is having difficulty acquiring the sound system for adequate representation. The second type of child evidences a reduction in complexity of structure related to syntax and morphology and the hearer assumes that the child has difficulty acquiring the conventions of the system. The third type of child has difficulty with even the basic semantic development so that the child's language is confusing and difficult to follow.

The three types of children are all experiencing difficulty in acquiring the representation of the semantic system. As described in Chapter 7, this inability to represent semantic development may be a result of the incoming message stimuli not being organized or attached to the appropriate lexical markers at this phase of semantic development. A case study for each of the three types of language disorders will be presented with the theoretical relationships explained. Goals and objectives will be provided based on theoretical assumptions and language analysis. (For more information on how to do a qualitative analysis of a language sample, see Lucas, 1980.)

## Case Study One—Phonology

Once a child has acquired the prelanguage sociocognitive processes for language tools to be developed, and once the child has made a transition into the language phase based on the processes functioning to produce a sufficient frequency of utterances, the child is ready to demonstrate language tools that represent the earlier semantic acquisition. Some children continue to acquire semantic knowledge but are unable to attach the auditory marking by caregivers to the knowledge. As a result of this inability to code the underlying information, they are unable to produce a conventional sound system. It should be noted that even though such a child's language system *appears* to be intact except for the sound system, such an assumption is not feasible according to a pragmaticism methodology. The surface coding (phonology) cannot be unilaterally interrupted; there have to be other problems within the system that disrupt not only the phonology but other parts of the language tool.

As noted in Chapter 7, there are four possible reasons for breakdown: the child is unable to receive sensory stimuli because of an acuity problem, for example; the child is unable to group the basic information of the received stimuli; the child is unable to organize stimuli into groups of features; or the child is unable to group features into concepts. Which of these four possibilities represents the child who has severe phonological problems? Since the child is unable to group auditory features into a code that represents the conventions of a given society, the child must be experiencing some processing deficits with auditory information. These deficits could exist on their own or they could be the result of earlier problems with auditory acuity, as appears to be the case with some children having chronic middle ear pathology, chronic otitis media.

The child who has difficulty with organizing features has problems with all aspects of the code. He or she will experience failure in tying semantic features into morphological representations such as the ''s'' for plural marking or the ''in'' for a spatial dimension. With this inability, phonological problems are really problems with the underlying semantic organization so that the child who is unintelligible is also the child who omits functors and morphological inflections. This child may also exhibit problems with acquiring the higher semantic concepts for space, time, quality, and quantity since he or she cannot organize the features well enough to manipulate their representative concepts. If this theoretical explanation is sound, one should be able to closely analyze those children who have phonological problems and find these concomitant deficits: morphological deviations and omissions, limited semantic development in the areas of time, space, quality, and quantity.

Because intelligibility is so obvious to a hearer, the clinician often works on the child's sound system thinking that unless the hearer can understand the child, the child can't make any progress. From the point of view of a pragmaticism methodology, there is some logic to this notion. The child who is unintelligible is not going to have the same effective ways of changing the environment as a child who is intelligible. Therefore, the ability to perform speech acts as a learning system is impaired and the child's advanced language development is restricted. However, there are some illogical components to this notion of working on making the child more intelligible by evaluating and treating the phonological system. If the child has a problem in the underlying organization of semantic features into a conventional code, the child has a semantic problem, not a phonology problem.

The application of a pragmaticism methodology to the remediation of language disorders assumes that the therapy is going to remediate the problem not the symptom. Therefore, the therapy should emphasize semantics and not the coding or tools, the phonology. The therapy for the child who is unintelligible would deal with the underlying semantics responsible for the poor use of conventional signs.

Despite encouragement to deal with semantics there will still be some people who decide to work on phonology. Anyone insisting on this approach to the unintelligible child should incorporate some of the recent phonological analyses (e.g., Ingram, 1981; Ling, 1976). Furthermore, semantics should be incorporated into the phonological work. For example, if the child says "sue" for "shoe," a contrast is made between the two words by using a picture to depict the visual representation of each word. This semantic contrast appears to be much more effective with young children than the repetitious models.

It is not that children do not need phonological work. A child's production simply cannot be analyzed without considering the auditory semantic contribution. There are children who may have many errors in the sound system who have acquired the minimum amount of expansion and modulation of language tools. These children need refining help that may come more effectively through semantics than through work on the sound system.

Children who are mostly unintelligible do have deficiencies in modulation and expansion, either because of insufficient features to begin these processes or insufficient use to increase them. Too often, the psycholinguistic approach overlooks the child's real problem when intelligibility is affected. For example, a five-year-old child was brought to a university clinic and the clinician did a very thorough phonological analysis of the child's actual production as compared to expected production. Exhibit 10-1 provides a segment of the child's language. However, after some confusion on scheduling, the parents went to a private clinic. Several months later the child was referred to a multidisciplinary team. The child was found to be performing as age expected on psychological and physical batteries. The private clinician had referred the child to this team when he realized that the problem was not just in the sound system. The child had evidenced other problems. An examination of the original sample and the present language usage indicated that the phonological approach to the child was clearly inappropriate.

This child's inability to attach auditory input to a code rested in deficiencies in the semantic system. The phonological deficits were only a symptom of the underlying auditory processing. Chapter 7 described the breakdown points and the primary reasons for semantic development problems. For this child, the semantic features auditorily coded from speakers were not being organized, with the result that functors, morphological inflections by modulation and expansion, were not occurring. Furthermore, this child had made negligible progress in therapy or in academics. A child does not do poorly in class if the only problem is phonology. Too many children like this are seen for phonological or articulation therapy when the real problem has to do with the way the child's system functions for communication.

Based on the information regarding the child's communication skills according to a qualitative analysis of semantics, appropriate goals and objectives were developed. For example, "(1) The child will expand through modulation more complex relationships to include functors representative of underlying semantic development." The materials for this child's language intervention included pictures that could be verbally marked by the clinician. For example, the clinician would point out available relationships within a picture, then provide the child with the opportunity to imitate the semantic relations. From these imitated productions, the child would be provided an opportunity to use the relationships within a speech act. Remember that according to the pragmaticism theory the person who performs an utterance act with the semantic constituents of a speech act is learning how to use language to further development. For example, the clinician shows the child a picture and says, "The man is chasing the truck." The clinician then has the child imitate this utterance and the child has by imitation produced an utterance act—probably similar in specifications to an assertion type of speech act when used with another child in a group. The actual production by the child feeds the

**Exhibit 10-1** Phonological Analysis of a Child with Semantic Disorders

| INTERPRETATION | | ANALYSIS | | |
| | | | Substi- | |
| Transcription | Target | Syll | tution | Process |
| --- | --- | --- | --- | --- |
| I didn't see a yellow one.<br>aɪ dɪdn si ə jejowʌn | t<br>(dɪdn) | cvcc→<br>cvc | −/+<br>j/l | DFC (delete<br>final con)<br>liquid gliding |
| One time I went to go and<br>wʌn taɪm aɪ went tu go æn | d(æn)<br>l(jejo) | vcc→<br>vc | −/d<br>j/l | DFC<br>gliding |
| I see yellow playdough.<br>aɪ si jejo penoi: | pl,d<br>(peno) | cvcv→<br>cvcv | pl/p<br>n/d | cl. red.<br>(cluster<br>reduction)<br>nasalization |
| Yeah, I did.<br>jea, aɪ dɪd | | | | |
| I make one, a log?<br>aɪ mek wʌn, ə lɔg? | | | | |
| A little snake?<br>ə lɪd! nek? | sn (nek)<br>t<br>(lɪd!) | cvc→<br>cvc | n/sn<br>d/t | cl. red.<br>voicing |
| Push hard?<br>pɪs hard? | v, ʃ<br>(pɪs) | cvc→<br>cvc | i/v | vowel<br>tensing<br>stopping |
| I don't know.<br>aɪ dont no | | | | |
| I did tear it up.<br>aɪ dɪd tɛr ɪt ʌp | | | | |
| Little more?<br>lɪd! mor? | (lɪd!)<br>t | cvc→<br>cvc | d/t | stopping |
| This like this you do?<br>Dɪs laɪk dis ju du du? | t<br>(du) | cv→<br>cv | d/t | voicing |

system, creating a need to be synergistic in nature—an active need to learn more about the system.

The objectives for this child's therapy included the number of opportunities the child would be given as well as the type of expansions that the clinician would model for the child to imitate. Eventually, the objectives emphasized productions in a variety of different contexts to produce a variety of different effects without the model. For example, "Given 20 opportunities to spontaneously produce through expansion and modulation a speech act, the child will perform five different types of speech acts with the essential language elements regarding morphology being met."

The clinician may want to specify the types of speech acts as well as the types of language essentials that would have to be met in terms of morphology. The critical factor for this therapy is that the expansion and modulation be varied so as to maximize the range of semantic development underlying the utterances. If there is no variety the child may learn a structure as a response and not as a language tool for communication. For example, if a picture is shown to the child and the child says "eat sammich," the clinician would want to expand on this utterance and have the child say it to someone else in the group or to "try again" with the clinician. The clinician might say, "Yes, the boy is eating his sandwich." When the child tries it again, the child says, "The boy eat sammich." This time instead of expanding on the utterance, the topic needs a new predication so the clinician says, "The boy likes to eat sandwiches for lunch." The utterance type has been changed by the addition of meaning in a causal relationship that is more advanced than the original thought object. The child now is requested to add to the former utterance with the clinician changing the meaning and subsequent structure each time something is said about the picture.

To summarize: the child with a language problem involving phonology is considered unintelligible because he or she is not able to organize auditory information into concepts, nor is the child able to represent, because of the auditory problems, the acquired semantic information. Therefore, the child omits the modulation and expansion that represents the changing semantic development. Therapy should emphasize the semantic organization rather than the phonology problems. The semantic development may be facilitated by directing a child through utterance acts that can be used as a speech act when the imitation is removed. The primary focus is always on the semantics and not the structural components of the language code. This latter point means that the child will probably need additional visual cues other than just pictures. Visual cues include not only the picture but the face, the use of pointing to demonstrate relationships, and the use of any other visual representations such as the orthographic or written word paired with the picture.

## Case Study Two—Syntax and Morphology

Whereas the phonological problems presented in the first case study dealt with the underlying problem of coding auditory features to represent relationships, the second case study is of a child who exhibits a reduced complexity in morphology and syntax without the concomitant phonological problems. The child's underlying semantic relationships are not well established. The child is not having difficulty with attaching features but rather organizing the features into appropriate signs to represent the underlying semantic notions. This child is a four-year, eleven-month-old male who has been referred to a university speech and hearing clinic (Russell & Arwood, 1982) for problems with ''being understood.'' The following segment of utterances are consecutive and are considered ''representative'' of the entire language sample obtained on this child.

1. Tom sat in yard eating his a cookie.
2. Tom walking over his a wagon.
3. He walking over to his a wagon.
4. In the nest
5. Tom, kitty watch bird gettin' in nest.
6. That gonna take picture.
7. Cookie crumbs for birds.
8. Birds, Tom gave cookie crumbs.
9. That [pointing to another child]
10. Birds can fly away.
11. Pussy cats . . . birds fly away
12. Big birds
13. He goin' build house.
14. Use the blocks and build a house!
15. We goin' build a house.
16. For help
17. We goin' build a house.
18. That house
19. I need help.
20. Got fence on it
21. Put that block right there.
22. Buildin' house
23. Can't get that out
24. Gotta build one too
25. Gotta make that car go now
26. Comin' in the car
27. That house is big.
28. I can't find that block.
29. Can't get that
30. Can't get it
31. Get that out in this car
32. Put that in that man.
33. Put that in that car.
34. Tall house
35. That old
36. Got that car goin' in there
37. Couch done fell
38. Cow felled
39. Go cow
40. That cow can't
41. Can't get that outta my hand
42. Backing up
43. Get that car, cow.
44. Cow can't
45. Car backing up
46. Put these away
47. That guy big

On another day, the following segment of language was obtained from the same child:

1. That monsters are dancing
2. Max being bad boy
3. (unintelligible) chasing a dog
4. These a gre up in Max's room
5. Big ol' monster blowing smoke at Max
6. Monsters are coming after Max
7. That big monster has one [smile] on his face

These utterances suggest some problems in the underlying semantic basis resulting in the child's inability to appropriately mark utterances to agree in number, tense, etc. However, when the context (not provided with the language sample) is considered, there are some other types of semantic disorders. This child, Jimmy, was unable to identify the basic topic of conversation as demonstrated by inappropriate answers to questions and as demonstrated by his off-topic utterances (see Lucas, 1980). For example, when he was shown a picture of a story book and asked "What is Grover doing?" he inappropriately answered, "That my cow." He produced numerous off-topic (Lucas, 1980) utterances when a story was being presented or during other language group activities. For instance, during a story about a family going on a picnic, he made a comment about his boots and about an airplane that was not present.

Once during a snack time while the other children were requesting snacks, Jimmy said, "Oh, it bit me" when there was no apparent referent for that utterance. These off-topic utterances along with his inability to answer questions indicated a lack of ability to scan the speaker's utterances and determine the underlying meaning of the referent.

Jimmy also exhibited some word-finding difficulties. For example, he would often repeat parts of utterances as if scanning for more information to organize into lexical tags. These repetitions would often be followed by unintelligible utterances suggesting that he could not organize the features. For example, "Here go, uh, cow eat, eat boy up . . . [unintelligible] I, I [unintelligible] cow eat him up, cow eat." He also used a lot of "fillers" (Lucas, 1980), words with indefinite meanings such as "it," "that," and "one." Even when the hearer asked for clarification, the child often had difficulty specifying the referent.

In addition to problems with referents and the inability to organize features into appropriate lexicalization, Jimmy also demonstrated some problems with organizing basic semantic features. This inability to organize semantic features resulted in semantic word errors. For example, he referred to a "duck" as a "kitten" and to a "horse" as a "cat." Although he obviously had the idea that these were animals, the fact that Jimmy had the referents confused suggested that he did not possess all of the basic semantic features of the lexical tags. Therefore, he could not distinguish between the tag for "duck" or the tag for "kitten." This ability to appropriately tag the common types of referents is a task that most children could do at age three. Jimmy (ca. 4 years, 11 months) is chronologically beyond the age at which he should have acquired this ability to organize semantic features.

There is additional information from the language sample that suggests that Jimmy was unable to organize semantic information. Syntactic (word order) errors were produced such as "Bowl in that dough" instead of "Dough in that bowl." The unconventional ordering of words is a disorder related to an inability to put semantic information into appropriate relationships. As the child put a pan in the oven, he said, "Put that oven in the pan." The real semantic relationship was the child (agent or possibly instrument if the child views himself that way) putting (action) the object (objective recipient) into the oven (recipient of the object). If Jimmy had developed the necessary semantic features for agents, actions, objects, instruments, location (recipient of the object), and so forth, he would have had no problem with conventional word ordering.

The inadequate semantic basis was also observed in Jimmy's lack of age-appropriate morphological modulation and consequently poor expansion. He omitted many types of functors and qualifiers from his language as well as inappropriately used some functors. For example, he tried to put an article into his utterances and consequently had some redundancy of meaning. For example, he said, ''. . . his a cookie.'' This inappropriate use of functors coupled with the omission of functors was related to the semantic complexity of the utterance. If the utterance expressed several relationships, the ability to use certain modulations would decrease. When the utterance was a repetition of a previous utterance or when it was a standard rehearsed utterance, Jimmy would modulate appropriately. For example, he missed the meaning of the functors in ''Tom sat in yard eating his a cookie.'' This utterance was complex in meaning compared with an utterance such as ''I can't find that block.'' Jimmy's underlying semantic basis was so weak that when ideas or propositions were predicated sufficiently, he was not able to modulate and thus represent such changes in meaning. He had moved into Phase Two of language but was not able to make the modulation and expansion processes work sufficiently because the underlying semantic features were not sufficiently developed. Jimmy had acquired structures without their corresponding meaning.

In considering the quality checks of the Language Assessment System protocol (Appendix B), Jimmy's flexibility and productivity were limited. The goal for intervention with Jimmy would have to take into account the lack of flexibility because of the underlying semantic deficits. The objectives would have to include specific areas of remediation. A goal with objectives might be written as follows: ''To increase the semantic relations for reduction of specific semantic disorders including semantic word errors, difficulty identifying the referent, off-topic comments, and word-finding difficulties. Given a picture with specified semantic relationships, Jimmy will produce 10 semantic relationships about the topic. Given the semantic relationships, the clinician will expand the utterance to include age-appropriate modulation. Given an expansion, Jimmy will imitate the modulation so that age-appropriate utterances are produced. Given the imitated productions, the clinician will expand the utterances to include other semantic concepts.''

Note that the goal followed by the objectives also included procedures and methods for keeping the child on the topic yet provided for spontaneous productions to be increasingly more complex semantically. It is important that the child's language remain semantically appropriate. Therefore, this child required a structured topic. Activities that encourage free play or open-ended topics could only invite the child to talk about nonrelated ideas. The purpose of therapy with this child, as it is with most children that have semantic problems, was to keep the child's ideas organized. Since the child did not have the necessary language tools to talk about his environment, the clinician tried to organize him so that whatever was uttered was truly representative of the signs used.

Like the child in Case One, Jimmy required the maximum amount of visual presentation. Pictures and other forms of visual cuing would expand on semantic relationships for increased semantic development.

## Case Study Three—Limited Productions

The third type of problem that may be found in the second phase of semantic development is exhibited by the child who has not developed many language skills. The child's surface representation is quite deficient because almost no expansion or modulation has occurred. For such a child, structure is very limited in nature as is flexibility and productivity. Joan, a nine-year, four-month-old female, was referred for a speech and language evaluation. The following segment of language is considered representative and was taken from 100 consecutive utterances that were collected over two separate testing occasions. The two sessions were required since Joan's frequency of utterances was so low.

1. That is my sister.
2. That is my sister.
3. That is my class.
4. A kid got bite right where it hurts.
5. A boy got bitten by a geese right where it hurts.
6. We were feeding them.
7. We were feeding them.
8. I never got bit by the geese.
9. I never got bitten by the geese.
10. What is her name?
11. They clean up the messes.
12. They drop their trays.
13. They drop their trays on purpose.
14. They drop their trays on purpose.
15. That is _____ _____ _____ [three unintelligible terms]
16. Susan and Bill are best friends.
17. Susan and Bill are best friends.
18. That Bill, I love him.
19. Her sister is my best friend.
20. She is not in
21. She is not in this book.
22. This is in in my sister.

23. They are in my sister class.
24. They are in my sister's class.
25. This is fifth grade class.
26. There are more.
27. There are chickens, about fifteen chickens.
28. Now there about 25.
29. The mama turkey and the daddy turkey and the goose who broke his leg, they hang out together.
30. All the time we're in barn I see the animal.
31. An, we kill two baby turkey.

The most significant characteristic of the preceding language sample is the child's constant attempt to revise a previous utterance to include modulated and expanded utterances. During the time between about three years of age and five years of age, many children try to revise an utterance to match a conventional form. However, at nine years of age the revising is no longer a typical pattern. At this point the child is demonstrating difficulty with the organization of semantic features and the attachment of those features.

In view of the restricted use of language and the inappropriateness of some of the higher semantic concepts, it appears that this child has been building structure at the expense of semantic development. It should be noted that some of the child's attempts to revise utterances may be a product of the child being in a language therapy situation that emphasized structure. The child's overall ability to use language tools in a productive and effective manner is limited by the following semantic problems: (1) an inability to relate a predication to a proposition so that there is a variety of ways to represent basic semantic relations; (2) the lack of appropriate things to say as demonstrated by a low frequency of utterances and by the same content being reiterated; (3) a lack of on-topic comments as indicated by the child leaving a topic about school to talk about a book (perhaps associated); and (4) the production of unintelligible utterances representative of the child's inability to formulate organized relationships into appropriate tags. Each of these four points will be separately explained in the following paragraphs.

The child's inability to relate a proposition to a predication means that she is not able to say a variety of things about a topic. This is the result of her lack of semantic feature acquisition. In other words, the child receives sensory information that becomes organized into features that do not get organized into related feature bundles. Therefore, the child's lexicalization does not occur as a process and expansion and modulation are not needed to refine the basic semantic features acquired. There are insufficient relational features for proposition-to-predication relationships. This inability to relate features manifests itself in the limited variety of utterances because of the limited variety of relationships. It also manifests itself in a lack of variety regarding lexical tags. The child tries to say different things using the same basic referents and revising the referents. However, since the child does not have a variety of relations, her topics become limited. The more limitations placed on the child's production system, the more limitation placed on the child's learning system. The synergistic system that was not functioning for the child to acquire features for relational organizations limits the system's overall capability of learning.

This child has a lower semantic level than the children of the two previously described cases. Like many children with deficient feature organization, she has ineffective communication. The phonological child and the child with the deficient way to acquire advanced semantic skills to stay on topic have effective ways to communicate, that is, effective ways of affecting the environment. The child with the very low semantic level has very few ways to affect hearers.

There are other children who may demonstrate more form but be just as deficient as Case Three in terms of semantic development. The primary characteristic of these children, regardless of the surface form, is the insufficient number of utterances within a given context. These children lack enough information about the environment so that their utterances are either very rigid and stereotyped repetitions or they are few and far between and even these are often inappropriate. The therapy for such children must utilize context to allow the child to perform speech acts that will have an effect on someone in the environment. This type of production then forces the child's nonsynergistic system to learn about the conditions of the speech act, thus increasing the knowledge about underlying semantics. The child gains the experience of the utterance act being attached to the effect or consequences; thus, the child has a purpose for communicating an increased number of appropriate utterances.

The third problem that this Case Three child exhibited was an inability to stay on topic. A child who doesn't stay on the topic is demonstrating a deficiency in underlying semantic information. If the child had the knowledge about the referent organized, the child could scan others' utterances as well as his or her own utterances and be able to stay on the topic. Many children have a lot to say but don't know when enough has been said because they don't have enough meaning attached to whatever is spoken.

The child's fourth problem, unintelligible utterances, represents the basic problem in the acquisition of semantics: the child is having difficulty organizing auditory features into lexical tags representative of the intended signs. The four problems that the child demonstrated were a result of the same underlying problem. Remediation should be aimed at the child's appropriate organization of auditory features—features attached to relational notions and represented by specific referents modulated and then expanded.

The goals and objectives for Case Three are written for a lower semantic level than were the goals and objectives for Case One and Case Two. The goal would emphasize the child's development of semantic relationships. This low level is chosen because the child is not really operating at a higher level, even though her sentence structure may appear to be at a higher level. For example, the sentence "A boy got bitten by a geese right where it hurts" appears to reflect fairly complex structure, but the use of "a" is indefinite, as is the phrase "right where it hurts." A lack of specificity is observed throughout the sample. The child does not have enough semantic development to support these structures. Most of the child's utterances are expansions by stereotyped phrases such as "right where it hurts." Other types of rigid structures included "on purpose . . . " or "by X." Most of the child's utterances were a basic X is Y proposition to predicate relationship. Most three-year-old children show more variety in the use of language than does this nine-year-old child (see Chapter 5).

The product of a very restricted semantic development is a child who cannot affect the attitudes, beliefs, and/or behaviors of other people. The goal for such a child might be written as follows: "Given a manipulative activity, the child will produce an expansion of basic semantic relationships to perform the speech acts of requesting, asserting, calling, ordering, and stating information." The objectives would include the specific number of opportunities and expected level of performance: "Given 20 opportunities to request, assert, call, order, or state, Joan will produce 15 semantic relationships in a speech act attempt. Given the speech act attempt, the utterance will be expanded structurally to include more complex semantic representations. Given the expansion, Joan will be given another opportunity with all semantic conditions for a speech act met for the performance of a more complex act." The methods and procedures could be extended. The primary concern in providing intervention for this child is that the basic semantic relationships are put into a situation that requires her to perform speech acts. The performance of the speech acts will increase the frequency of the utterances as well as add variety to her very limited sign system.

In summary, children who are in Phase Two of semantic development require some development of underlying semantic relationships either through marking the relationships with visual cues or manipulative activities such as drawing a picture for which the child must perform specific speech acts in order to participate in the setting.

## METHODS AND PROCEDURES

The preceding section presented three cases and their corresponding goals and objectives for intervention based on the language *use* of the child. Note that although only the language tools were provided, the interpretation was made from the Language Assessment System (Appendix B), which determines the quality of the system through an examination of how a child uses language tools, when the language tools are used, and for what reasons the language tools are used.

The methods and procedures for children in the second phase of semantic development vary according to the goals and objectives developed for them. There are basically three types of therapy that could be used with children in this phase: (1) The child is provided with modeled examples of certain semantic relationships expressed with appropriate form for imitation. The imitations are then changed to meet a higher level of semantic development representative of modulation or expansion. (2) The child is provided with opportunities for performing semantic relationships within a speech act that will alter the clinician's activities in some way. (3) The child is provided with a combination of manipulation activities and semantic relationship practice. Each of these three types of therapy will be discussed separately.

## Semantic Relationships

The term "semantic relationship" is being used to denote the use of a proposition-predication relationship that describes something or says something about a topic. The major problem in having a child imitate these relationships is that the semantic relationship will eventually be expanded into a speech act. A speech act cannot exist unless the sincerity semantic condition is met. Imitation violates the sincerity condition. Therefore, the more natural the therapy model, the more likely that the child will not already know what is expected. For example, the clinician looks at a picture, points to a boy throwing a ball, and says, "That boy is playing baseball." The notion of baseball may not be obvious to both the clinician and the child. The clinician can then ask the child to tell another child about the relationship. Since the concern is about relationships, the child need not produce a grammatical construction or even the same relationship that the adult clinician presented. However, the utterance of the child needs to be related to the original topic, baseball or playing.

If patterns (repetition of sincerity-violated utterances) are used, the child has the semantic basis for the utterance but not the ability to attach the appropriate lexical tags. The child in the phonological case presented in this chapter might do quite well with a pattern type of therapy. However, the other two children would become more inflexible and more rigid in their productions. The main concern of the clinician should be to keep the therapy process as consistent with the principles of semiotics as described by the pragmaticism methodology as possible so that the system reflects the use of sociocognitive processes in a dynamic interaction between a speaker and a hearer.

The semantic relationships that are built are marked by the utterances of the clinician in context, that is, with activity pictures, play, or manipulation types of materials. The utterances of the clinician are always synergistic; they take what the child says and are manipulated to include more semantic complexity. As the semantic complexity is increased, representation of the semantic development is increased, as evidenced by increased complexity of the structures. This interactive process is often described in terms of models.

Models or productions for the hearer to follow are explained in the literature (e.g., Lucas, 1980; Muma, 1971). These models are used in context with many of the synergistic qualities of the language kept intact. Some children who are in the language phase of development may also need as many visual properties of the system as possible. Therefore, printed words, sign language (manual language tools), color-coded cards, pictures with sufficient semantic information are used to help them acquire the necessary relationships.

## Speech Acts

Some children need many opportunities to affect hearers. These children usually have very restricted semantic development even though their language tools seem to be structurally higher—either because they talk constantly about nonsense or they talk very little about anything meaningful.

In order to have the opportunity to affect a hearer, the speaker must be given materials that require participation (see Lucas, 1977; Lucas, 1980). By participation, the opportunity to affect others allows the child to develop the underlying semantic constituents of a speech act.

## Semantic Relationships and Speech Acts

Some children are unable to use the pattern type of therapy because they have restricted semantic development but they are not so restricted that they do not need some assistance in organizing their language skills into some formulation. These children are capable of working with manipulative materials that are also structured around certain types of acts. For example, the activity might be playdough and the clinician might provide the opportunity for the child to perform speech acts to get the playdough, to get more playdough, to get other toys, etc. The clinician also provides the child with the opportunity to increase semantic knowledge about the activity through various types of models. This third type of therapy will usually work for any child in the second phase of semantic development because it provides a natural setting for altering the child's use of language tools for communication.

## PROGRESS

The synergistic component of the second phase is contingent on the following development: (1) The child must have a high enough frequency of effective speech acts for a need to modulate and expand in order to refine the semantic system; (2)

The child must have sufficient expansion and modulation for extension into lexicalization to occur; and (3) The child must have sufficient opportunity for the performance of speech acts in all settings.

The synergistic principles must be kept in mind if progress is to be recognized. There is a significant difference between a child who has just entered the second phase and a child who is leaving the second phase in terms of language functioning.

The child entering the language phase has basic semantic feature organization for semantic relationships that quickly become refined through expansion and modulation. They are represented in a variety of speech acts by the time the child is three years of age (see Chapter 5). These speech acts are also performed very frequently—probably on an average of more than one per minute if the opportunity is provided.

The child who is leaving the language phase has acquired basic concepts that can be manipulated in the use of a speech act to demonstrate learning about very complex semantic notions such as time, space, quality, and quantity. This child demonstrates enough language tools to be able to function on most tasks that do not require advanced reading and writing—that is, to be self-sufficient, whereas the child entering the second phase will need a structured and protected environment since language will not be a tool.

The real tool for being able to function as a citizen is developed in the second phase. The ability to refine this tool for academic learning occurs in Phase Three. As previously noted, there are many people that never develop language tools beyond the second phase who function in society quite well. If the clinician can get a child through most of the second phase of development so that the child has access to productive and flexible communication, the clinician will have accomplished a goal that is appropriate.

---

**REFERENCES**

Ingram, D. *Procedures for the phonological analysis of children's language*. Baltimore: University Park Press, 1981.

Ling, D. *Speech and the hearing impaired child: Theory and practice*. Washington, D.C.: Alexander Graham Bell Assoc., 1976.

Lucas, E.V. The feasibility of speech acts as a language approach for emotionally disturbed children. (Doctoral dissertation, University of Georgia, 1977). *Dissertation Abstracts International*, 1978, *38*, 3479B-3967B. (University Microfilms No. 77-30, 488)

Lucas, E.V. *Semantic and pragmatic language disorders: Assessment and intervention*. Rockville, Md.: Aspen Systems, 1980.

Muma, J. Language intervention: Ten techniques. *Language, Speech and Hearing Services in the Schools*, 1971, *5*, 7-17.

Russell, S., & Arwood, E. *An explanation of a language disordered child's functioning*. Unpublished research project, Texas Tech University, 1982.

## Chapter 11

# Intervention for the Linguistic System

*Relativity—The presence,*
*Productivity—The existence,*
*Little is asked that does not act.*

## Chapter Objectives

1. Explain the linguistic principles involved in semantic development.
2. Explain how semantic principles relate to the planning of goals and objectives.
3. Explain how the goals and objectives are determined from the language assessment.
4. Explain the emphasis of intervention for the child who has difficulty acquiring a linguistic system.
5. Explain the relationship between language intervention and intervention for a child who is acquiring a linguistic system.
6. Describe the techniques used to facilitate linguistic development.
7. Explain how to determine progress for this type of intervention.
8. Write goals and objectives for a child who is trying to master the linguistic system.

## INTRODUCTION

The prelanguage phase of semantic development emphasizes the child's ability to communicate, the language phase of development emphasizes the use of language tools, and the linguistic phase of semantic development emphasizes the linguistic principles for advanced academic learning. These linguistic principles include semanticity, redundancy, maximum displacement for productivity, and flexibility. Three case studies will be presented with the goals and objectives for planning intervention. Each case presents a child who has made enough semantic progression to be between the language phase and the linguistic phase. None of these children would be considered to have a system functioning adequately for advanced learning.

## CASE STUDY ONE

This seven-year-old female is talking with a clinician about what she likes to do during the summer. The following utterances were recorded along with the clinician's utterances. The clinician says, "Tell us what you do when you go swimming."

1. I eat before I go swimming the first time in the morning.
2. But in the afternoon I don't eat.
3. I can't eat before I go in the afternoon, but in the morning I can.
4. Before I go swimming—
5. I have to wait for my mama to get finished one hour.
6. I have to eat in hour.
7. It ain't dangerous.
8. There is a bump here on my gums. (Is that from swimming?)
9. I don't know.
10. Up here, it's up here.
11. It hurt my tooth (Does the bump hurt?)
12. Only when I touch it. (Let's go back to talking about swimming.)
13. Before you chew gum in your mouth.
14. Like if you swallow some water it might get stuck in your lungs. (You can't chew gum when you swim?)
15. The gum
16. You can chew gum.
17. You can after an hour. (Tell me the whole story again)
18. Eat breakfast then go to you swimming lessons and then in the afternoons wait one hour before I can chew gum (Do you wait an hour before you swim?)
19. OOOOH! That's right.

20. My mom said we had to wait one hour before we went swimming.
21. I get dressed in my swimming suit and eat.
22. And then I wait for my mama.
23. One hour . . . etc.

The previous segment of language was believed to be representative of this child's ability to use linguistic principles. As previously noted, the child who is between five and seven years old can typically give very accurate and detailed stories consisting of a series of propositions and predications. However, this child is having difficulty putting ideas together in a relationship to describe the event of going swimming. This child is not able to series a number of propositions and predications.

A close analysis of the various utterances in relationship to the context indicated that she had the following semantic language disorders: semantic word errors related to the semantic feature acquisition for space and time as evidenced by the inability to sequence an event according to temporal relationships; an inability to coordinate relationships as evidenced by a lack of terms related to connecting ideas; an inability to follow a specific line of conversation by relating to the predication as evidenced by the inability to determine the accurate relationship of such ideas as not going swimming after eating as opposed to not chewing gum while swimming.

These disorders resulted from the child's inability to acquire the necessary semantic information about certain semantic concepts so that the maximum amount of semanticity or lexicalization could facilitate the ability to use ideas related to the maximum amount of displacement (time). In other words, the child had progressed sufficiently past the second phase of language development in order to possess sufficient amounts of semantic information for refinement, but she was not able to progress far enough into the linguistic phase to represent the advanced semantic concepts with appropriate sign markers.

This child is different from the children in the case studies presented about language disorders in that she has mastered a variety of structures through modulation and expansion of basic semantic relations; however, this child did not acquire enough information during these processes to evolve a linguistic system. Why didn't this child acquire sufficient information to build an appropriate type of linguistic system?

Chapter 6 discussed the principles of a linguistic system and the corresponding assessment for children with problems in this phase of semantic development. The primary consideration is one of feature acquisition. Why would this child acquire sufficient features to function in the first two phases and not enough to function in the third phase?

A closer analysis of the language segment indicates that the language this seven-year-old child used was adequate except for those areas of semantic development that require a considerable amount of organization of auditory information. These areas require a manipulation of concepts in order to organize the features into more advanced signs. Like most of the children in Phase Three, this child had problems in advanced semantic concept development because of an inability to organize large groups of features into concepts.

The notion that auditory features were the problem rather than visual features is based on an assumption about the way information is coded from environmental stimuli. As previously described, space and time markers as well as other perfect symbols, signs that are manipulated to create new signs (for example, the word "justice"), are received by auditory not visual or tactile sensory input. The child who has difficulty with organizing such features shows the kinds of problems that were observed in the explanation of swimming lessons. The goals for such a child would emphasize remediation of those specific semantic disorders through the development of semantic features related to advanced semantic concepts.

It is important to recognize that the problems of the child who does not progress into a full linguistic system require specific remediation as opposed to facilitation. For the seven-year-old child, the goal might be written: "To remediate specific semantic disorders related to an inability to organize advanced semantic features into space, time, quality, and quantity concepts." The objectives would provide specific information about the types of performance that would be expected as well as the type of criteria. For example, an objective might be written: "The child will produce two propositions about a picture that are linked with appropriate temporal markers including 'and,' 'because,' 'on,' 'during,' ' while,' 'when,' etc." The numerous temporal markers are listed because they are all relational and will be acquired only as the child uses a variety of them to mark the various relationships.

When the therapy includes a variety of ways to mark a variety of relationships in time and space, it has a better chance of being synergistic in nature. If the system is synergistic, the child is able to produce a variety of speech act types in order to learn more information. The number of opportunities for these types of performances as well as the amount of time could also be put into the objective. For example, "Given 10 opportunities to perform a speech act with all conditions met about a series of sequence pictures, the child will produce at least three assertions connected in time by three different markers."

One objective would not be sufficient. It would be necessary for the child to work on sequencing ideas, anticipating the next logical step for increasing problem solving that involves displacement, using more semantically advanced or complex notions in novel utterances, learning to identify the important features of an event rather than the detailed or insignificant features, learning to find different reference points so as to determine other ways to displace a referent for increased concept development, and so forth.

Most of the children entering into the linguistic phase of development require a good deal of structure within the context in order to develop the internal mechanism related to displacement. When given the opportunity to tell a story or to participate in a conversation, these children often become involved in minute detail at the expense of the primary referent. Unless the topic and context can be structured so that the child does not have open-ended conversation, the child will continue to have problems identifying and staying with the referent. Attending to inappropriate detail is a symptom of the main problem—not being able to relate perceptual features to lexical tags so that the manipulation of concepts for the creation of new tags might take place. An example of this will be observed in the next case. The child in the last case did get off the topic and began talking about a bump on the gums. The bump did not look significant and it certainly didn't contribute anything to the conversation topic of swimming.

Since the product of the linguistic phase is a synergistic system for advanced learning, intervention should emphasize the organization of language tools into the use of concepts to learn other skills. For example, asking a child to indicate the next logical step in a series of sequence cards provides the child with an opportunity to problem solve through an event.

By going through an event the child acquires the internal association of time that is marked and then followed with speech acts by the child. The child's production of the time-marked speech acts is a temporal act that is coded for permanent storage. When the child is asked to tell a different story about the sequenced cards, the child is required to adjust his or her reference point and to assume a different perspective. This ability to utilize different perspectives or different reference points is a prerequisite to being able to manipulate concepts for advanced semantic displacement. Keeping the child on the topic by verbally redirecting the child back to the main proposition with a comment such as "We were talking about swimming" provides the child with additional organization. The child who also can't sequence any series of ideas but does expanded labeling (for example, "The dog is big," "The cow is here," and "I like horses") also needs verbal models in addition to the structure of the task and verbal redirecting.

All activities for this child should emphasize visual learning as a means to get around the auditory deficit in the organization of features for development of advanced semantic concepts. The child will eventually have to utilize auditory information in order to experience the maximum amount of semanticity and displacement. Therefore, intervention activities must attempt to connect visual learning with the auditory area. This is usually accomplished by asking the child to verbalize all directions, sequences, answers to questions, etc. In verbalization the child is performing a speech act that is simultaneously changing his or her ability to learn in future situations. Again, this processing by the child is the synergistic aspect of the system.

It is important to recognize that there is a difference in prognosis, therapy type, and expected outcome for the three phases of semantic development. During the first phase, the prelanguage person could demonstrate prelanguage behaviors and be chronologically any place from birth to adult. The rate at which this prelanguage person was able to perform a task would determine the rate at which change would be made. A preschool child who is prelanguage and learns rapidly would only need the opportunity, the right facilitation techniques, and someone to monitor progress. However, an adolescent who is still prelanguage and has had many opportunities will learn very slowly. The prelanguage child who can learn rapidly might be able to demonstrate the various processes under certain facilitation and therefore begin to show linear or at least some type of synergistic learning of other skills. The same is true for the language child.

If the child is a rapid learner and if the time that certain processes can be engaged has not passed, the child will demonstrate an ability to engage these processes by direct organization. The child will demonstrate the quick learning characteristic of a synergistic system—one piece of learning leading to another piece of learning and so forth. If the child has passed the time when most of the processes should have been engaged (usually by seven to eight years of age), the therapy is trying not so much to get the processes engaged but to intervene to try to get the child to compensate for problems.

The difference between being able to get the child into an active, accelerated path of learning and having to work on compensatory skills is quite dramatic. For example, a child might be diagnosed at eleven years of age. This child will make different progress through skills from the seven-year-old who was talking about swimming. The eleven-year-old will be learning to compensate for his or her lack of ability to organize features, whereas the seven-year-old will be allowing learning to facilitate other learning so that the child's system actually compensates. It is quite alarming to a beginning clinician who puts two children with language to linguistic problems in the same group at the same level at the beginning of the year only to find that the two children change differently over the course of the year. The younger child gets the processes started and as some clinicians have said, ''It is like a light!'' They begin to learn on their own. The other child struggles with each step, learning with each step, but the quality of progress is remarkably different for the two children.

Whether the child is taught to use specific semantic skills in certain situations or whether the child begins to process information in a synergistic fashion, the therapy for a child such as was described in Case One should emphasize temporal and spatial organization. There are some specific techniques and activities presented in Lucas (1980).

## CASE STUDY TWO

This eleven-year-old male, Adam, is describing how to play basketball. Adam exhibits as much difficulty in acquiring the linguistic principles as the child in the first case study. The primary difference between Case One and Case Two is that

Adam is older and the problems are persisting. Academics have become almost an impossibility. The following segment of representative utterances seem even more semantically disordered considering his chronological age.

The clinician said, "Start from the very beginning and tell me how to play basketball." He had already tried one time without much referential clarity.

1. There's girls and boys basketball in Old Town [name of town]
2. And that's where, that's where my school is.
3. First off there's like the Cougars and oh, let me see.
4. I don't know very many teams.
5. Our group is called the Cougars.
6. There's two teams, one the Cougars are playing against and the other team is trying to win.
7. An, whoever gets the most points wins.
8. There's a basketball, you dribble it like this [demonstration].
9. Throw it through the hoop and you get a point.
10. And there's a great big ol' point thing. Clinician asked, "Do you take turns?"
11. No you get fouls when somebody knocks you over. Clinician asked, "Does someone just hand you the ball?"
12. No, they throw you the ball.
13. Well, there's two teams.
14. The Cougars throws somebody on their team the ball, and they, whose close to them, they shoot and if they miss, miss they get the ball and that's a rebound.
15. And then they throw it back up. Clinician asked, "What happens on a rebound?"
16. Well, you catch it and it didn't make it, so you throw it back up.
17. But if the other team catches it, they have to go down to the other side of the courtfield.

After these utterances, the child tried again. The third time through the child told the clinician that basketball ("It") was "sorta like wrestling, but there's a ball and there's a o.k." He tried to draw the game and to demonstrate the game. The child finally listed just about every possible thing related to basketball but none of these "things" or ideas were related or connected by spatiotemporal, quantifying, or qualifying terms.

He was asked to describe what he likes to play at recess and the listing continued with very little connecting of ideas. For example, "We skip rocks and play [redundant], we also throw rocks at each other, splash um in the water and platter all the water on each other." This last utterance demonstrated the child's ability to provide detail but not necessarily according to the appropriate relationships. In this last example, it is unclear what or who the recipient of the action might be since "platter" [splatter] and "splash" have slightly different meanings. Furthermore, the child was asked about what he does at recess but he does not give a specific answer. Instead, the child mixed the detailed and general ideas together illustrating his problem with understanding semantic feature organization for semanticity.

If the child were able to organize ideas into a concept, his language would be efficient and semantically would be at its maximum. In other words, the child's ability to semantically organize information would result in a need to refine the lexical tags already used. This need to refine would result in an escalated semantic development. When the semantic development becomes so involved in the refinement process that the child begins to use concepts, there exists a great need for space, time, quantity, and quality terms. This need produces the development of these higher semantic skills.

Adam was unable to acquire enough features, probably the auditory ones related to displacement, to develop the semantic concepts related to space, time, quantity, and quality. This can be observed in his use of lexical tags such as "courtfield." The use of the word "court" was explored to see if the coach used this word or if the family used this word. The child had created a semantic neologism to express his semantic interpretation of the place of play. Adam also used other types of neologisms and auditory misperceptions throughout the evaluation. If the child had had sufficient use of semantic features, he would have appropriate use of commonly used words.

The inability to use these words appropriately also affects the ability to identify referents or to use specific referents. It would probably be more accurate to say that the lack of ability to organize semantic features for concept development affects the ability to identify the referents (feature grouping and identification) and to use specific referents. The ability to use specific referents in a story or conversation requires that the speaker be able to relate the ideas or referents together. The relational terms involve space and time as well as quality and quantity. These terms are relative to some referent. If the child has difficulty in acquiring the auditory marking of this relativity, these terms do not develop. The child is not able to verbally describe the relationship between two referents, two ideas, two predications, and so forth.

Even though Adam did a good deal of talking, part of this talking time resulted from his inability to relate ideas and thus to understand when he had said enough. His own use of referents was lacking in semantic depth—he didn't know what they included in meaning so he kept talking. Whenever a child has to keep talking or trying to revise previously uttered ideas, the child is trying to reauditorize the words he has spoken in order to gain information from their use. This circular type of talking lacks the flexibility and productivity of a true linguistic system—one that provides synergistic development or learning just by the performance of a speech act. With Adam, and most children in this struggle to acquire higher semantic concepts, the inability to meet the semantic constituents results in utterance acts that are not connected into a series of speech acts called a speech event. The product for these individuals is a language system that is not the most effective for communication.

For intervention, the goal would stress the ability to organize ideas into a series of speech acts for a speech event. The goal for Adam might be written as follows: "Given a series of sequence picture cards about an activity such as basketball, this child will produce an appropriate series of proposition-predication relationships through the use of spatiotemporal markers including: 'first,' 'second,' 'then,' 'if,' 'when,' 'because,' 'so,' 'during,' 'between,' 'meanwhile,' 'while,' etc.

Case Two is similar to Case One in that there is a need to keep the child verbally redirected to the topic, reverbalizing all components of the utterance act, and producing a variety of different speech acts. Both children would benefit from being directed through classroom assignments since all class activities require the following of directions—a linguistic, not a language task.

Children with semantic problems resulting from auditory deficits in organizing semantic features do quite well with the simple directions of the kindergarten and sometimes first grade teacher. However, when these children reach the second grade, they have great difficulty following auditory instructions that require the manipulation of symbols for compliance. Case Study Three describes an eight-year-old male who is repeating first grade. This child couldn't even handle the easier instructions.

## CASE STUDY THREE

Case Study Three was repeating the first grade and failing for the second time when he was brought to a clinic for a speech and language evaluation. Like the other children described in this section, Case Study Three was believed to have a learning or motivation problem but not a language problem. These children were referred to the speech and language clinic because the parents had no other options.

The following segment of language is believed to be representative and was taken from the language sample obtained through conversation and by looking at pictures. This particular segment is selected from the conversation only.

The clinician said, "Tell me about a day in school. What do you do from morning until you get home from school?"

1. Half of my class stays in *are* other class and some people go in the other room. (The clinician asked, "What do you do first?")
2. Reading—no.
3. Math, when I think—I forgot. (The clinician asked, "Why do you go to the other rooms?")

4. Reading.
5. We got a book that we spell in.
6. I forgot what's next.
7. We go outside and we *do* recess.
8. I have science at school.
9. We go outside and then we *do* a science book.
10. Then we have lunch and then pass papers.
11. If the bell rings that means we have to get out.
12. Go outside—
13. Then we—school's over we go outside and play.
14. I play soccer all the time. (Clinician said, "Is that all?")
15. We run.
16. I'm teaching a friend to run. (Clinician said, "I wonder how you teach someone to run?")
17. We're going to run.
18. Go fast, pick up your feet and run.
19. I bike ride a dirt bike. (Clinician said, "Is that how you got that?" and pointed to a scrape.)
20. I fell on the bumps-on-they make.
21. These bumps I jumped on one and fell.
22. You know on the side and fell back ("You hit the bumps?")
23. I jumped. ("You did?")
24. No I was on—no I went on—
25. On a dirt bike. ("How did you scrape your nose?")
26. On the dirt.
27. My helmet did it. ("How?")
28. It moved right here (He demonstrated)
29. They gave me a point. (The clinician said, "What kind of bike is it?")
30. A dirt bike.
31. It got spray painted blue, white and yellow, no, pink.
32. It's number 16.

The most apparent problem that this child demonstrated was the inability to tell about his day at school even though it has been the same sequence with the same teacher in a very structured private school for almost two years. Why couldn't the child sequence these relationships?

Either the child does not have the ability to process the incoming information or he is unable to organize the information. This inability affects the sign development of symbols for demonstrating a knowledge of the environment. If the child does not have the ability to process incoming stimuli, he would show a slow rate of learning in all areas outside of academics as well as in academic subjects. Since this child does very well at all kinds of sports and physical tasks, he is able to learn from the environment. The incoming stimuli are being received and processed. However, if this child is given a verbal instruction such as "Stand over there!" he stands in that spot and doesn't move even though all the other children are running all over the field. Therefore, the problem must be in the ability to take different reference points. The result is a child who understands only literal interpretations of tangible referents. The child is unable to change organization of the semantic features for concept manipulation. If no one says anything to this child, he does very well in any nonverbal task. His sister, who is two years older, is in an accelerated program. This child can compete with her in anything that is based on motor performance but not academics. The report of the psychologist also indicated a significant difference between the boy's performance on a verbal intelligence subtest and a nonverbal intelligence subtest.

If this child has not been able to alter points of reference, why is he so good at nonverbal games? Even more perplexing is the question, "Why does he have so much language if the verbal system is so impaired?" This child's breakdown is between Phase Two and Phase Three; he was able to acquire the basic structural components of Phase Two for language development but was not able to engage those processes that require maximum displacement and semanticity. Therefore, he stopped making progress at that point—end of Phase Two.

It should be noted that a child may be able to expand basic ideas through the use of markers or conventional structures that are used in the environment without a thorough understanding of the underlying meaning. Therefore, a child could be taught to put words together but unless the meaning is well established, the ordering of the words as well as the relationship between words will not be well represented. This child did exhibit some of these problems. For example, he said, "I fell on the bumps-on-they make." This utterance has some meaning for the child but to the adult hearer the utterance could mean a variety of different relationships. Maybe the "bumps-on-they make" is a semantic neologism referring to the bumps. Maybe the bumps were made from the dirt bike or maybe the bumps make bumps when the child falls, which is a complete reversal of the action recipient from the first interpretation. Clearly, the child did not have the underlying relationships well established. He could not describe the relationship between his scrape and the bumps in the track in terms of who was being scraped and what was being bumped or was part of a bump, etc. Therefore, the child could be lacking in the ability to take on different perspectives and thus not be able to develop relationships even though he could begin to acquire language skills. This child is an excellent example of how unimportant language skills are compared to the acquisition of semantic development represented by sign development. The child needs the semantics in order to be able to acquire the perfect symbol development.

This child's problem could be approached from the discussion in Chapter 7 about the four levels of semantic development: (1) sensory reception, (2) feature perception, (3) feature organization, (4) concept manipulation. The child has been receiving sensory (auditory) information or there would be little development of verbal skills, and what speech the child would have acquired would be deficient in phonological development. The child also has been able to organize some of the sensory input into features or he would not have the intelligible speech that demonstrates expanded utterances with modulation.

This modulation and expansion also suggests that he has been able to organize some of the features for language skill development. However, at this latter place of semantic development, the sample shows some problems. For example, he said, "It got spray painted . . ." instead of using the verb "It is . . ." or "It was . . ." In fact there are several errors in the use of specific words. He uses the word but the way that he uses the word suggests he is missing some of the displaced types of information. For example, several of his utterances do not clearly demonstrate the recipient of the action as opposed to the agent of the action. He said, "We *do* recess." Recess as a noun can't be done by a person. The meaning of the verb "do" as opposed to "have" is not well defined for this child. The recipient of "do" is an object, whereas the "have" would indicate a possession of an event. The child could be "absorbed" by the recess but the child can't act upon a recess since it is not an object of an action. The word "recess" is confusing for this child since it is not a tangible object or action. Furthermore, the word "recess" could be used as an action or an event, which could also affect the child's ability to make fine distinctions in meaning. The problem with the verbs is also a result of the inability to take different perspectives or to displace oneself for the acquisition of nontangible concepts.

One of the easiest ways to identify a problem with the ability to change perspectives and thus to refine the meaning of nontangible notions is by examining the sample for redundancy. The children in the other two case studies in this chapter as well as this child exhibit some redundancy in semantics. For example, this child said, "We got a book that we spell in." This utterance could be refined to "spelling book" thus eliminating the extra words—the redundancy. This child also said at one point during the evaluation, "If the bell rings that means we have to get out," which could be semantically refined to "When the bell rings, it's time for recess." Notice that the refinement process eliminates the redundancy and allows for increased specificity of the referent.

These types of children experience much difficulty in making themselves understood because the refinement process has not narrowed the meaning of specific referents. For example, in the previous illustrations the intent was assumed by the hearer. The clinician assumed the child to mean "spelling book." However, there is always a chance that it was not a typical "spelling book." The child was not capable of refining the meaning so that a specific referent could be used or qualified.

Redundancy of meaning also occurs when the child cannot connect ideas with the appropriate predications or transitions. These transitions usually occur by saying something about the topic through use of qualifiers, quantifiers, and/or spatiotemporal terms that relate by predicating the proposition. If predications do not exist because the child is unable to acquire the auditory features that represent the notions of displacement and semanticity, the child will not be able to refine the referential meaning. For example, the child said, "We go outside and then we do a science book. Then we have lunch and then pass papers. If the bell rings that means we have to get out." It may be assumed that the child had just given most of the school sequence to the clinician. However, this assumption is false. The child gave only those acts that were of importance to the child. The notion that passing papers had any relationship to previous work or new work is not recognized or expressed by this child. He did not use a predication or transition about what is done outside to get the hearer from going outside to doing some work inside. The ordering of ideas through relationships is not well developed because the child is not able to organize the features for the acquisition of concepts. Therefore, the fourth level of semantic development, concept manipulation, is never really attained.

When concept manipulation does not occur, the child's language lacks the advanced concepts of displacement and semanticity. This third child was not able to use any of the advanced space, time, quality, and quantity terms even though he was eight years old. In fact, during the discussion, the child spent a great deal of time on the spray painting of his bike and he never did figure out what color it was.

Now that the place of breakdown, between Phase Two and Phase Three, is determined, and the problem is assessed—that the child cannot organize the features because he cannot take a different perspective, nor can he recognize nontangible differences in meaning—the intervention may be planned. The goal for this child is much the same as the type of goal for the other two children in this chapter. The goal might be written as follows: "The child's specific semantic disorders will be remediated by increasing semantic development." Semantic development may be increased through the use of objectives that might be written as follows. "Given 20 pictures, James will produce two propositions about each picture, connect the propositions by appropriate markers, and then add a third proposition." For example, "The girl is big" and "The girl is my sister" might be combined to form "The big girl is my sister." Although the meaning is slightly changed, the combination allows the child a way to learn how to connect relationships.

Activities that demonstrate changes in perspective and thus illustrate relationships would be good. These types of activities include following directions for making an object; sequencing routines using appropriate connecting or transitional markers of space, time, quality, and quantity; working through the solution of a problem; telling more than one story for a picture or a set of pictures; and the like. The clinician constantly monitors what the child says by putting in the appropriate markers for suitable predications that the child can practice by saying to another child in the group, writing a story, or retelling the story. When the child gives the corrected relationships back to the clinician, the child's performance becomes part of his or her system. Correct performances mean appropriate speech acts—ways to effectively affect the attitudes, beliefs, and behaviors of the hearer.

## SUMMARY

The children in the linguistic developmental phase necessitate the maximum amount of organization by adults in order for them to use their language skills to organize their own actions. Given this organization through directed performances of speech events, they learn to compensate for problems in their language system. Because most of these children are beyond the seven- or eight-year age limit for synergistic qualities to be facilitated, the child will demonstrate ways to compensate for further learning rather than a system that learns by learning.

---

**REFERENCE**

Lucas, E.V. *Semantic and pragmatic language disorders: Assessment and remediation.* Rockville, Md.: Aspen Systems, 1980.

## Chapter 12

# The Classroom: A Dynamic Context

*To teach is to learn*
*What the teacher has to give.*
*To learn is to teach*
*What one has to receive.*

## Chapter Objectives

1. Provide a description of language development as it relates to classroom activities.
2. Explain the advantages of a group setting for language development.
3. Explain the basic techniques used in the classroom for facilitating language.
4. Explain the basic principles that the teacher can use when developing class assignments.
5. Explain the differences among the various levels of language development.
6. Give several examples of various language activities for the classroom setting.
7. Explain the relationship between language and academic subjects.
8. Explain the relationship between the child's language usage at home and the child's usage in the classroom.

## INTRODUCTION

The purpose of this chapter is to describe some of the principles that can be utilized by the classroom teacher as well as by the language clinician while working with language-disordered children in a group setting.

## CLASSROOM LANGUAGE

The principles involved in facilitating or remediating problems in the classroom are based on the theoretical assumptions provided in the earlier chapters of this book. These principles include the following:

- Make language activities dynamic in nature.
- Make language serve a purpose for the child.
- Make the language activity operate at the child's semantic level of development.
- Develop materials that are semantically appropriate, that is, cognitively appropriate.
- Make the purpose of language activities assist the child in learning to communicate better.
- Make the language activity relate to the child's semantic needs, not the adult's needs.

Each of these principles will be discussed in the following sections of this chapter.

### Dynamic Language Activities

Since language appears to be a dynamic series of processes that function interactively, the language activities in a classroom should also be a series of dynamic processes. Which processes can be facilitated and how? The answer rests with the age of the children involved. If the children are in an infant stimulation group, those processes that are described in the prelanguage section of this book are facilitated. However, if the child is acquiring language tools, the activities should reflect language development and those processes should be facilitated. And, of course, if the child is in a school-related resource or regular classroom, the child's activities should reflect the linguistic processes.

The preceding information is true if the child is having difficulty with a breakdown that is close to his or her regular acquisition time. If the child is much older than would be expected for certain processes to occur, the processes cannot be facilitated. In other words, facilitation can only occur if the child is still around an age in which such processes would be occurring. Outside the typical range of expectation, the child will acquire certain skills by being taught through an intervention approach but the processes cannot be facilitated.

In the previous chapters about intervention, goals and objectives were discussed for each type of child in the three phases of semantic development. Sometimes it is difficult for the classroom teacher or classroom clinician to understand how to apply these goals and objectives to classroom activities where the preacademics and academics take precedence. The relationship between those academic types of tasks and the child's dynamic language system is pertinent to understanding classroom activities.

The system that has been proposed is one that is semantic or meaningfully based. In other words, every activity that requires language skills is based on semantics. Therefore, the activity must relate to the principles or processes that make the system dynamic in nature. The task provided the child in the classroom setting should take into consideration how the underlying principles will facilitate communication functioning for the child. If a task is not pragmatic in nature, that is, if it does not meet the semantic principles of a pragmaticism methodology, it will not determine what a child can perform on a given task and will not help the child function. For example, if a teacher holds up "vocabulary" cards for the children to name, the children will demonstrate "how to name." Since naming does not have the dynamic properties of a true speech act, the child has not demonstrated anything better than the specific task. The child will not improve in communication. However, if the children are divided into two groups that require exploration and solving of two problems, the dynamics of language will be exercised.

For the task to be dynamic in nature, the activity must be one that allows the child to affect the hearer in some intended manner. This type of activity allows for the maximum interaction between a speaker and hearer within a context. The dynamic aspect of the system is exhibited when all of the speech act principles discussed in earlier chapters have been met in that interaction. The child attempts to solve or manipulate a situation that requires communication to be used to its maximum effectiveness.

## Activities That Serve a Purpose

Activities should be designed so that the child's language use serves some sort of purpose. For example, if the child is allowed to make up his or her own topic every time the teacher is discussing something else, the child's language does not meet the intended purpose of communication. Usually when a child comments or affects the teacher in an inappropriate way, the child is really saying something about needing attention or not being able to follow the referent of the immediate topic. For example, the teacher is talking about cows and the child says, "I watched Mr. Jones on T.V.'' The teacher tells the child that they are talking about cows.

The child's inappropriate comment received attention, which was the child's purpose perhaps, but the child's utterance act did not improve the quality of the communicative act. Because the child did not meet the sincerity condition of seeing Mr. Jones (the child wanted some attention), the child's inappropriate comment will also not function as a speech act to facilitate further learning.

These types of inappropriate uses of utterances or inappropriate utterance development as in the case of off-topic discussions do not serve a purpose for the child. The activity must be organized so that the child can use language in order to learn from language use.

A child's inability to follow a teacher's activity suggests that the activity is too difficult for the child to act on appropriately. Such a child usually does not have the underlying semantic features of the conditions necessary to understand the teacher or to follow the task. When semantic features are not well organized in the task for the child who does not have them internally well organized, the child will not be able to demonstrate much purpose since he or she will not be able to stay on the topic. Basically, the child does not understand the complexity of meaning that has passed, nor does the child know or understand the nonverbal complexity of meaning so as to know when to talk or be silent.

In order for the teacher to make the activity as purposeful as possible, the child who is continuously off topic needs to be verbally redirected back to the present topic. If the child remains off topic, the teacher may want to violate the child's sincerity rule and try to answer the child's utterance act as if some speech act had been performed. For example, the child says, ''I watched Mr. Jones on T.V.'' The teacher might say, ''Susan, tell me you need some help with your paper.''

These techniques for making a task as purposeful as possible for a child who is continuously off topic can be put into the following order: When the child is off topic, the teacher verbally redirects by saying something about the topic, such as ''Johnny, we are talking about plants right now.'' If the child is also showing confusion or frustration by nonverbal facial and body posturing, the teacher may want to try to guess the intent. For example, ''Oh, Johnny, you mean you need some help on your paper. Ask me for help.'' Notice that the teacher actually directs the child through the performance of a speech act so that the child may learn from the process. For more information regarding the use of speech acts, see Lucas (1980). In addition to verbally redirecting and/or guessing the intent, the teacher may want to tell Johnny that he can talk about Mr. Jones at a specific time when it is appropriate to talk about that subject.

When the language used in any activity becomes purposeful, as in the case of being directed through a speech act, the child has better communication and a better chance of learning how to use language tools. The opportunity to use language in a purposeful manner means that the child gets a chance to experience the relationship between language skills and their representation. Success at affecting the hearer helps the child develop the necessary semantic relationships. The teacher who provides many opportunities for the child to use language is providing exercises in relationships.

There are many ways to provide opportunities for verbally solving environmental problems (Lucas, 1980). An example of an environmental problem might be walking into the classroom after lunch to find that the chairs are missing. It is important that the teacher recognize that the relationships that exist provide the experience base for language development. In other words, the child's productions within the context to affect the environment provide the basis for the language to improve. Any unnatural attempt to facilitate things for the child to say is so artificial that the child never develops the necessary sociocognitive prerequisites. Furthermore, advanced linguistic development does not fully evolve under artificial conditions. By definition of a synergistic system, the semantic conditions would not be met and the system could not expand to its fullest capability.

## Semantic Level

If the teacher's activities are to be appropriate, the child's semantic level must be considered. The child who has difficulty acquiring language skills needs to have materials that are appropriate at the child's level of cognition and learning—the semantic level. Social and chronological variables are secondary to the semantic level of development.

There are certain considerations for the teacher of language-disordered children that can be addressed without having to devote too much extra time and without having to include extra adults. The following suggestions are for the classroom teacher to use in meeting the semantic, cognitive needs of the handicapped child within the classroom setting. The suggestions are not meant to increase the child's language skills but to allow the classroom setting to be less frustrating for the teacher as well as the language-disordered child.

- *Keep Instructions Short*

Most language-disordered children cannot effectively handle instructions or directions that are more than two semantic units in length or complexity. The reason these children have such difficulty is that their language has the basic skills for communication but not the linguistic components that allow for advanced displacement. This means that the underlying semantics that allows for temporal ordering of ideas for instructions or directions are not developed beyond the basic two proposition-to-predication notion. The surface capabilities of these children have little to do with their underlying inability to connect more than two semantic units together for following directions. The child who has language problems has not acquired the same underlying semantic displacement as the typical child and does not understand the relationships involved in a sequence of directions.

For some children, even two semantic unit directions are problematic. Examples of directions that have two semantic units include the following: "Circle three of the letters"; "Put a circle around two of the objects"; "Find two of the pictures that match and circle them"; "Throw away your milk carton before you take your seat"; "Put your coat in the closet before you sit down." Each of these directions will be analyzed according to the number of predications about the proposition.

The first example, "Circle three of the letters," has two predications of the proposition. The first predication is that the child must be able to recognize the letters and the second predication is that the child is to circle those letters. This direction could be simplified by breaking it into two simpler units—simpler in semantic complexity. Put your finger on a letter (one proposition and one basic predication). Put your finger on the next letter (one proposition and one predication with a possible hidden predication of next). Circle the letter, and so forth. Even though the child had been given what appeared to be a simple two-semantic-component direction, the components had other parts. In other words, the two basic propositions also had predications increasing the complexity of the direction. This direction could be semantically simplified by reducing the predications to one per proposition.

For the second example, "Put a circle around two of the objects," the child has to recognize two of the objects (referent implied) and then be able to manipulate concepts well enough to circle each of the objects. Since language-disordered children cannot handle implied or nontangible referents, the instructions need to be simplified as in the preceding example. The simplification should include the referent in a simple proposition-to-predication relationship. For example, "Put your finger on the dog. Now put another finger on a different dog. Circle the dog. Circle the second dog." This could be made simpler if the person giving the instructions has the child circle the dog after each identification.

The third example is almost a three-proposition direction: "Find two pictures that match and then circle them." It is implied that the child must find two pictures (already the manipulation of more than one referent), the two pictures must match, and then the child must be able to circle the pictures that match. Again the directions can be broken down into simpler proposition-to-predication relationships. "Put your finger on this picture [demonstrate]. Look for a picture like this one," etc. Since language-disordered children have difficulty with the terms denoting "first" or "next," for example, visual cues such as pointing add semantic information, making the task easier for the child. Visual cues can be as simple as pointing to the picture that the child should circle or as complex as the orthographic representation of an idea.

The fourth direction, "Throw away your milk carton before taking your seat," is an instruction that a teacher might give between tasks or activities. Again, most children will have no difficulty handling this instruction because they pick up on the salient component, throwing away the milk carton. However, the child who has trouble utilizing information from the teacher's instructions may not respond to this type of command and thus be reprimanded for noncompliance. The semantic components of this instruction include the act of throwing away the milk carton followed by a complicated idiomatic expression. One child was seen trying to squeeze behind a large lounge room chair and standing there when all of the other people were sitting because the child had been told to "take a seat."

Language-handicapped children cannot deal with multiple meanings like those required with an idiomatic expression. Multiple meanings require an ability to manipulate concepts, a linguistic ability that language-handicapped children do not possess. Therefore, a language-disordered child will follow the part about the milk carton or pick up on the "seat" and sit down but will probably not perform both acts. The direction could be simplified by omitting the idiom, saying "Jimmy, throw your milk carton in the garbage can. Now, sit down in your chair." Utilizing the specific referents provides more semantic information for the child, thus making the task easier.

The fifth and last example of directions that could be simplified is "put your coat in the closet before you sit down." Again, the child will attend to the first or second part of the direction depending on what is being processed into meaningful units at the time the instruction is given. The teacher has no way of knowing what is being processed unless the teacher is willing to ask the child to verbally give back the instructions (see verbal redirection in this chapter).

- *Be Specific*

From the previous discussion, it should be apparent that the teacher can simplify the number of propositions and predications but still may have a complex idea embedded in a direction or instruction. Therefore, it is important that the teacher provide referents in these instructions as well as delete any multiple meanings, idioms, indirect requests, or polite forms. The language-disordered child cannot deal with any instruction that is not accessible in referential meaning.

An example of an indirect form might be a request that is a polite command: "Johnny, why don't you pick up your book?" Even though this request is given with a command intonation pattern, the language at the surface level provides an option for Johnny to either pick up the book or not pick up the book. Children in the preschool and early primary grades as well as language-disordered children should not be given these unrealistic options. The polite request was really intended as a command. The difference between the surface function of the utterance and the intent is a manipulation of concepts, multiple meanings, and variations in paralinguistic variables. The language-disordered child has not acquired the linguistic system that allows for these types of manipulations.

Children without language problems can usually handle indirect requests by the time they are seven or eight years of age. This age range is not surprising since the linguistic principles for a synergistic system of learning are also acquired usually by the time a child is seven or eight. These linguistic principles continue to help a child refine the semantic system until the child is capable of manipulating symbols of displacement at the adult level of knowledge.

The indirect form requires the same semantic prerequisites as the inferred or implied referent. The relationships among implied referents require a manipulation of concepts that is quite difficult for a language-disordered child to develop. The implied referent is easily handled by putting the referent into an utterance. For example, instead of saying, "Put your book up," the teacher would say, "Put your book on that shelf." The teacher might specify the shelf by pointing to it. The deletion of idioms also removes all inferred referents. Idiomatic expressions include "Take your seat," "Don't be goofy," "Sit on it," "Keep it to yourself," "Don't be so crazy," etc., where the referents are hidden among the past or previous experiences of the speaker and the interpretant. New expressions in particular often take an idiomatic form: "Gag me with a spoon," "Punch your lights out," "off the wall," "bonkers," "to the max," etc.

- *Use Reauditorization*

Since children cannot demonstrate what they are processing except through their actions in response to certain stimuli, the teacher who wants to know whether or not a child is processing certain bits of information might have the child tell the teacher what the teacher said. For example, the teacher tells the child to go get a book. For the teacher to know whether or not the child processed this command, the teacher would ask the child to restate the directive. The teacher might say to the child, "Tell me what I said." What the child says back to the teacher will be what the child processed as the directive. The child could still make an error in an attempt to comply with the request, especially if the child's language is so unorganized that he or she cannot attach the act to what is being processed. For example, the child starts to go get the book and before the child can get the book looks at the other children playing. Internal language says something about playing and the child never makes it to the book. Many language-disordered children who have poor internal control of what is processed and held in semantic memory for being acted upon have difficulty complying with directions, finishing homework, doing class assignments, or recognizing when they have done what was asked or when they have left a task incomplete.

The ability to comply with an instruction is quite different from the ability to process the instruction as it was given. When the child repeats an instruction, the teacher can at least determine whether or not the child is picking up the entire utterance or only a part of the utterance. If the child has not processed the complete instruction, the teacher will want to simplify the instruction, have the child repeat it, and possibly add some visual cues to the instruction.

For most children, the completion of academic work in the classroom is often not dependent on knowledge about the task but on the ability to understand what the task requires them to do. Many language-handicapped children are notorious for not completing assignments, for answering questions in the wrong way, for misbehaving, for knowing how to do work but never doing it without a struggle, and the like. All of these problems are better handled through simple instructions at the child's semantic level, providing specific referents, and utilizing reauditorization.

In addition to assisting the child in following instructions, reauditorization also assists the child in developing language skills by making an association between experience and actual utterances. Therefore, reauditorization actually assists the child in the connection process between what is asked and how it is done. Theoretically, the child who reauditorizes the teacher's input is coding the act as if the child had performed the speech act. This performance increases the semantic condition or knowledge for the child, thus organizing the system for the child.

- *Use Visual Cues*

Since most language-disordered children have difficulty with the auditory processing of information, visual cuing will assist them in acquiring the basic semantic relationships. It should be restated that the child has the auditory difficulties not because of a specific problem with audition but because the auditory system is the way to process semantic information that is displaced in space and time. Auditory processing allows the linguistic principles discussed in Chapter 6 to be acquired. Since the language-disordered child has difficulty acquiring linguistic properties, increasing input through the auditory mode will not help. The child needs extra semantic information through another mode. Visual representation of language tools assists the child in extending his or her semantic base.

Visual cues for increased semantic information come in all forms. A teacher's finger guiding the child's gaze to significant relationships in play and in pictures may help to develop the meaningful attributes of referents. Pointing, gestures, facial postures, pictures, color-coded cards, frame markers for reading, and orthographic symbols are all visual cuing devices.

Many teachers have expressed a concern about allowing a child to use fingers for reading or for counting. The visual cuing is not meant as a crutch but as a way to provide the child with more information about the relationship between the auditory and visual signs. Remember that signs are ways to represent the child's cognition or thinking. Without learning the relationships between signs and levels of referring, the child will not be able to demonstrate a higher level of learning. If auditory signs are not related to visual relationships, the child will never make the transition between the sign and the representation. This child will only learn how to do "sight" reading or visual types of learning.

Reauditorization when added to the visual cuing for completion of a task greatly assists the child in making the auditory sign representation. Anytime the visual cue is added to the auditory task, the integration is being done for the child. After the task is completed for the child, the child must be requested to complete the task for the teacher. For example, drawing a picture during art allows the child to express through an artistic mode those perceptual integrations. However, asking the child to show his or her picture to another child requires some form of communication. The cuing from the teacher to say something about the picture to the other child forces the drawer to use at least an auditory mode of communication in the form of an utterance. The child's utterance produced with the semantic conditions of a speech act being met changes his or her learning and integrates the information about the picture with information about the context. All classroom activities can include visual and auditory cuing to assist the language-disordered child in making the transition between the visual and auditory integration of semantic information.

- *Use Appropriate Semantic Levels of Materials*

In addition to the teacher trying to get verbal directions or instructions down to the child's semantic level of processing, the materials must be geared for the child's level of semantic development. Materials that relate to the child's experiences can be processed more easily than materials that are novel. A language-disordered child who is to write or tell about a picture that has semantic relationships never before experienced will be limited by a lack of language tools. The typical child will use language tools to learn about the task before proceeding but the language-disordered child has no such resource.

The visual materials should also provide a variety of sign levels with the maximum communication available for the child to derive semantic features. For example, a line drawing or an impressionistic sketch provides the minimum level of communication and forces the child to take on the responsibility for understanding inferred information. The more semantic information that is included in a picture, the easier it is for a language-disordered child to relate the picture to his or her own experiences.

Pictures that are void of background information and foreground reality are more difficult for the language-disordered child because semantic features are limited. For example, if the people in the picture are cut off at waist level by a desk or a car in front of them, the child has to visualize completed bodies in order to understand the relationships in the picture or be able to take on another's perspective. The language-disordered child needs to have available as many of the semantic features for added information as possible.

Felt boards and story charts often have minimal information unless some other process such as an activity is used to demonstrate relationships prior to using these materials. Movies are also devoid of these relationships unless the child has previous experiences related to the movie material to develop or to create relationships. Furthermore, movie material is not stored or ulitized by language-disordered children unless it is divided into smaller pieces that allow the child to actively respond between segments. Self-tutorial centers or computers allow children to respond after each presentation and therefore enable them to make maximum use of processing time.

- *Emphasize Social Interaction*

Since language tools are a representation of semantic level according to the child's need or purpose, classroom language activities should provide opportunities for socialization. Opportunities for social language require the child to interact in an activity by asking for materials, actions, or verbally participating with other children. The remaining section of this chapter will discuss specific types of classroom activities that incorporate the theoretical principles discussed earlier in this book.

## ACTIVITIES

Developing activities for facilitation of language within a group or classroom setting must include consideration of the aforementioned techniques as well as the theoretical rationale for the activity. Programs are developed on the premise that all children and educators learn alike. The premise behind developing specific language skills separate from commercial programs is that the educator understands the theoretical rationale and can make the activity serve the needs of the children as well as the educator. The following activities are meant as catalysts for the educator to develop other activities based on the theoretical principles presented in the first chapters of the text.

### Semantic Relationships

One way to facilitate various relationships between and among objects, actions, and events is to use pictures that depict the relationships. The teacher or clinician then facilitates productions of the relationships. For example, instead of presenting pictures for vocabulary development in which the teacher asks the child to name objects, etc., the teacher could use pictures with more detail about activities to illustrate relationships.

The teacher talks about the various activities in the picture by attaching the various relationships to the topic. For example, the teacher might say, "The dog is barking. The dog is a friend's pet. The pet's name is Rufus." These relationships are used instead of labels. The adult's structures are varied so that there is little emphasis on the construction and more emphasis on what the agents or instruments do, where they do it, how they do it, and why they do it. These attachments of the relationships with the picture allow the teacher to make the integration for the child. The child always gives the information back to the adult so that the adult can be sure the child is learning by the active processing.

**Constituents**

Relationships and their semantic features can also be built through constituent types of tasks. The constituent is the referent that is missing in a question. For example, "Who is that?" is missing the referent "who." By being able to answer questions, the child soon learns to scan for referents and to select the referent from others' speech. Being able to pick out a referent allows the child to acquire more information, thus facilitating the processes that expand and modulate language skills into a more productive semantic system.

Questions should not violate the sincerity rule any more than any other task. Therefore, a group situation is an ideal way of getting questions developed. The teacher asks a question and someone answers the question. Then the teacher has the child ask the same question of another child so that there is an interactive question-asking situation. Again, the forms should vary, with some attention being given to the complexity of the answer. For example, some questions require a very simple one-word answer such as a what or who. Questions that ask for an explanation are much more complex because of the semantic information required in the answer.

**Stories**

One of the best ways for the facilitation of a synergistic system is to get the child to produce stories. A story implies that the child can appropriately connect at least three propositions. The connecting of propositions is easiest when the child has had experiences with the topic, has had instruction through each step of the story, and has had some practice talking about the individual components of the story. For example, "The farmer plants the seeds. The seeds begin to grow." The story could be continued in as much detail as the children are capable of performing.

It is important that the children get a chance to verbalize these steps for the teacher with as many visual aids as needed. Children with language problems will have a tendency to give extended labels without any description of the connecting relationships (see Chapter 11). The teacher's purpose is to keep the children expanding on their ideas and thus expanding their ability to use language tools for further academic learning. The children should always repeat a segment of a story that they did not appropriately sequence.

## Games

Playing games requires an incredibly complicated set of tools for explaining the rules and regulations. Therefore, how to play a game can be used to develop the relationships within a speech event through the successful performance of speech acts. The child should have some experience at playing the game before the rules are expected to be verbalized since language-handicapped children tend to use more visual than auditory language skills. When the rules are presented in a sequence, the teacher should provide ample visual cues. Giving vocabulary or what parts of a field or game are called does not facilitate the language of a language-disordered child. The child learns meaning by the relationships in context. Therefore, the game is presented in context. Group games or sports such as basketball, baseball, soccer, football, or even checkers work well. These types of games require a set of rules for definition. Furthermore, the rules must be in the appropriate sequential order for the child to explain how the game is played.

## Academic Subjects

The child's academic subjects are usually excellent sources of activities for developing language, provided that the teacher keeps instructions at the child's semantic level, the academic material at the child's semantic level, and allows the child to act on the academic material in an active, verbal manner. For example, a child may have a reading assignment. The teacher can use the assignment to make sure the child understands the instructions.

If the child does not understand the instructions or if the child is having difficulty with the topic, the lesson can be broken into stories with the parts of the story printed along with pictures for visual cues. This way the child begins to make a written-to-verbalized association or integration for a better language basis. For example, a reading assignment might be about Eskimos. The child is having difficulty with the assignment so the teacher breaks the story into segments, that is, into the basic propositions and predications. Some children will also need more visual representation along with the simplified story to understand the relationships. The teacher might draw a stick figure so that the child has the visual cue plus the written word.

The reverse of this process can also help a language-disordered child. A child who does not yet read might get more information from the pictures in sequence if the printed word is provided than if only the picture is provided. It does not hurt the child who has not learned to read to begin to make visual configuration discriminations.

## Artwork

Artwork allows the child to follow directions as well as to present what he or she has produced by using specific speech acts to convey the child's message. Many types of artwork can also require some interaction as the child participates in getting materials, making objects, etc. Art is an expression of the child's semantic development and will correspond to the child's development of signs, provided the child has had ample opportunity to perform the art tasks. This is true up through most of the primary grades.

## Summary

Language facilitation in the classroom is contingent on the teacher's knowledge of how language develops. Once the teacher recognizes that the child with language difficulties is really having problems with one of the four levels of semantic acquisition, the teacher can arrange materials to meet the child's needs. Once the teacher recognizes that a child's current phase of semantic development will only be advanced by the development of sociocognitive processes such as expansion, modulation, or displacement, and not by tasks or structures, the teacher can understand the child's problem and plan appropriate lessons and interventions.

## PARENT AND PARAPROFESSIONAL PROGRAMS

One of the most important principles of the theoretical approach of pragmaticism to the assessment and intervention of language disorders is that it is based on an interactive system in which parents can play an important role in the child's language development. The literature (e.g., Snow & Ferguson, 1977) has described the importance of social interaction or stimulation on the infant's development. Pragmaticism methodology assumes that there is a social reciprocity between the child and the caregiver. This social process will be described as it pertains to intervention.

### Prelanguage Phase

The child in the prelanguage phase counts on the parent acting as an interpretant for the child's use of signs. In remediation, the parent is taught to respond to those physical, nonverbal behaviors that the child is encouraged to use. The parent's response is then a means of changing the child's behavior into an indicator. As noted in the discussion of prelanguage assessment (Chapter 8), the indicator represents the beginning of the other sociocognitive processes for facilitating semantic development. With some multiply handicapped children, nonverbal skills are not typical and the parents need to be taught how to look for consistent behaviors that they can make into an index representative of some information.

As the child gathers the information, the parent is taught to provide feedback about the child's communication attempt both nonverbally and verbally. The nonverbal information provides opportunities for the child to continue with the interaction and the verbal responses provide the child with some feedback about the communicative value of the message.

**Language Phase**

Once the child has begun to indicate about various needs in the environment or about various relationships within the environment, the parent's feedback usually increases the child's semantic development. The nonverbal behavior of responding with smiles, frowns, head changes, and the like is encouraged so that the child has a maximum number of opportunities to initiate communication. One of the primary concerns of using parents and paraprofessionals (aides) to assist with language development is that these people usually do too much for the children, especially those in the prelanguage and language phases. Therefore, the parent is taught to respond to and not necessarily to lead in the child's communicative acts. Responses are best provided by nonverbal means rather than verbal means.

The child who could indicate in the prelanguage phase now needs more help with relationships. If spontaneous imitation can be facilitated, the parent and aide are encouraged to use it in a variety of situations as a technique to get the child to produce certain types of utterances representative of certain types of needs. Most of the techniques described in the intervention chapter on language can be used by parents or paraprofessionals.

**Linguistic Phase**

Parents play naturally in the prelanguage phase while facilitating the child's meaningful behaviors. During the language phase, parents can use a variety of models to facilitate semantic development through any experience. In the linguistic phase, the parent is asked to keep the child's routine set and described on a calendar. The parent is asked not to teach the child at home but to be a parent. This is not as drastic a change as might be expected from the previous phases in which the parent played a significant role in the teaching. In Phases One and Two the parents provided semantic development by contextual interaction; however, for Phase Three, the parents have a tendency to try and teach those academic subjects that the child is having difficulty mastering because of semantic deficits. Many children resent their parents trying to be teachers.

The teacher, parent, and paraprofessional should recognize that language as described in this text is a tool that develops from the semantic system. Unless the child has the semantic prerequisites for use of the tools, the child will not develop an adequate system. Even though parents and teachers are always concerned with the child's progress, it is unrealistic to consider the progress of the tools (language structure) unless the child's communication progress is paramount. Teaching the tools is always at the expense of the child's creativity for further learning. Chapter 13 will describe some of the other ways that the semantic system functions to facilitate communication.

---

**REFERENCES**

Lucas, E.V. *Semantic and pragmatic language disorders: Assessment and remediation.* Rockville, Md.: Aspen Systems, 1980.

Snow, C.E., & Ferguson, C.A. *Talking to children.* Cambridge, England: Cambridge University Press, 1977.

Chapter 13

# Application of a Synergistic Model of Communication

*Fondle our dreams into hope and*
*Raise our consciousness into metaphoric bliss—*
*Here rests the future!*

# Chapter Objectives

1. Describe the purposes of a synergistic model as it pertains to the study of human behavior.
2. List five different areas of study for which the synergistic model may be applied.
3. Describe the significance of applying a synergistic model to other disciplines.
4. Describe the characteristics of a synergistic model.
5. Explain the extension of pragmaticism methodology to other disciplines.
6. Explain how semiotics pertains to other disciplines.
7. Explain how semantic principles affect the development of new ideas in new disciplines.
8. Explain the importance of concept manipulation for the development of new disciplines.
9. Explain the purpose of using a pragmaticism methodology to explore new developments in human behavior.

## INTRODUCTION

The method of pragmaticism introduced by Charles S. Peirce dealt with the use of signs to evoke certain consequences in a hearer. These consequences determine the type of representation to be an icon, index, or symbol sign. The more semantic development the speaker and hearer share, the more complex is the representation. The interpretant's representation of the speaker's sign usage results in certain social and cognitive consequences of behavior. These consequences could be verbal or nonverbal and thus the effects could include the attitudes and beliefs of the hearer as well as overt behaviors. The behavior of the speaker could also be represented in any number of different verbal and nonverbal ways depending on the degree to which the speaker's behavior is meaningful to the hearer. Based on this review of pragmaticism, it could be said that pragmaticism methodology deals with the consequences of human behavior as the result of preceding changes in human behavior.

Any discipline that studies human behavior must consider the interactive consequences shared by two people. Therefore, the pragmaticism methodology or philosophy could be applied to other areas outside of communication disorders. It is important to understand the total consequences of sign usage in order to recognize the significance of the pragmaticism methodology. The purpose of this chapter is threefold: (1) to introduce the reader to the power of pragmaticism philosophy as it relates to the ability to change consequences by sign usage, (2) to introduce the reader to other disciplines that are considering the methodology as part of their practices, (3) to reemphasize the importance of a synergistic system in the remediation of language disorders.

## PRAGMATICISM PHILOSOPHY

Pragmaticism refers to the use of signs to affect a hearer's attitudes, beliefs, and/or behaviors. In order to demonstrate the power of semantic consequences on a speaker's attitudes, beliefs, and/or behaviors; the reader will be asked to participate in some exercises. The rules of the exercises are the same ones that were used throughout the book: (1) The participant is an active speaker, that is, the speaker is producing the utterance act and not just visually speedreading the following exercises. (2) The speaker performs each utterance act as a speech act with the four semantic conditions of preparatory set, propositional content, sincerity, and essential elements met. The author will establish the preparatory set and will provide the propositional content but the reader will have to meet the sincerity condition. (3) The speaker will expect changes in the hearer. Since the speaker will also be the hearer (reader) for these exercises, in order for the sincerity condition to be met, the speaker will have to expect changes in himself or herself.

## Exercise One

The reader will be asked to vocally read a question as an utterance act. Then the reader will provide an answer to the question in an honest, that is, sincere, manner using an utterance act. After the question has been answered, there will be some discussion and the reader will be asked to perform another utterance under specified conditions. The question for the reader to respond to with an utterance act is "How do you feel about today?"

The reader should have given an honest answer to the question. Under most situations, the question would have elicited a neutral response. Examples of a neutral response include the following: "Fine," "It's been O.K.," "I don't know." Sometimes there are slightly negative responses such as "I've seen better days," "It wasn't a terrific day!" "Well, if it hadn't been for the 'kid' who bit me, it would have been O.K." There are also slightly positive answers, such as "Boy, it was a pretty good day!" "Well, I got paid so I guess it was better than average," "I really liked the sunshine for a change." Very seldom does a speaker have a very negative or a very positive reaction to a neutral question like "How do you feel about today?"

Assuming that the reader had a slightly positive or slightly negative or even a very negative response to the given question, the author would like the reader to perform a second utterance act. If the reader had a *great* day, the effect may not be as great as with other readers, but please go ahead and do the exercise. The reader is to perform an utterance act that will be provided for the reader to repeat using a prepared proposition. In other words, the preparatory set and propositional content will be provided; the reader is to perform the utterance with the appropriate sincerity and essential elements so that the utterance will eventually become a speech act on one of the repetitions. To make the utterance into a speech act, the speaker's (reader's) performance may have to be made with careful selection of essential elements. Let's begin with this second utterance act.

The reader is to say the following utterance (vocally): "I feel great about today!" Now, the reader is to repeat this utterance five times. If the reader has not met the sincerity condition by the time the utterance has been repeated five times, the speech act *has not* been performed and, of course, there are no noticeable changes or consequences in the hearer (reader). Therefore, the reader is to again say "I feel great about today!" but this time to utter these words as if the reader really means them. The reader is to try to make the condition real so that the sincerity rule is met by altering stress of the utterance or any of the other essential elements.

If the reader has said the utterance "I feel great about today!" with the appropriate essential elements to meet the sincerity condition of the speech act, there should be some changes or consequences in the speaker (reader and hearer). To assess those changes, the writer will ask the reader to honestly·answer the following question one more time: "How do you feel about today?" The reader's answer should be more positive than before. The extent to which it is more positive depends on how well the conditions of a true speech act were met and how much the person could change. If the person had a fairly good day, there would be less opportunity to change than a person who had had a rotten day. The following explanation is provided so that the reader may better understand the changes.

If the reader met the sincerity condition that the reader really wanted to tell the hearer (reader) that the day had been great, the speaker's (reader and hearer) cognition about the day would have to change to be believable. Even if the reader didn't want any feelings to change, they would have changed with repetitions of an utterance that met the speech act requirements. If the reader could not produce the utterance with appropriate essential elements to convince the hearer that the utterance was a specific type of speech act, then the utterance act did not have a desired effect and would have to be considered an incomplete attempt at performing a speech act.

Experiments like the previous exercise have been used with a semantic differential (Osgood, Suci, & Tannenbaum, 1957). A semantic differential is a scale on which a person provides a judgment. For example, a person is asked to rate a teacher from 0 to 7 on how well the teacher communicates. Zero might be a negative judgment and 7 might be a positive judgment. Values would be attached on the scale so that the negative judgment of 0 might represent "very poor" and 7 might represent "excellent," with halfway between the two numbers being "adequate." Once the judgment was made, the subjects would be asked to perform a previously assessed utterance judged to be neutral with either positive or negative expressions and actions. When the subjects are again rated on the differential, they once again would show a shift in judgment in the direction of the utterances. For example, a teacher might be rated by one subject as being a very poor communicator. The subject would then be asked to say "She says very nice things about all of her students. I like those nice comments." This might be repeated several times. The subject would then fill out the sheet with the many different judgment values for a number of different ratings. Since teacher one would be mixed with the other ratings, the subject would not remember the way he or she responded. The result of this type of experimentation was always in favor of the utterance that was repeated several times after the judgment was made.

The reason for the change in attitudes for the reader and for the subjects who performed convincing tasks is that the person eventually changed an utterance act into a speech act on one of the repetitions. A speech act is an *active process*; it changes the attitudes, beliefs, and/or behaviors of a hearer if all of the semantic conditions of the utterance act have been met. If the conditions are not met, it is not considered a speech act. The semantic conditions for the speech act "I feel great about today!" in which the speaker is letting the hearer know how good he or she feels about the day are described in Exhibit 13-1.

**Exhibit 13-1** Utterance Act: "I Feel Great about Today!"

| | |
|---|---|
| Preparatory Set: | The speaker has been asked how the speaker feels about today. There is a shared assumption that the question was asked with sincerity and that the hearer is able to respond to the question. |
| Propositional Content: | The speaker performs an X(Y) utterance act. X is the proposition of feeling and Y is the predication "great" about today. The proposition of the question could change with the predication. |
| Sincerity Rule: | The speaker does want to tell the hearer Y about X. |
| Essential Elements: | The speaker performs the utterance act with all of the essential elements that would be required to affect the hearer in a specified manner—in this case, of letting the hearer know about the speaker's feelings. It was assumed that the hearer did not previously know how the speaker felt so that the performance is a speech act as defined in Chapter 5 as a statement of information. |

After this discussion, if the reader does not feel any more positive about the day, there was not a complete speech act performed. Instead of a speech act, the reader performed an utterance act with semantic rule violations. If the violations were such as to change the effects on the hearer, a different speech act may have been performed. For example, if the reader said, "Gee, this is really a stupid exercise. I don't need any more irritation today!" followed by saying the utterance with very negative essential elements such as a falling contour with stress emphasis on "very," the result may have been the opposite effect. The reader may have felt more negative after the exercise rather than more positive. The speech act may have met the requirements of violation for sarcasm, a violation of the sincerity rule that changes the representation of the surface message.

Whether the change was positive or negative, the reader should have felt the power of the active process of a speech act performance. Prior to the discussion of this power as it pertains to human behavior, a second exercise will be utilized.

**Exercise Two**

This second exercise will again utilize the speech act to illustrate the power of the semantic system in the consequences of human behavior. This exercise will take the speech act and place it in the context of other speech acts for a speech event. The reader is asked to consider the various meanings of each of the parts of the speech event.

The preparatory set will be established by describing a situation. The day is a cold, wet wintry Thursday. The reader has been at work since 7:30 A.M. The children at school were tired of staying indoors because of inclement weather and were beginning to act out. At 11:30 A.M. the principal asked the reader to serve on lunch duty. During lunch a child threw a plate of spaghetti at another child but the plate hit the reader's favorite wool suit and the stain wouldn't come out by sponging. The director of special services asked the reader to attend an "emergency" meeting with some parents who were dissatisfied with the school's program. The parents stayed until 6:00 P.M. The reader's family was expecting guests for dinner and the reader's spouse was to take the roast out of the freezer and begin the thawing and the cooking process at noon for the guests who were to arrive at 7:00 P.M. The reader arrives home at 6:30 only to find this message: "Since you were tied up at school, I've gone to play tennis—see ya' around 10:00 P.M." The spouse has forgotten about the guests, roast, etc.

Now for Exercise Two, the reader is to use a number of utterance acts to express how the reader feels under these conditions. When using the utterances, the reader is asked to assume the fictional identity of the character. The reader is to assume that he or she is the person who had the children acting out, had a wool suit smeared with spaghetti sauce, an extra long and difficult parent meeting, and a spouse forget to prepare for guests and who won't be home for the guests.

Once the reader has considered how to respond to this situation, the reader should utter those messages that would express the fictional character's feelings. The utterances could be directed to one's self or to a fictional spouse.

The following is a hypothetical set of utterances performed under the aforementioned conditions: "I can't believe it! This has been an incredible day. Where's the phone? Where are the yellow pages? Where is that tennis court!?"

Each of these utterances will be described in terms of its effects on the hearer. In this case, the speaker and hearer are the same. Basic wants and desires are not as easily met but there should be two effects. One effect is material and it includes a solution to dinner or finding the spouse. The other effect is more intangible. The speaker's utterances are working the speaker through the anxiety, frustration, anger, and any other feelings associated with this event.

If the speaker is aware of the power of these speech acts, the speaker is able to self-induce the desired or intended effect. This use of a speech act to affect a speaker's intentions on an individual basis is akin to modern counseling programs. The changes in the speaker who is also the hearer may be optionally controlled.

There are two effects on the speaker. The first effect of the previously uttered speech event was to alter the situation so that there would be a solution to the basic problems. The utterances suggest that the speaker was going to find a phone book to call for some prepared food and also to call the tennis clubs in order to find the spouse. These particular utterances are fairly neutral in that they are an attempt to find a solution. However, the second effect on the speaker who is also the hearer is a change in attitude about the situation. The person is verbalizing the necessary change, with the result that the person's anxiety may be dealt with in a suitable fashion. This type of change in attitude or belief is a second effect.

The speaker or hearer in this situation could have produced different types of utterance acts that would have had different types of effects. For example, the person could have said, "This is the worst day of my life. I just don't know what I am going to do. I can't believe that anyone could be so insensitive as to forget an important thing like this. When I get hold of that insensitive tennis player, I'll strangle 'em." This second set of utterances has a very negative effect on the speaker who is the hearer. The pragmaticism methodology states that "to say is to do"; therefore, unless the sincerity rule is violated intentionally, the person who utters this type of set will probably act out negative behaviors. It is unlikely that the person will do something as drastic as "strangle" but the speaker will act on these words in either negative verbal or negative nonverbal ways. It is not the purpose of this section to determine whether such a negative act would be good or bad but to demonstrate the power of the utterances on a hearer.

If the speaker who performed the negative utterances uses this as a release so that the opposite effect is incurred, that is, if the person realizes how ridiculous it is to think that this is the worst day in his or her life or that physical harm could result, the speaker may laugh about the situation once these utterances have occurred.

A woman once recounted how she had thought of taking her life many times until one day she called a crisis line. The person on the phone never said a word while the caller enumerated everything that was not right with her life. After she had described her terrible life, she began to laugh because she realized that her utterances had placed a judgment on the situation. When a person laughs about a situation, the sincerity rule is violated and the effects of the negative utterances are very different than the surface value of the meanings might suggest. If a person is aware of the power that such negative utterances may have on other people or on the speaker's self, the speaker may opt to alter the types of utterances in various situations in order to alter the types of effects.

## COUNSELING

The notion of a speech act within a speech event to alter a speaker's self as a hearer or someone else's reaction to utterances is a critical concept in counseling therapies (Hansen, Stevik, & Warner, 1977). In one type of counseling therapy known as Gestalt therapy, the following assumptions are employed (Passons, 1975):

1. Man is a composite whole who is made up of interrelated parts. None of these parts, body emotions, thoughts, sensations, and perceptions can be understood outside the context of the whole person.

2. Man is also part of his own environment and he cannot be understood apart from it.
3. Man chooses how he responds to external and internal stimuli; he is an actor on his world, not a reactor.
4. Man has the potential to be fully aware of all his sensations, thoughts, emotions, and perceptions.
5. Man is capable of making choices because he is aware.
6. Man has the capacity to govern his own life effectively.
7. Man cannot experience the past and the future, he can only experience himself in the present.
8. Man is neither basically good nor bad. (Hansen et al., p. 145)

Within Gestalt therapy, a person can direct his or her own development. It is suggested that this direction is in part a result of language manipulation. Through verbally recognizing the structure of the situation, the client is to ''. . . recognize that the impasse exists in his mind and that he does have the ability to resolve his own impasse. In effect the counselor is telling the client, 'You can and must be responsible for yourself' '' (Hansen et al., p. 155).

Many Gestalt techniques are speech act performance directives. For example, the counselor tries to get the client to change words that carry one effect to different words, as in the change of ''can't'' to ''won't.'' The semantic aspect of these two words is very different. If the speaker says ''can't,'' he or she is saying that the situation is out of the speaker's control. If the speaker says ''won't,'' that means that the situation is within control. Therefore, the effect of a ''can't'' utterance act is different from a ''won't'' utterance act. Once the utterance meets the requirements of a speech act, the person by producing the speech act either takes responsibility or denies responsibility.

The Gestalt types of therapy take an affective approach, whereas many reality or rational therapies take a logical, verbal approach. The rational therapies also use the client's utterance acts. For example, the rational therapies take the client's excuses or illogical statements and explain the irrational components. Therefore, the client's language is changed to represent more of a rational approach to the situation. For example, the client says, ''I can't deal with this, I'm going to have a drink.'' This type of statement would not have the desired effect of solving the person's problems. From a rational approach, this utterance act would suggest that the person was running from responsibility, which would be illogical since running would not solve any problems.

There are a number of self-help books utilizing these counseling therapies. The person needing the help is able to change attitudes, beliefs, and finally behaviors by changing the way in which the situation is verbalized and thus acted upon. For example, several books by Dr. Wayne Dyer, such as *Your Erroneous Zones*, explore the consequences of a person's behavior on someone else. ''You made me do it'' has a different effect on the hearer from ''I should have put the cat outside, then I wouldn't have fallen over the chair while we were talking.''

The counseling therapies and the self-help books have one thing in common: language is the primary vehicle used to change the current situation or to improve future situations with parallel contexts. If language is the primary tool for such change, it appears significant to recognize the parallel with a pragmaticism methodology. Pragmaticism methodology encourages change by the use of signs or language, with the components being specified by modern philosophers (e.g., Searle, 1969) as speech acts within a speech event.

The significance of a pragmaticism contribution is that the criteria for change can be specified when the speech act is analyzed according to the semantic components. The semantic conditions determine the effects. If the effects need to be changed, the semantic conditions can be analyzed for components to be changed. The consequences of human behavior are in essence the consequences of the signs according to the specifications of the semantic conditions. Therefore, if the person's effect is different than intended, the analysis should explain why the effect is so different. Perhaps the essential elements are ambiguous. The person says a positive content utterance such as ''I like your dress'' while frowning. A videotape analysis of a similar situation would assist the speaker in monitoring his or her use of essential elements. The speaker may use content that is interpreted as having different meaning than intended. Therefore, the speaker should analyze the various interpretations of those words according to the semantic conditions specified by the preparatory set and the essential elements.

An inability to perceive the interpretation differences between conventional use and the speaker's individual use may lead to questions about a person's ability to function adequately in society. The inability to function appropriately might result in changes that would be considered asocial and unacceptable by the legal justice system.

## LAW ENFORCEMENT

At the beginning of this chapter two exercises were presented for the reader to get a feel for the power that the use of a speech act may have on an event or situation. There is probably no other discipline in which the power of a speech act is as great as in the legal profession in which criminals and accused innocents vie for a ''say'' in their consequences.

The power of the system is seen in the verbal development of a case and the decision regarding the consequences is a verbal interpretation of the proceedings. Even though evidence may be concrete, the means by which the evidence becomes part of a case is verbal and the power of the jury, judge, lawyers, witnesses, and police officers rests with their ability to verbally interpret as well as produce appropriate speech acts within a speech event.

The question of whether or not a person is guilty also rests with the conventions of what society defines as guilty. If a person accused of stealing a stereo is found to be guilty, that person's guilt is governed by society's determination of what is meaningfully "wrong." However, the guilty person may claim to be not guilty and in fact, according to the meaning surrounding that person's notion of guilt and nonguilt, the person may not really be guilty. For example, the person "picked up" a stereo that was sitting in an unlocked car. To that person, the stereo was just sitting there and if the owner wanted the stereo then the owner should have locked the car; otherwise, the stereo was for anyone who came into the situation. To the person found to be guilty of stealing, possession of the stereo means ownership and so that person did not believe himself to be guilty. However, by society's conventions, the person had "stolen" the stereo.

If the meaning of a situation is different from what would be expected by a larger group of society, there could be two or more interpretations of the term "guilty," for example. The person who believes himself to be "not guilty" and verbalizes such an idea through the performance of speech acts will believe that society is unjust and that there is no doubt that he is not guilty of the crime. In other words, the person believes and acts as the person performs.

Have you ever wondered how some people could lie so well? The concept of the active process of a speech act explains the person's ability to lie. It is apparent that the person who lies is really convincing himself or herself that the situation is as the act is performed. Therefore, there may come a time in which the person cannot determine what the standards of society are compared to that person's standards. In this latter case, the person who would be considered a criminal by the majority of society would be considered a hero by the faction that sees the acts according to the speech act performances of the criminal.

A person who has difficulty lying is really having trouble performing a speech act that meets the essential elements of the lie. In other words, if the words of the essential elements are different from the underlying propositional content or preparatory set, such a person might grin more than usual while performing the utterance act or might not give enough eye contact and so forth. The hearer interprets the person's utterance act as a violation of sincerity in the literal sense— the person is telling a lie.

The power of the speech act to change attitudes and beliefs of people who are considered to be acting inappropriately according to society's conventions may act in favor of society's rules or against society's rules. An incredible amount of "persuasion" can occur with the performance of a specific speech act. When the semantic conditions are set for a certain effect, the amount of people who are persuaded in that way will be comparable unless the hearer's interpretation involves a change in the effect. For example, the ability of leaders to affect the people depends on control of the semantic conditions—the preparatory set, the propositional content, the sincerity element, and the essential elements.

Adolph Hitler was one of the masters of persuasion. He required constant performances of utterance acts that sooner or later became speech acts that would move an entire nation to perform acts that the rest of the world would someday find deplorable. For example, even the salute to the country and to Hitler was an utterance that when given under the right semantic conditions would have a nationalist effect. The people would feel a closeness of identity and unity that could only be "right" under specific conditions. There were probably many individuals who worked for Hitler regime that *believed* they were doing what was truly *right* and *necessary*. There were probably others who thought about their acts by verbalizing whether or not their acts were *really* right. Such doubt would alter effects that were being produced through the speech act performance at rallies or the speech act performance of nationalist songs in the streets. The constant production kept most of the doubts at a level in which the people believed more in what they were doing than not. The constant performance of nationalist types of speech acts kept the people from using such doubts to change behavior through their own performance of opposing speech acts.

The beliefs of Hitler's people were conditioned through the performance of speech acts within speech events much like the suicide acts performed by the Jones followers in Guyana. The ability to follow others' commands or beliefs depends on whether or not the hearer is able to verbalize the act according to the hearer's own system of values. If a hearer has no set of beliefs about values, he or she is very vulnerable to being affected by someone else's speech act performances. Many of the Jones followers were individuals who had been experiencing difficulty with family or society. The chance to believe in a system of values was a powerful form of persuasion for these people. The opportunity to say and act accordingly provided for a peaceful, nondissonant existence.

The following of leaders and the willingness to perform according to the leader's wishes is greatly dependent on the hearer's interpretation of the speech acts in speech events. The more the speech act provides for the hearer, the more likely will the hearer follow. Provision for the hearer's needs, wants, and lack of mental turmoil may occur through verbal means by the utterance of acts within a specified set of semantic conditions.

Research using a semantic basis of analysis is needed on individuals who commit crimes or who may be considered as acting differently from the expectations of society. If the linguistic phase of development is necessary for the person to perform according to all possible ways of understanding displacement, then it may be possible that many children who begin having semantic problems continue into their adolescent or adult years not understanding the total picture of a situation or possibly the second or third meaning of the detail. For example, it is recognized that many criminals are considered intelligent but are often characterized as asocial or behaviorally deviant. Perhaps these individuals have specific semantic disorders.

The most apparent difference in the language of many individuals diagnosed as having "personality problems" or "psychological problems" is the lack of semantic organization. This is *not* saying that an individual with semantic problems has psychological problems or will become a criminal—but rather that the semantic system is governed by sociocognitive processes. Often the individual with a psychological problem is actually referred to the clinician for a speech and language evaluation since the lack of organization of the sociocognitive processes will result in a semantic deficit. One hears this lack of organization in the speaker's utterances and believes the person has a speech or language problem.

In terms of rehabilitation or remediation, counseling procedures that utilize the semantic organization of the speech act could in fact be used to change a person's ability to think or act. Therefore, the criminal or the socially deviant person could be helped through the performance of appropriate speech acts but they could also perpetuate their problems through the performance of inappropriate speech acts.

The freedom to say what these individuals want to say in ways that the individual wants to say it may do more damage to the speaker than it does good. With children who are off topic or who become tangential, the primary therapeutic strategy is verbal redirection. However, for adults, our society seems to believe that everyone has the freedom of speech—guidelines for the content of that speech in terms of language have not been defined.

The adult is expected to use content and to interpret content according to society's uses, but if that person has difficulty processing the information for an organized functional semantic system, the product is disorganized and may not function adequately by society's standards. Since the law of the system is governed by linguistic processes of maximum semanticity and displacement, the ability to interpret words that are nonreferential according to another's use would be very difficult for a person with semantic deficits. The ability to learn would not be affected. Therefore, a person with the disorganized semantic system would appear to be different through his or her actions or behaviors. If the differences were so great as to be considered aberrant, that person might be hospitalized or treated for an inability to deal with "life" as society expected.

It would seem appropriate that the adult who begins to show signs of being off topic or tangential needs verbal redirection much like the child. This adult is also showing problems with organization—if the person can be redirected so as to produce appropriate speech acts, then his or her acts corresponding to the speech acts would be appropriate. Whether or not socially deviant individuals are placed in the confines of a jail or a hospital for criminal or noncriminal acts, the freedom to speak may jeopardize their freedom to recovery. The structure of the speech acts must be considered more important than just the opportunity to talk. If these people are to be helped, the opportunity to perform socially acceptable speech acts must occur. Speech acts representative of socially unacceptable effects or consequences would hinder appropriate change in the person's behavior.

## ARTIFICIAL INTELLIGENCE

Much time and effort has been spent trying to determine what "intelligence" really means. Now that people in special education and regular education are beginning to feel comfortable with the way that intelligence measures are being used, there is a new field of "artificial" intelligence. This is more accurately described as "the way to make a machine function like a person"—to think, to act, to change the consequences of an act. Computers have been programmed to do most functions that people can do except program new and novel solutions to a situation, much the same way that a speech act is used by a speaker to effect a hearer.

It is fairly obvious that the computer can do everything *except* spontaneous programming. Limited programming is possible through writing a program for the computer to program. However, for the computer to have a spontaneous thought object created from previous experiences for representation through a speech event is still unlikely—though perhaps not impossible.

Winograd (1980) has looked at speech act theory as a possible solution to finding a natural language for the computer. Winograd suggests that there is already available information regarding linguistic structure, linguistic structure and the world, and cognitive processes. His recent interest is in a fourth area: human action and interaction, specifically, "An utterance is a linguistic act that has consequences for the participants, leading to other immediate actions and to commitments for future action" (p. 229). If this statement has a familiar ring, it is because Winograd's need to find a natural language for computer artificial intelligence has led him to consider speech acts as presented by Austin (1962) and Searle (1969). He stated: "The challenge was to see what it meant to look at language as a whole from the perspective of speech acts—as action rather than structure or the result of a cognitive process." He decides that:

> Some day in the future there may be a field called "cognitive science" whose boundaries are defined by a narrow and common approach and domain, just as there are fields of "anatomy," "physiology," and "pathology" dealing with the physical structures and functioning of the human body in their own domains. This narrowly defined cognitive science would deal with those aspects of language, thought, and action that are best understood in the domain of information processing. At the moment though, this is not the case. As indicated by this volume and the nascent professional society it represents, "cognitive science" is a broad rubric, intended to include anyone who is concerned with a phenomena related to mind. I believe that the kinds of issues I have been led to in looking at language are relevant to a broad segment of cognitive science as generally interpreted, and a serious consideration of them

may call into question many of the assumptions at the heart of our current understanding (p. 209).

## COMMUNICATION DISORDERS

The discipline that can benefit from all of the aforementioned research is communication disorders—a science of why, how, and when communication does not occur as it should. The communication disorders professionals involved in speech, language, and hearing sciences have been concerned with subcomponents of communication for most of the field's history. It is time now for the field to consider a "cosmopolitan" perspective—a willingness to incorporate the knowledge and methodologies from other disciplines.

It might be argued that the field would not exist if it were not for the knowledge of other disciplines; however, in the area of language, it is crucial that "firsthand" knowledge be obtained through the methodology, not the components. If a person wants to "know" about pragmatics, the pragmatist's works should be studied, critiqued, reviewed, and analyzed by the same philosophical notion. Far too much time has been spent in the past decade considering new taxonomies for studying language "use," or what is often called "pragmatics," without utilizing a pragmaticism methodology. Taxonomies or classifications are secondary to the properties of a concept. The properties or characteristics should determine the concept so that a researcher ascertains the criteria for studying an act prior to the research.

Arriving at research conclusions based on the interpretations drawn from psycholinguistic componential analyses is contradictory to Peirce's notion of pragmaticism. Pragmaticism suggests that a concept is its existing properties. Therefore, to study pragmatics might mean engaging in a philosophical consideration of its existence through the self-performance of speech acts. A clinician's ability to evaluate the effectiveness of therapy is the essence of a pragmaticism methodology. A clinician who plans to use a particular activity, such as "over-the-shoulder game" (Muma, 1970) should use the pragmaticism methodology to critique the effectiveness with a client. Since the child has to take on another person's perspective to play this game, only those children who have already developed a linguistic system would be effective players. In other words, it is a task or game designed without concern for the child's semantic functioning by an adult thinker with a linguistic system. *Any* therapeutic task or procedure may be evaluated by using a pragmaticism methodology. If the activity or therapeutic approach does not meet the semantic constraints of a speech act, the effects will be negligible.

The power of the speech act is apparently part of the truly human makeup—currently safe from the minds of the computer. If or when the computer can be programmed to perform true speech acts, the computer will have the same intelligence potential. The potential will include the ability to purposefully affect the attitudes, beliefs, and behaviors of hearers. The logic of the computer will reflect the precision of the speech act semantic criteria as interpreted by the hearer. The interesting component to this inventive notion is that the computer will never have control since the human can decide whether or not to be affected in a certain way by the computer. In other words, the interpretant can control the context and the subsequent performance of speech acts.

Based on the discussion of the field of communication disorders coupled with the notion of using speech acts for programming computers, one significant conclusion can be stated: *If the adult controls the interpretation, the adult denies the child the freedom to perform speech acts, to express his or her intentions, to be an active learner.* For example, there are many children in our schools who are provided for in every way possible. They are handed paper, pencils, crayons, and they go home as if programmed by a teacher to respond. These same children come to the language specialist to work on tools without an internal mechanism to support the tools. They leave the clinician with greater tools but no way to use them. Until the field of communication disorders is willing to work on the power of the speech act, children will be denied their right to express their full intelligence potential. Until clinicians and teachers are willing to allow their children to manipulate their environment in ways that are truly human, truly species specific, children will be denied the power of different kinds of speech acts within speech events for a linguistic system. Until the field of communication disorders is willing to deal with communication and not just speech or language, children and adults will be denied their right to have their "say" in their mode, in their "way."

## SUMMARY

There are some basic principles regarding pragmaticism methodology that should be restated:

- In any given context, the situation is totally novel.
- Any similarities or differences detected within a context are determined by interpretation.
- Interpretation of recognized features is based on the meaningfulness of the features.
- Features are semantic in nature and increase in complexity over periods of use and recognition.
- Semantics governs the way the interpreter may understand any given communicative act.
- The value of the act for communication is totally dependent on the active process of the interpretant.

- The communicative value dictates the type of effect on the interpretant so that a performance is an act that changes the hearer's attitudes, beliefs, and/or behaviors.
- The hearer may also be the speaker.
- The effects on the hearer and speaker are not expected to be the same but there should be shared semantic elements.
- Shared semantic elements are the conventions of the society for verbal and nonverbal information.
- The semantic elements include the propositional content, the preparatory set, the sincerity, and the essential components of the speech act.
- The speech act is the unit of analysis for use of signs according to the pragmaticism methodology.
- Pragmaticism methodology is a study of the sign consequences.
- The complexity of the signs may be divided into icons, index signs, and symbols.
- The three types of signs may in turn be analyzed according to the functional and perceptual properties of the organized semantic features.

Each of the aforementioned principles has been explained in the preceding chapters. The purpose of this chapter has been to tie these properties into the consequences of human behavior so that the reader may understand the power of the speech act as it relates to children who seldom, if ever, perform speech acts. From the discussion of this chapter, it should be apparent that there is a need to research and study the effects of speech acts on the consequences of society as well as handicapped children and adults.

---

**REFERENCES**

Austin, J.L. *How to do things with words*. London: Oxford University Press, 1962.

Dyer, W.W. *Your erroneous Zones*. New York: Avon Books, 1976.

Hansen, J.C., Stevic, R.R., & Warner, R.W. *Counseling: Theory and process* (2nd ed.). Boston: Allyn & Bacon, 1977.

Osgood, C.E., Suci, G.J., & Tannenbaum, P.H. *The measurement of meaning*. Urbana: University of Illinois Press, 1957.

Passons, W.R. Gestalt therapy intervention for group counseling. *The Personnel and Guidance Journal*, 1975, *51*, 183-189.

Searle, J.R. *Speech acts: An essay in the philosophy of language*. Cambridge, England: Cambridge University Press, 1969.

Winograd, T. What does it mean to understand language? *Cognitive Science*, 1980, *4*, 209-241.

# Prelanguage Assessment System

## INSTRUCTIONS FOR ASSESSMENT SYSTEMS

The purpose of the three assessment systems is to provide a criteria-referenced checklist for considering those skills that are representative of the prelanguage, language and linguistic areas of development. The representative skills are chosen from the theoretical principles discussed in the text. It is on the basis of a pragmaticism methodology that the dynamics of the system override the static measure. Therefore, the quality of prelanguage, language, and linguistic system functions is paramount.

Prelanguage assessment is accomplished by observing a child interact in a play setting with two different persons. Language assessment is completed after a representative segment of the child's language skills has been analyzed for consistency and inconsistency. The linguistic assessment system is utilized after a language sample emphasizing conversation has been collected.

## PRELANGUAGE ASSESSMENT SYSTEM

*Section I.* Directions: Record and briefly describe by giving examples the nonverbal behaviors used to indicate communication.

*Index Determination—Means of Communication*

1. Eyes (gaze, observation, blink, other _____ ) _____

2. Motor (point, gesture, reflex, symmetrical movement or asymmetrical movement, other _____ ) _____

3. Vocal (production quality typical or atypical, type of vocalization typical for age range, quantity typical for age range) _____

*Opportunity for Communication (Nonverbal)*
    4. Interaction (give examples of types) ⎯⎯⎯⎯⎯⎯⎯⎯⎯⎯⎯⎯⎯⎯

    5. Joint Activity (give examples) ⎯⎯⎯⎯⎯⎯⎯⎯⎯⎯⎯⎯⎯⎯⎯⎯

    6. Semantic Feature Acquisition (give examples) ⎯⎯⎯⎯⎯⎯⎯⎯⎯⎯

    7. Semantic Notions (give examples) ⎯⎯⎯⎯⎯⎯⎯⎯⎯⎯⎯⎯⎯⎯

    8. Intent or Purpose (give examples) ⎯⎯⎯⎯⎯⎯⎯⎯⎯⎯⎯⎯⎯⎯

*Mode of Learning*
    9. Visual Alternatives (boards, displays, objects) ⎯⎯⎯⎯⎯⎯⎯⎯⎯

   10. Auditory Alternatives (meaningful, nonmeaningful) ⎯⎯⎯⎯⎯⎯⎯

   11. Motor Alternatives (latency, change) ⎯⎯⎯⎯⎯⎯⎯⎯⎯⎯⎯⎯

   12. Vocal Alternatives (differentiated, nondifferentiated) ⎯⎯⎯⎯⎯⎯

*Section II.* Directions: Since many children operating at this level have multiple problems, the following list of items needs to be considered. Record the presence of any of these items and briefly describe, by example, any effect on communication behavior.

*Concerns*
    1. Seizures ⎯⎯⎯⎯⎯⎯⎯⎯⎯⎯⎯⎯⎯⎯⎯⎯⎯⎯⎯⎯⎯
    2. Tactile Defensiveness ⎯⎯⎯⎯⎯⎯⎯⎯⎯⎯⎯⎯⎯⎯⎯⎯
    3. Self-Stimulation ⎯⎯⎯⎯⎯⎯⎯⎯⎯⎯⎯⎯⎯⎯⎯⎯⎯
    4. General Stimulability (health, medication, sensory deficits) ⎯⎯⎯⎯

*Section III.* Directions: Since motor development is important at this stage, indicate any problems with the following that interfere with communication mode.

*Motor Ability*
    1. Relaxation ⎯⎯⎯⎯⎯⎯⎯⎯⎯⎯⎯⎯⎯⎯⎯⎯⎯⎯⎯⎯
    2. Freeing the Shoulders (gesturing, pointing, writing, etc.) ⎯⎯⎯⎯⎯

    3. Freeing the Hips (walking, running, climbing) ⎯⎯⎯⎯⎯⎯⎯⎯⎯

*Section IV.* Directions: To determine prognosis, the time to learn or to acquire semantic abilities is important. Record by example the following information.

*Learning Time*
    1. Time to Learn a Task ⎯⎯⎯⎯⎯⎯⎯⎯⎯⎯⎯⎯⎯⎯⎯⎯
    2. Influence on Time to Learn a Task ⎯⎯⎯⎯⎯⎯⎯⎯⎯⎯⎯

**Exhibit A-1** Sample Data Sheet

SPEECH EVENT NUMBER _____

CONTEXT AND MATERIALS _____

CHILDREN _____

| SPEECH ACT | LINGUISTIC CONTENT | PARALINGUISTICS | NONLINGUISTICS |
|---|---|---|---|
| | | | |

3. Semantic Complexity of Completed Tasks _____

4. Use of Icons, Indices, Symbols (give examples) _____

*Section V.* Directions: Record all verbalizations on a data sheet (see Exhibit A-1). Provide the following information.

*Purpose*

1. Did the utterances show purpose? _____ If so, indicate intentions. _____

   If not, why? _____
2. Give examples of the illocutionary force indicating devices that the child used (prosody, intonation, stress, loudness, mood of the verb, etc.). _____
3. Did the child have a desired effect on the hearer? _____ Give examples. _____

*Semantic Development*

4. List the types of semantic notions that were used. _____

5. List the frequency of each type of semantic relationship. _____

*Processes*

6. Did the child use spontaneous imitation? _____ If so, how many of the utterances were spontaneously imitated? _____

7. Did the child show any increase in verbalizations that were modeled with a rising intonation? _____ Give examples. _____

8. During spontaneous imitation did the child ever show modulation or an expansion? _____ If so, give examples. _____

*Effects*

9. What was the child's total frequency of utterances? _____
10. How much time did it take to obtain these utterances? _____
11. What materials were used to collect the utterances? _____

*Section VI.* Directions: With the data recorded, answer the following quality checks by giving examples for each in order to determine the interpretation of the data.

1. Did the child's verbal and nonverbal behavior demonstrate a variety of objects, actions, and events in a variety of relationships?

2. Did the child use a variety of intonational patterns (interrogative, declarative, and imperative) to express a variety of intentions?

3. Did the child use utterances that were appropriate to the context?

_____

4. Did the child *initiate* communication verbally? _____

_____

5. Did the child only respond to others' actions or did the child initiate communication nonverbally? _____

_____

6. Did the child create new contexts either verbally or nonverbally?

_____

7. Did the child use echoic utterances that lacked the flexibility found in spontaneous imitation? _____

_____

8. Did the child use a variety of semantic notions to function differently in a variety of contexts? _____

_____

9. Did the child establish a person-to-person relationship or did the child only prefer objects?

_____

*Section VII*. Directions: Interpretation of the data requires a summary statement indicating where the child is functioning and what is the next step of development.

*Summary*

_____
_____
_____
_____
_____
_____

# Language Assessment System

## THE LANGUAGE ASSESSMENT SYSTEM

*Section I*. Directions: Record the child's utterances and the contexts on a data sheet like Exhibit B-1 and then answer the following.

*Identifying Data*
    1. Total Number of Utterances _____
    2. Total Time to Collect Utterances _____
    3. Frequency of Utterances (1/2) _____
    4. Materials Used _____

*Listening to the Child*
    5. List two or three typical utterances. _____
    _____
    6. What characterized these typical utterances? _____
    7. What types of processes were evident? (modulation, expansion, overextension, overgeneralization) _____
    _____
    8. Are these processes engaged for sufficient frequency? _____
    _____

*Section II*. Directions: The analysis of the results requires an integration of ideas. Answer the following by giving examples (quality checks).

*Child's Language*
    1. Does the child's language contain action, objects, and events in a variety of relationships?
    _____
    2. Does the child use a variety of forms to express a variety of functions? _____
    _____
    3. Are the child's utterances appropriate for the context? _____
    _____

**Exhibit B-1** Sample Data Sheet

SPEECH EVENT NUMBER _____
CONTEXT AND MATERIALS _____

CHILDREN _____ _____

| SPEECH ACT | LINGUISTIC CONTENT | PARALINGUISTICS | NONLINGUISTICS |
|---|---|---|---|
| | | | |

4. Does the child answer questions appropriately or does the child just respond? _____

_____

5. Does the child initiate or create new utterances in new contexts?

_____

6. Does the child use forms that are rigid? _____

_____

7. Does the child use a variety of complete speech acts? _____

_____

*Section III.* Directions: If the child possesses any of the following language disorders, give examples. If not, skip this section.

*Child's Disorders*
1. Auditory Misperceptions _____
2. Off-Target Responding _____

_____

3. Syntactic Errors _____

_____

4. Semantic Word Errors _____
5. Word-Finding Problems _____
6. Neologisms (not overextensions) _____
7. Topical or Referential Identification Problems _____

_____

8. Topic Closure Difficulties _____

_____

9. Tangentiality _____

_____

10. Echolalia _____

_____

11. Verbal Perseveration _____

_____

12. Phonological Problems _____

_____

*Section IV.* Directions: In order to determine overall communication effectiveness, answer the following questions and give examples.

*Communication Effectiveness*
1. When the child is speaking or attempting to communicate does the child use gaze or eye contact to signal readiness or to identify the referent? _____

_____

2. Can the child respond appropriately to questions when engaged in play or other activity?

_____

3. What does the child do with a picture book? _____

_____

4. Does the child use an abundance of gesture and pantomime to convey messages? _____

_____

5. How do the significant people in the child's environment affect communication? _____

_____

6. How does the child follow routine? _____

7. Does the child consistently wait to be given materials, snacks, or play toys rather than asking for them? _____

8. Does the child make snacks or play toys rather than asking for them? _____

8. Does the child make utterances that are inappropriately stressed or with insufficient intensity? _____

9. Does the child attempt to solve problems physically rather than verbally? _____

*Section V.* Directions: To determine the child's ability to improve with environmental changes, answer the following questions and give examples.

*Prognosis*

1. Does the child produce more complex structures by elicited imitation? _____

2. What level of semantic complexity can the child utilize before the language skills decrease?

3. Does the child's use of language skills improve under different levels of semantic complexity? _____

4. Do models assist the child in developing certain processes? _____

5. Does patterning assist the child in complexity? _____

*Section VI.* Directions: A summary for interpreting the child's language skills should be written below.

*Interpretation Summary*

_____
_____
_____

# Linguistic Assessment System

## THE LINGUISTIC ASSESSMENT SYSTEM

*Section I.* Directions: Record the child's utterances and the corresponding contexts on a data sheet. Give examples with each answer.

*Identifying Data*
    1. Total Number of Utterances _____
    2. Total Time to Collect Utterances _____
    3. Frequency of Utterances (1/2) _____
    4. Materials Used to Collect Data _____

*Listening to the Child*
    5. List two or three typical utterances. _____
    _____
    _____

    6. What characterizes these typical utterances? _____
    _____

    7. Is there evidence of linguistic processes? (semanticity, displacement, redundancy) _____
    _____
    _____

    8. Is there evidence of a complete or incomplete linguistic system?
    _____
    _____

*Section II.* Directions: The collected data must be analyzed according to its quality. Answer the following quality checks and be sure to give examples for each answer.
    1. Does the child use a variety of speech acts? _____
    _____

    2. Does the child sequence ideas by using spatial and temporal markers?
    _____
    _____

3. Did the child explain the directions of a game sufficiently for the hearer to play the game if necessary? _____

_____

4. Does the child answer questions appropriately or does the child just respond? _____

_____

5. Does the child use forms that are rigid or stereotyped? _____

_____

6. Does the child use an increased number of fillers ("uhn," "um," for example) when the semantic complexity of the task increases?

_____

_____

7. Does the child initiate or create new utterances in new contexts?

_____

_____

8. Do the child's language forms show a variety of structural complexity? _____

9. Does the child answer each of the following types of questions:
   a. What + object? _____
   b. What or who + action? _____
   c. Where + address? _____
   d. Where + place? _____
   e. Where + action? _____
   f. When + do action? _____
   g. When + does action? _____
   h. Why + what or who? _____
   i. Why + cause? _____
10. When given the opportunity does the child ask a variety of questions?

_____

_____


*Section III*. Directions: If the child demonstrates any of the following language disorders, give examples of the ones evidenced.
   1. Auditory Misperceptions _____

_____

   2. Off-Target Responding _____

_____

   3. Syntactic Errors _____

_____

   4. Semantic Word Errors _____

_____

   5. Word-Finding Problems _____

_____

   6. Neologisms (not overextensions) _____

_____

   7. Topical or Referential Identification Problems _____

_____

   8. Topic Closure Difficulties _____

_____

9. Tangentiality _____

10. Echolalia _____

11. Verbal Perseveration _____

12. Phonological Problems _____

*Section IV*. Directions: To determine the extent of the learning language problem in acquiring a linguistic system, the child's academic profile should be studied. Answer the following questions by assessment or by others' assessments.

1. Does the child read at grade level? _____

2. If there are reading problems, what kinds of errors does the child make? _____

3. Does the child have writing difficulties? _____

4. If the child has writing difficulties, explain the relationship of errors to the types of oral language errors. _____

5. How does the child describe his/her problems? _____

6. What is the relationship between the child's description and the child's learning pattern as evidenced by oral language skills?

_____

*Section V*. Directions: Based on this data, interpret the child's method of learning and the resulting restrictions or limitations on the linguistic system.

*Summary*

_____
_____
_____
_____
_____

# Semantic Conditions of Speech Acts

1. Requests for objects (similar to request specifications, Searle, 1969, p. 65).

| | |
|---|---|
| Propositional Content Rule: | Future act (A) of H (hearer). |
| Preparatory Rule: | a. H is able to provide A. S (speaker) believes H knows what A is and that H has A. |
| | b. It is not obvious to both S and H that H will provide A in the normal course of events of his or her own accord. |
| Sincerity Rule: | S wants H to do A. |
| Essential Rule: | Counts as an attempt to get H to do A. |

The following elements are included as a necessary part of the essential rule for the H to be appropriately affected:

(1) S's body orientation is toward the H in order to ready H for the utterance.
(2) Eye contact or name is used to signal H.
(3) Appropriate linguistic markers indicating either—
    (a) an interrogative form
    (b) an imperative form
(4) An utterance which specifies what the H is to do.
(5) Appropriate loudness for the H to respond.

2. Requests for action.

| | |
|---|---|
| Propositional Content Rule: | Future act (A) of H. |
| Preparatory Rule: | a. H is able to do A. S believes H is able to do A. |
| | b. It is not obvious to both S and H that H will do A in the normal course of events of his or her own accord. |
| Sincerity Rule: | S wants H to do A. |
| Essential Rule: | Counts as an attempt to get H to do A. |

The following elements are included as a necessary part of the essential rule:

(1) S's body orientation is toward H in order to ready H for the utterance.
(2) Eye contact or name is used to signal H.
(3) Appropriate linguistic markers indicating either—
    (a) an interrogative form
    (b) an imperative form
(4) An utterance which specifies what the H is to do.
(5) Appropriate loudness for the H to respond.

3. Assertion.

| | |
|---|---|
| Propositional Content Rule: | Any proposition (p). |
| Preparatory Rule: | a.  S has evidence (reason, etc., for the truth of p). |
| | b.  It is not obvious to both S and H that H knows (does not need to be reminded of, etc.) p. |
| Sincerity Rule: | S believes p. |
| Essential Rule: | Counts as an undertaking to the effect that p represents an actual state of affairs. |

The following elements are included as a necessary part of the essential rule for the utterance of an assertion:

(1) A falling contour representative of a declarative form.
(2) A form of p is X which does not follow by direct imitation is used (otherwise S would know that H is already aware of p).
(3) The utterance is given with appropriate loudness.
(4) Eye contact is given to signal the H or observation is used to signal H.
(5) Body orientation between S and H is within a front plane position.

4. Denial.

| | |
|---|---|
| Propositional Content Rule: | Past A done by H is in the p form of not X. |
| Preparatory Rule: | a.  S does not believe that it is in his or her better interest to do as X indicates. |
| | b.  The p is obvious to both H and S. |
| Sincerity Rule: | S does not want to do X. |
| Essential Rule: | Counts as an attempt to deny H's p. |

The following elements are included as a necessary part of the essential rule for a denial:

(1) The previous action or p of the S is implied through gesture or is linguistically specified.
(2) Use of emphatic stress or loudness for H to respond.
(3) The utterance is negatively marked.
(4) Eye contact is used to signal H.
(5) Orientation is toward the H or toward the action being denied.

5. Statement of Information (differs from Searle's assertion).

| | |
|---|---|
| Propositional Content Rule: | Any proposition (p). |
| Preparatory Rule: | a. S knows of p to be fact or evidence of fact.<br>b. It is not obvious to H what p is. In fact, it is obvious to S that H does not know p. |
| Sincerity Rule: | S believes that H needs the information and cannot get the information elsewhere. |
| Essential Rule: | Counts as an attempt to state the information. |

The following elements are included as part of the essential rule for a statement of information:

(1) A falling contour representative of a declarative form.
(2) Appropriate loudness for the H to respond.
(3) Content is factual for the H.
(4) Eye contact signals the H or observation signals the H.
(5) Orientation of the body is toward H.

6. Requests for Information.

| | |
|---|---|
| Propositional Content Rule: | Future A of H. |
| Preparatory Rule: | a. S believes H knows X and H is able to tell S.<br>b. It is not obvious that S will find out without asking H.<br>c. S wants H to tell X. |
| Sincerity Rule: | S wants H to tell X. |
| Essential Rule: | Counts as an attempt to get H to tell X. |

The following elements are included as part of the essential rule for requests for information:

(1) The utterance is marked with a rising contour.
(2) The utterance utilized a specific lexical item indicating a constituent question or an interrogative reversal for a yes/no question.
(3) Appropriate loudness is used to signal the H to respond.
(4) Eye contact signals H or observation signals H.
(5) Body orientation is either toward the constituent or toward H.

7. Calling.

| | |
|---|---|
| Propositional Content Rule | Future A of H. |
| Preparatory Rule: | a. S believes that H will not notice or do A without S telling him or her.<br>b. S believes it is in his or her better interest to have H do A. |
| Sincerity Rule: | S wants H to do A. |
| Essential Rule: | Counts as an attempt for S to get H. |

The following elements are considered as a part of the essential rule for calling.

(1) The H is specified by name or signaled by some other linguistic marker or notification.
(2) Orientation is facing H.
(3) Eye contact or observation is made during or as a part of the utterance.
(4) The utterance specifies how the H is to perform or respond.
(5) The loudness is adequate for the H to respond.

8.  Rule Order.

Propositional
Content Rule:          Future A of H.

Preparatory Rule:      a.  S believes that H does not know the rule of the situation.
                       b.  S does not think H will know A unless S tells him or her.

Sincerity Rule:        S believes H should know the rule.

Essential Rule:        Counts as an attempt for S to follow H.

The following elements are considered part of the essential rule for the rule ordering to count:

(1) The utterance is given with a falling contour of an imperative form.
(2) The utterance is given with adequate loudness for H to respond.
(3) Body orientation is toward H.
(4) Eye contact signals H or observation signals H.
(5) The utterance specifies what H is to do.

The semantic descriptions of the previous eight speech acts were taken from Lucas (1977). The following semantic conditions are for the speech acts identified by Rostamizadeh (1981).

9.  Speculation.

Propositional
Content Rule:          Future A of X.

Preparatory Rule:      S "believes," "guesses," or "thinks" that H and S cannot know X as a
                       fact.

Sincerity Rule:        S does not expect an overt change in behavior but expresses X as an
                       assertion.

Essential Rule:        Counts as an attempt for S to understand H.

The following elements are considered part of the essential rule for speculation.

(1) The utterance is given with a falling contour.
(2) The utterance is given with adequate loudness for H to receive the utterance.
(3) Body orientation is toward the H.
(4) The utterance uses a speculative performative (verb).
(5) The act cannot be obvious to either H or S—that is, it should not be a known fact and specified
    that way in the essential elements.

The pretend statement of information, pretend rule order, pretend request for action, and pretend request for information are the same as their nonviolated sincerity counterparts. Of course, the difference is that it should be obvious that the sincerity rule is violated since neither can act on the "meaning" at the surface level.

## REFERENCES

Lucas, E.V. The feasibility of speech acts as a language approach for emotionally disturbed children. (Doctoral dissertation, University of Georgia, 1977). *Dissertation Abstracts International*, 1978, *38*, 3479B-3967B. (University Microfilms No. 77-30, 488)

Searle, J.R. Speech acts: An essay in the philosophy of language. Cambridge, England: Cambridge University Press, 1969.

Rostamizadeh, M.B. *A comparison of two dyadic conditions for speech act types in three-year-old children.* Master's thesis, Washington State University, 1981.

# Glossary

**Additive principle of discrete units**—The more discrete characteristics of language tools that a child exhibits, the more complex is the child's language.

**Cognition**—the physiological organization of sensation into the basic thought object.

**Communication**—the conveyance of an intended message so as to act to alter a hearer's or receiver's attitudes, beliefs, or behaviors.

**Concept**—the organization of semantic features to be represented by a symbol sign.

**Constituent rules**—semantic properties of a speech act including propositional content, sincerity, and essential rules.

**Context**—from a pragmaticism methodology, context refers to the immediate environment of the speaker and hearer, including past experiences that each one brings to the situation.

**Conventionality**—the state of awareness of sign relations between a speaker and a hearer.

**Conventions**—the mutually used tools of sign representation between any given speaker and hearer.

**Deixis**—a purposeful exchange of information; requires a maintenance of interaction.

**Discrete complexity assumption**—the more complex the system as demonstrated by the addition of discrete units, the more intact is the system.

**Displacement**—a linguistic principle that accounts for the various degrees of referring in sign usage; the more the features are assumed the greater is the displacement.

**Echolalia**—a language disorder resulting from an inability to attach meaning to perceptually organized features.

**Essential elements**—the language and paralanguage requisites for an utterance to be interpreted as a specific speech act (e.g., loudness, signal devices, specific lexical usage, mood of the verb, tense, intonation pattern).

**Expansion**—the sociocognitive process of adding features through modulation resulting in more complex structures.

**Extension**—the temporal continuum of a term, as in overextension and underextension; the features are applied to other situations or the characteristics are represented by the same concept of features.

**Facilitation**—the use of naturalistic models to provide opportunities for utilizing sociocognitive processes.

**Features**—meaningful bits of information related to perceptual and functional characteristics of a referent.

**Felicity conditions**—the speech act exists only when all semantic conditions are met; the felicity conditions are those semantic requisites.

**Fillers**—nonmeaningful words or phrases that replace a pause in the production of a proposition/predication type of relationship.

**Flexibility**—the use of a particular type of utterance produced in a variety of situations.

**Functors**—nonreferential words such as articles, prepositions, and auxiliary verbs.

**Icon**—the representation of a sign only by relationship.

**Illocutionary act**—the intent of the utterance act.

**Illocutionary force indicating devices**—essential elements of a speech act that help to determine the intent; in English these include stress, mood and voice of the verb, etc.

**Index**—a sign or representation of a specific event by nonverbal or verbal means.

**Indicator**—a nonverbal device interpreted by the observer, because of its consistency, as meaningful.

**Intension**—the specific semantic features of a term as opposed to the continuum of features in extension.

**Interpretant**—the determiner of meaning in any given message; includes the nonverbal and verbal message.

**Intervention**—the imposition of change on a child's system from the use of clinical models and techniques.

**Knowledge**—the representation of thought through sign; occurs as the result of semantic feature development.

**Language**—the tool of verbal communication; i.e., syntax, morphology, phonology according to the semantic development.

**Language delay**—the assumption that a child who does not evidence certain language tools is developing in the same way as a non-language-handicapped child, only slower.

**Language disorder**—the nonsystematic, nonsequential development of a language product as the result of a deviant system

**Language phase**—a period of semantic development characterized by the use of newly acquired syntax, morphology, and phonology tools.

**Lexical tag**—the attachment of a term (tag or word) to previously organized perceptual features representative of a concept.

**Lexicalization**—the addition of new terms to a child's repertoire; the addition of signs to represent concepts.

**Linguistic phase**—a period of semantic development characterized by the principles of semanticity, maximum displacement, and limited redundancy.

**Mark** (-er, -ing)—the attachment of meaning to an object, action, and/or event because of a consistent indicating device.

**Modulation**—the sociocognitive process of changing a system by semantic feature addition resulting in grammatical changes in the language.

**Native speaker assumption**—the adult knowledge of what characterizes that adult's own system.

**Neologisms**—newly created words.

**Paradigm**—a working or operational model.

**Peirce**—Charles Sanders Peirce (1839-1914) was considered the "father of the pragmatists."

**Perception**—the organization of sensory-received stimuli into usable features.

**Performative**—a verb that performs an act when uttered, as in the case of "promise," "vow," etc.

**Perseveration**—repetitious, nonpurposeful verbal and/or nonverbal behavior related to an inability to sort semantic features.

**Phonology**—principle governed sound system of language.

**Pragmaticism methodology**—the study of the way that signs are used to produce given consequences.

**Pragmatics**—a modern "generic" term for how language is used.

**Pragmatists**—philosophers in the late 1800s and early 1900s who studied the consequences of life.

**Predication**—the referring agent (Y) of a proposition (X).

**Prelanguage phase**—a period of semantic development characterized by nonverbal communication.

**Preparatory set**—the semantic conditions of a speech act specifying assumed, shared, or unshared meaning.

**Presupposition**—the conceptual information about any given context.

**Processes**—dynamic semantic interrelationships.

**Productivity**—a variety of novel utterances representative of a variety of uses.

**Proposition**—a referred, intended notion (X), much like a basic topic conveyed to a hearer.

**Propositional content**—the representation of a message.

**Psycholinguistic methodology**—the study of those language tools that are acquired, produced, and comprehended.

**Reauditorization**—self-repetition of vocal material.

**Redundancy**—the overlap of symbol usage.

**Reference points**—the changes between speaker and events, between speaker and hearer, or hearer and others; the child acquires sufficient features to begin to consider others' perspectives or objects' perspectives.

**Referent**—the shared semantic concept of a speaker and a hearer.

**Referring**—an act of sign usage dependent on the availability of shared semantic information.

**Refinement**—a narrowing of features for the specific use of a lexical tag.

**Semantic features**—the physiological organization of sensory information into meaningful units.

**Semanticity**—a linguistic principle in which meaning is refined by increased complexity of sign usage.

**Semantic memory**—the auditory processing of semantic features into symbols.

**Semantic notions**—the semantic relations and semantic functions; meaningful objects, actions, and/or events in relationship to their functions.

**Semantic relationships**—a proposition-to-basic-predication of a given object, action, and/or event.

**Semantics**—the study of meaning—verbal, nonverbal, and contextual as interpreted by a hearer.

**Semiotics**—the study of the use of signs.

**Sensation**—the receptive use of the stimuli of the sensory organs (eyes, ears, skin, etc.)

**Sign**—the representation of meaning as interpreted by the hearer.

**Sincerity rule**—condition in which the speaker does intend the propositional content as performed or uttered in a speech act.

**Sociocognitive processes**—the social need to refine semantic development through a series of synergistic changes.

**Spatial terms**—symbols representative of displacement in space, through the horizontal, vertical, or diagonal planes.

**Speech act**—the unit of semiotics consisting of the semantic constituents of an utterance act for the changing of attitudes, beliefs, and/or behaviors.

**Speech event**—a series of speech acts.

**Spontaneous imitation**—a sociocognitive process of lexicalization in which the child is able to replicate part or all of a previously used utterance for the purpose of refining semantic feature usage.

**Symbol**—the representation of semantics at the highest level; the referent is represented by a verbal sign.

**Synergistic model**—the pragmaticism methodology used to describe the dynamics of language, cognition, and socialization.

**Temporal terms**—symbols of time displacement.

**Thought object**—the basis of cognition; explained by Peirce as part of a theory of cognition.

**Utterance act**—production of words in series.

# Index

---

*Note:* Subheadings are listed in order of appearance in the book rather than in alphabetical order.

# About the Author

ELLYN V. ARWOOD received her doctorate of education as Ellyn V. Lucas from the University of Georgia in speech and language pathology. She has been a clinical supervisor at the University of Illinois and the University of Georgia for students dealing with a wide range of language-disordered children. She has been an assistant professor at Washington State University and Louisiana State University, and was recently promoted to associate professor at Texas Tech University, where she has acted as the clinical director of speech and hearing services, a program accredited by the Education Training Board and by the Professional Services Board of the American Speech-Language-Hearing Association.

Dr. Arwood is the author of *Semantic and Pragmatic Language Disorders: Assessment and Remediation* as well as numerous papers dealing with communication disorders. She has conducted many inservice and workshop programs in language methods and procedures throughout the United States and Canada and has been invited to serve as keynote speaker at several conventions.